Success

...swimming in a sea of

By

Steve Gammill

Published by
Trafford Publishing

Order this book online at www.trafford.com
or email orders@trafford.com

Most Trafford titles are also available at major online book retailers.

Printed in Victoria, BC, Canada.

ISBN: 978-1-4269-0258-1 (sc)
ISBN: 978-1-4269-0259-8 (hc)
ISBN: 978-1-4269-0260-4 (eb)

Our mission is to efficiently provide the world's finest, most comprehensive book publishing service, enabling every author to experience success. To find out how to publish your book, your way, and have it available worldwide, visit us online at www.trafford.com

Trafford rev. 11/13/2009

 www.trafford.com

North America & international
toll-free: 1 888 232 4444 (USA & Canada)
phone: 250 383 6864 ♦ fax: 812 355 4082

Also by Steve Gammill

Your Legacy: Meaningful Estate Planning

To
Terry Fine

Terry Fine, doctor of dentistry, passed away in 2008. His profession was that of a scientist. His life, including his professional life, was that of a servant, and a humble one at that. I first met Terry when I came to Grand Junction, Colorado in 1991 and needed a dentist to replace Dr. Ed Cooper, my dentist during all those years I lived in Albuquerque, New Mexico.

My respect for Terry grew to encompass far more of his person than just his gentle hands. Terry truly cared about the persons in his world. That was evident not only in how he treated those he was serving professionally, but by his relationships with his staff and his colleagues. His chapter in this book reveals that aspect of his hub, the foundation of his person, far better than I could describe.

In 2006 a small group of men and women in Grand Junction formed what was to become the Grand Junction Time To Think Council, and Terry was invited to become a founding member. The purpose of the Council is to meet monthly and to offer to its individual members the great benefit of the very best, deepest, richest, and independent thinking of each of the Council members on a given topic or issue.

Terry felt humbled to be asked to join; the Council felt honored that he accepted. That's who Terry was.

The Council meetings typically last about two hours and involve lunch together. During one of our earliest meetings, after about 15 minutes Terry disappeared out into the hall. Upon returning, he apologized and told us he had to call his office to reschedule a patient: Terry had forgotten that we would not be finished by one o'clock p.m. and he had scheduled a patient for one and-a-half hours after the meeting began. Even though our Council was yet untried and possibly unworthy of a busy physician's rescheduling his patients, Terry had made a commitment.

He was one who honored not only his commitments, but individual people as well. When I was considering writing this book, Terry was a very strong supporter. His encouragement did not stem from any earned merit of mine or of the project; he supported it because *I* thought it worthwhile. And his encouragement went far beyond simply saying positive words. I asked him if he would like to be the first interviewee for the book. He thought he didn't have much of value that would be meaningful to others, but he agreed simply because it was my project and he wanted to support me. "If you want me to do it, then I'll do it," he said, "I want to support you." So Terry was the very first contributor, and his chapter is found within the covers of this book. Over the time it took to put this project together, and right up until his death, he frequently asked about its progress and what problems I might be experiencing.

Terry Fine, a true friend and mentor to many.

Table of Contents

The descriptive identification found in this Table is deliberately brief. Each contributor to this book has told his or her own stories reflecting who he or she is. The interpretation of that should be left to the Reader and not influenced by this Author's descriptive comments.

Acknowledgements

There are a great number of people who encouraged and supported me in the production of this book, especially in the personal and emotional support I needed in order to believe I could even do this. These people include, Rick Randall, Scott Farnsworth, Nancy Kline, Mary Harmeling, Harriet Carpenter, and the members of the Grand Junction Time To Think Council (Terry Fine, Laurinda Conrad, Michael Salogga, Travis Perry, Mark Ashman, Doug Mays and Jan Gammill). Without that consistent support, I would have given up long ago.

A special thanks goes to Mary Harmeling and Harriet Carpenter. Those two gave freely of their own personal time to read portions of the manuscript—not to provide editing, but rather to give me literary guidance in the very difficult task of making the stories flow for a reader while maintaining the individual personality, or voice, of the storyteller.

And then, of course, there's my loving wife, Jan. The entire project would have failed for lack of birth had it not been for her loving and consistent encouragement. Whether she is aware of it or not, she influenced my selection of contributors. She has a sense and an insight far beyond mine, and she knows people far more richly. She is my life partner, my wife, my best friend, and my teaching partner.

And there's one more point needing acknowledgement. I began this project believing I should make no introduction of any of the "characters," the contributors. That is because I wanted to carefully avoid influencing a reader's expectation for any given chapter. But then it was pointed out to me by many—by Mary Harmeling, by Harriet Carpenter, by my extremely patient editor, Bonnie Beach, and my wife— that readers who are unfamiliar with the individuals covered in these chapters will need some sense of who they are. So I've undertaken, in the Table of Contents, a very brief, hopefully quite bland, line or two, introducing each contributing person.

Preface

I heard an interesting story recently. In fact, I pulled it off the Internet and it is purely anecdotal. I didn't think to properly cite it or verify authenticity. The story originates with a television news magazine that aired in June of 2008, claiming that the Danes are the most contented and happy people in the world. Europeans ranked far below that, and we Americans were only about twenty-second. When asked, the Danes were surprised. They did not think they were the most happy and, in fact, claimed to not particularly enjoy talking with anyone. The Europeans and the Americans were equally surprised. They pictured themselves as happy, laughing, and thoroughly enjoying life.

Happiness may well have a lot to do with how one defines the word. Likewise, whether or not one is successful in life certainly depends on how one defines success. According to the same article, the Danes aren't particularly interested in the accumulation of material things and claim that happiness has everything to do with the quality of relationships. If we in America look around us, it's easy to believe that Americans are affected with the need to acquire "stuff." Who has the biggest house? Who has the most cars in the driveway that aren't junk? If those Americans whose life stories fill this book are representative, you may be surprised at what you hear.

I am the one who selected each of the people whose stories you will read, and while I don't claim to have been scientifically random in the process, I tried to approach selection with as little bias as possible. Frankly, I fully expected at least some to define the word "success" as involving the accumulation of financial wealth. And so I leave it to you, the reader, to draw your own conclusions as to my objectivity and whether you believe the definitions found in these chapters to be typical of the American people you know.

This book was written with two purposes in mind. The first, of course, is to explore the meaning of "success." Everyone interviewed for this book lives in the small corner of Western Colorado known as the Grand Valley. Some are relative newcomers, and some have lived there all their lives. The process involved my interviewing each of them privately and all were asked the same questions and in roughly the same order. It was important to keep my personal thoughts and definitions out of the conversation and, consequently, I asked as few questions as I possibly could to still keep the conversation going. I framed the questions in such a way as not to influence or guide the response.

The Oxford Dictionary and Thesaurus, published by the Oxford University Press, 1996, defines "success" as a favorable outcome or the attainment of one's aims or of wealth or fame. I could have gotten that information simply by asking the question, and that leads directly to the second purpose for this book—to spotlight the value of storytelling.

Without qualification, the telling of one's story is the single best and richest route to learning the heart of that person. Each of the questions I posed is specifically designed to elicit personal stories. In a book written in 2008 by Scott Farnsworth and Peggy Hoyt, *Like a Library Burning*, a Middle Eastern proverb is quoted: "When an old person dies, it's like a library burning down." That proverb is especially true if those old people have never shared their wisdom, their principles, their life's learning, and their values by telling their own histories. World War II veterans have traditionally been very reluctant to share their stories. As they leave us every year in greater numbers, the libraries are going up in smoke.

Listening to a life story, even one, will reveal important lessons and values of the storyteller, even though that may not have been the purpose in the telling—and that telling is far more interesting to a listener than a two-line response to a direct question. Listen to the following story from my own childhood,—and please note that I asked you to *listen*, not just to *read*—and see what you hear and learn about the storyteller.

In my conference room, which is where I normally meet with clients, I have a number of wall hangings that are of particular importance to me. One item is a piece of yellowed, quite old paper in a frame and behind a piece of glass. One day when I was probably nine years old I found myself downtown in a toy store—not that unusual for me. We lived in a small town—McCook, Nebraska—where my dad was the managing editor of the town's only newspaper, *The McCook Daily Gazette*. Of course, there was no such thing as a shopping center, so all the shopping we'd be doing was downtown, and that's, of course, also where the newspaper was.

Well, I was in this toy store, which was probably the dime store, and I discovered a wonderful red tractor. It was plastic, it was dark red, and my memory tells me it was about eight or nine inches long and three or four inches high. It had black rubber treads and looked like a Caterpillar tractor, except that it was red. It cost $4. I had $3, probably all I had to my name.

What was I to do but go across the street to the newspaper office and ask my dad to help me out? I have no idea what I was expecting he would say or do, because he was not the kind to just reach into his pocket and dole out money to his kids anytime they thought they wanted something. But I only needed a dollar.

He was in his office wearing his white shirt and tie with his sleeves rolled up and working away on something or other. I don't remember the conversation or how I pitched it, but I remember him turning to his typewriter. I don't think he said a thing. I wish I could describe the sound that typewriter made when he inserted the paper and rolled that black roller so that the paper was ready to receive the striking keys. This was a typewriter you would expect to see in a newspaper editor's office in 1949. It was pretty big, made a lot of noise—a rhythmic clacking noise—and my dad was a superb typist. He could really make those keys sing—clickety-clack, clickety clack—and there was always that "ding" when the typewriter would near the right margin, and then that short break in the clickety-clack when Dad would reach up with his left hand, push the silver return lever so that the typewriter carriage would return to the left-hand margin, and the rhythmic clickety-clack could begin again.

So it didn't take long for him to complete the task, and when he pulled the paper from the typewriter he handed me what was titled "Chattel Mortgage." It was two short paragraphs, double spaced and essentially said that I acknowledged borrowing $1 from the "party of the first part, Kenneth A. Gammill" and promised, as the "party of the second part," to repay "said debt" by Sunday, July 3, 1949.

The second paragraph said that if I didn't pay by the due date, plus 5 cents interest, I would release title to my new tractor and give up possession until such time as the debt had been paid or "at the discretion of the party of the first part."

My little sister must have been with me, or at least readily available, because she signed as a witness. She would have been only seven. I doubt I had the patience to run all the way home to find her and get her signature, so she must have been around at the time.

I know that I got the tractor, because I remember playing with it out in the front yard where I had quite a structure built in the dirt for my toy cars and trucks. I have no recollection of paying the debt or of having the tractor repossessed. I'm fairly certain, knowing my dad, that I did, in fact, pay the debt."

For many people, storytelling is a difficult undertaking, at least getting started. It sometimes can be too revealing, or it can bring emotion. In our culture, personal stories are sometimes considered poor form and storytellers suspect. Stories also constitute "anecdotal" evidence that somehow seems unsupported and, therefore, untrue. Oftentimes people claim that what they have to tell isn't of interest to anyone. Consequently, we learn to keep our stories to ourselves. Dr. Rachel Naomi Remen has written a wonderful little book about storytelling called, *Kitchen Table Wisdom*. In it she says, "I have discovered the power of story to change people. I have seen a story heal shame and free people from fear, ease suffering and restore a lost sense of worth. I have learned that the ways we can befriend and strengthen the life in one another are very simple and very old. Stories have not lost their power...stories need no footnotes.... I have become prouder to be a human being."

As you begin making your way along the pathways within these chapters, expect a joyful journey. You will definitely learn what some people believe it means to be successful in various aspects of their lives—professional success, financial success, success in learning and education, and personal success. And I hope you experience oh-so-much more.

This book has made me "prouder to be a human being."

—Steve Gammill

Jeff Taets

August 6, 2008

And it really struck a chord with me: if in my professional development I stopped learning and stopped gaining new experiences, I'm probably done. It's probably over.

I was grounded until three unsolicited people came to him and said I was a nice person. I was doing something good when they saw me. They couldn't be my friends— it had to be an adult in the normal course of life going to him and saying, "Hey, I saw your son doing something good,"— an unsolicited good report.

"Can you keep the farm?" It wasn't tied to a dollar amount such as, "We're going to make $X this year." No, it was tied to, "Can we do the things that we want to do and stay where we want to stay?" That was the measuring stick of financial freedom as a child.

Jeff, when you were growing up, what did you think it meant to be professionally successful, and what experiences led you to that definition?

I grew up on a small family farm in Iowa. My parents lived and worked on the farm together every day, and so did the children—my five siblings and myself. So we had an interesting perspective. We saw the successes and the failures. When the crops needed rain and everybody was down about that, we all were painfully aware. During the '70s, it was a prosperous economic time and we all knew it. In the '80s, it wasn't. There was a thing called the "farm crisis" in the early '80s, and some of my dad's neighbors up and down the road lost their farms, had to move to town, and get jobs.

During those times, I gained a lot of respect for my parents. No matter what, they were honest and they helped other people. Many times during the bad economic times, my dad would send me or my brothers to help somebody [even though] there was work to do at home. He sent us knowing that we were never going to get paid for that—he wasn't, and we weren't—but it was just the right thing to do.

We had a machine called the "haybine" that chopped hay and got it ready for a baler. And I ran that thing a lot. I can remember sitting at the table with my dad and him telling me that I'm going to XYZ farm and I'm going to ride that thing all day, burning his fuel, my time, depreciation on the vehicle. I was aware of all that stuff at [a very young] age. We weren't making a lot of money at the time—my parents worried about money just like those folks that we went to work for were. My dad knew that they wanted to pay but they couldn't, or maybe someday they would. This was a small community and people helped each other.

My life has taught me that talking about doing the right thing and doing the right thing are two different things. When times are good and money is plentiful, everybody is honest. But when times aren't good and money is not plentiful, when people [still] do the right thing—that's character.

What is your definition today of professional success?

Having the respect of my family, of my wife and my kids, my siblings, my parents; being honest, working hard, doing the right thing even when it's not the easy thing, and as a result of that, having the respect of the people I interact with every day.

That would be my definition. Doing the right thing, even when it's not the easy thing. Sometimes that means you have to make some hard decisions, things that would be a lot easier to just ignore—turn your head the other direction and pretend like you didn't see.

Can you think of an experience or an example of when you had to do that?

As recently as the other day, we had a vendor of ours that had said some things that were inappropriate about our financial institution and, incidentally, were not true. And those things had gotten back to me. It would have been really easy to pretend like I never heard it or to pretend like it wasn't going to hurt people. It would've been really easy for me to say nasty things about that company. I could've found many things to say. I didn't. Instead, I marched down there and I set the record straight with facts and truth and looked the people in the eye and said, "Our relationship is over." That wasn't fun. It wasn't easy. I didn't enjoy doing it at all, but it was the right thing to do.

I could have just called my staff [in] and said, "No more orders to XYZ Company." And, effectively, it probably would have been the same thing, but I'm a businessperson in this community. I run into people in the grocery store, at church, wherever. And frankly, I'd like to be able to look them in the eye and know that I did the right thing. It costs us some sleepless nights sometimes, but it's the right thing and that's the way it goes.

By your own definition, in what ways are you already a professional success?

That's a tough one. I believe that I have a lot of growth to do, but I am proud of the fact that I have taken my career from [being] an employee of a bank to an owner of a bank.

That was a goal since the day I decided to get into the banking business. In order to achieve that success, I had to, first of all, learn a heck of a lot about the banking industry, a lot about things that you don't see every day—law and regulations. One of my primary business partners is a very good friend of mine and [the others are my] brothers. We had to organize this company, and that was a lot of nights that I could have been spending with my family. And instead I was working on this, I believe, *for* my family.

And then at the end, we had to put our money where our mouths were. I had to risk my and my family's financial life by putting our money into the company and starting it. Not to mention going out to investors, who happened to be friends and business associates, and asking them to believe in my idea and to invest money in this company.

So I'm talking specifically about the organization of Timberline Bank. But that was a measure of the success I've had to this point. It was believing in myself enough to take a chance. It'd be a lot easier just to work for somebody else. And then, asking others to believe in me, knowing full well that they had the right to say no. And nobody likes rejection.

My wife believed in me, my business partners believed in me, and I believe strongly in them. So it was a solid risk and one worth taking. But having their support was a really big measure of what I've done today.

You are a young man, so what remains unfinished for you in achieving professional success?

I don't know that I'll ever say, "Aha! I'm a success. I've reached that level." I've had some success in my life, and I've had some things that weren't so successful. I think time may be the great equalizer—and time will tell whether I am a success or not. Every day [presents] new challenges and opportunities. I'm going to work hard and try to make the right decisions, even if they're difficult ones.

When you were a youngster, what constituted success in learning and education, and who taught you that?

The easy answer to that is grades. Good grades would be the measuring stick of success in learning. In my family, while they certainly wanted us to get good grades, that was never the primary focus.

I went to public school in Iowa. I was not the valedictorian of my class and I never really expected to be. My parents didn't go to college. I think they both would've liked to but at the time, it just wasn't economically feasible. They had a love for education and it was important. There had to be a really great reason for us to miss school. If you were sick, you were sick. You didn't watch TV. And if you were sick, you weren't working on the farm, either. You were in bed. If you weren't in bed, you were in school.

Even though my parents didn't go to college, it was expected that we all were going to because they worked [hard] to give us that opportunity.

So even as a young third or fourth grader, I knew I was going to Iowa State University and I was probably going to study business, maybe with an agricultural focus. The five boys and one girl in my

4

family blazed the trail. We went to the same college and we all lived in the same fraternity house, an agricultural fraternity.

I took college placement courses while a lot of my friends didn't. They were having a lot more fun in [the easy and] fun classes. I took some of those as well, but I also took advanced math and got a C. It would have been really easy to get an A in shop. When I was signing up for classes for my junior or senior year, I can't say I ever considered saying, "Hey, so-and-so is taking shop. I'm thinking about rebuilding an engine this year instead of taking advanced math." The question never even came up, because I had a real clear vision of where I was going.

I guess education [is necessary] to "get to the next spot." You have to learn to read in order to [understand] the math story problem; you've got to learn to do the addition to get to the multiplication; you've got to learn the multiplication to figure out division. It's just [the same] as building blocks. Maybe you won't get an A on every one of those fundamentals, but you've got to master [each] to get to the next level.

To what extent, if any, do you think that your participation in the fraternity at Iowa State affected your learning and education?

I would say to a large degree. I always kidded my parents about my education—and especially as I got into college—that I wasn't going to let classes get in the way of my college education.

But there's a lot more to it than class. I was in a lot of organizations and I learned about personal relationships and working on a team with other people. I learned far more doing that kind of stuff than I learned in the calculus or accounting classes. In our case, I was living with 80 guys that have varied backgrounds. They're there for different reasons. That part of my college education was far more of a growth experience than sitting in class. While I missed a lot of classes, I learned a lot about myself and about how to work with other people. And that's something I use every day.

What do you now think it means to be successful in learning and education?

I think it means that you're still learning. My first job out of college was with Norwest Bank in South Dakota. I was in a management training program, was going to classes every day, and learning stuff that wasn't really terribly exciting to me. One day, I sat down with one of the managers and he was asking me how it was going and how I liked it. And I said, " I want to *do*! I'm sick of sitting in these classes." I'll never forget [what] the guy said to me: "You know, in all businesses, if [management is] still sending you to classes and you're still learning—if we're making an investment in you—we feel that you're worth it."

And it really struck a chord with me: if in my professional development I stopped learning and stopped gaining new experiences, I'm probably done. It's probably over.

Before I graduated from college, just to kind of reinforce [my previous] point a little bit…I had eight offers to go to work in various companies, from sales to manufacturing to banking. I interviewed different companies. Prior to that, I'd done several summer internships and gotten exposure to different companies.

By far, the lowest paying job offer I got was in the banking industry—35 to 40% less than the highest. I remember thinking to myself that the reason I took the job in the banking industry is because I believed that I had the most to learn there; I believed that while a lot of industries will pay you a whole bunch of money to get you, you become kind of stuck. You're driving around in a car and trying to get people to use your product, as opposed to learning more and becoming a more rounded person.

So I made a bet on the banking industry. It was a big gamble for a young 23-year-old kid to make, and I still can't tell you that it was the right bet to make, but I felt there was growth potential there—[both] internal and external. And [at] this point, I'm where I want to be.

From your observations and experiences, what are some keys to achieving success in learning and education?

The keys to achieving success in learning are that you continue to learn and you continue to apply that in your daily life. I picked the industry I got into because I had the most personal growth in that industry. We now know in studies of the brain that [it] grows throughout your life.

The more you learn, the more your brain processes information, the less atrophy you have in the brain as you age.

So keep doing it—keep exposing yourself to new things. Nobody likes change, but change might be the one of the best things for you. We need to adapt, we need to learn. Every single day, I learn something new or I'm affected in a new way, [even if] it's [just] getting the newest cell phone. My old cell phone was great but two weeks ago, I got a new one. The old cell phone was like a comfortable old shoe. I knew everything that sucker could do but the new one can do more. When you give up learning new things, that's the beginning of the end in your growth as a human being, and your growth as a human being is everything.

My dad is 78 years old. Two months ago we bought him a computer. First one he's ever had. Last weekend, I taught him how—over the phone, mind you—to go online to a webpage called "Skype" and to video conference. I bet I spent six hours on the phone getting him there, and I'm really proud of him. The whole time I kept telling him, "You know, this is so good for you because you're doing something new. And when we're done, you're going to be able to look at your grandkids and talk to them over the computer for free." And at the end of the day on Sunday, we called [Skyped] each other. He could see my kids. I could see him and my mom.

Talk about change over a guy's lifetime. This is a guy who told me stories about riding to his dad's farm on a horse when he was young.

What are some examples of successful relationships that you've known?

I'm from a family that is very close. Geographically, we're not close—I have a brother in Europe who I consider one of my very best friends, and a sister in Minneapolis. Two of my brothers are my business partners and yet another brother [is] in my same industry. Even though we don't see each other very often, we're very close knit. I'm proud of each and every one of them. They're independent and successful in their careers. That would be my first call of success in relationships.

I also have a wonderful relationship with my wife. I'm very, very proud of her in her career, in being a good mother and in being a good wife. We're watching our kids grow up and I believe they see us as a healthy couple—they know what love is and they see a healthy relationship.

To the next level, I've been blessed in that I am in a business that I own and my business partners are my best friend and two of my brothers. [There are] many other folks that I consider colleagues, friends, and associates. We don't agree on everything. Some days, we don't agree on anything, but we talk it through and move on. I think it's all grounded in respect. You know, we work through issues and we genuinely enjoy being around each other.

What lessons has life taught you about how to achieve success in relationships?

I probably have learned the most from my failures with relationships. As a kid growing up, you say something you shouldn't say; you hurt somebody's feelings. I've had plenty of those learning experiences. You learn really quickly that you need to be careful. It's hard to be honest sometimes, but at the end of the day, that's really the foundation of a good relationship. It's hard to hear the truth and harder yet to tell the truth. But if you don't have a relationship based on that, you really don't have much.

People say, "To tell you the truth," and a lot of times [what follows] isn't the truth. As a kid when I said, "Trust me, Mom and Dad," that probably was a great time *not* to trust me. That is, I think, a huge foundation for success in personal relationships.

What remains for you to achieve in the area of relationships?

Well, lots. I think that the measuring stick for success in relationships is time. My best friend growing up I met in kindergarten, and he was the best man in my wedding. In September, he and his wife are meeting us in Las Vegas and we're going to spend the weekend together. He lives in Decatur, Illinois, and I live in Grand Junction, Colorado. That's a 32-year-old inconvenient relationship. They're wonderful people and I really, truly enjoy their company, but it's hard work. He's busy in his job and so am I; he has a family and I have a family. It's tough.

Even with my own family, it's not easy to spend time together, but you need to because relationships take a lot of work. Even relationships where you live together.

We celebrated my wife's parents' 50th anniversary this summer. Last summer, we celebrated my parents' 50th anniversary. It's our goal [his and his wife's] to celebrate ours someday with our kids. But just because people are in love doesn't mean they're going to make it work. It takes a heck of a lot of work and time is the key.

Going back to when you were growing up on the farm, what did financial success mean to you, and what personal experiences contributed to your understanding of that?

As a young person growing up, success to my family [meant] independence, truly. If you were not financially successful, you could not have independence. During part of my early years, farms were failing; people were losing their farms, and then their independence. During the really bad situations, some people took their lives. Farms were passed down from generation to generation—it's not only a job. That's why they call it a "family" farm. You lived, ate, and breathed that farm.

"Can you keep the farm?" It wasn't tied to a dollar amount such as, "We're going to make $X this year." No, it was tied to, "Can we do the things that we want to do and stay where we want to stay?" That was the measuring stick of financial freedom as a child.

I can remember when I was in high school and things were really getting tough financially on our farm. Some of our very best friends had lost their farms and there was a lot of talk in my family. I think I was the only one still at home. Everybody else was gone to college or married and on their own.

My parents were to the point where they were considering picking another occupation. There was talk of moving to another community. But it simply wasn't an option for me. I don't know if I had a vote or not—if it really came down to it, I'm sure I didn't—but I sure thought I did. I was extremely angry about the possibility of giving up that lifestyle, giving up that farm. It was the anchor, the rock. So, "independence" is my word.

What is your definition of financial success today, and do you think that other people share that view?

Today, my definition is the same. It's tied to different things, but it's the same.

I own my own business, and financial freedom is for that business to remain independent. That means to continue to be able to pay the people that are there working with me every day, to reward the shareholders, including myself, for the risk that they're taking in investing in that business.

At the core, what gets me up in the morning is that I want to provide for my family and for my retirement someday. It all ties into that independence factor. I am a small business owner—"entrepreneur" if you will—and at the end of the day, I make decisions to reward my shareholders [including] myself—so they can provide for their family, their retirement, and their dreams.

In your position as president of the bank, to what extent do you see people who you think are doing a poor job of shepherding their money?

You know, I don't know. You've really got to walk a mile in somebody's shoes. You may be handling your money in a different way than I am. And you may not agree with the way I'm handling my money. But at the end of the day, you've really got to spend a day in my shoes to know why I'm handling my money the way I am. I believe that to the core.

This is the best country in the world to get rich in. We have our problems, but nowhere else can you have the dream of financial independence, the dream of owning your own business, the dream of writing your own book. So I believe there [are] a gazillion different ways to get to that finish line, and I'm going to try really hard not to judge you for taking a different path than I am taking.

What advice can you share about how to achieve financial success?

Believe in yourself, bet on you. That is at the core of my being, financially. I've bought stocks in companies just because somebody told me it was a [good] deal. I'd say, in the high 90% of the time, that's not worked very well for me. However, when I bet on me or something I know a lot about, I usually do really well. Of course, do your research, don't be a fool, don't go headlong into something that you haven't really researched. But bet on yourself. I'll say that I've put my money where my mouth is in that regard: I've worked for Fortune 500 companies but given it all up to roll the dice on me. And that's worked out pretty good for me.

What remains for you to do in the arena of achieving financial success?

Lots. First of all, I have to stay the course. The bank that I helped form is four years old and we've got a long ways to go. We need to continue to grow. We need to continue to take care of our customers and help them grow themselves and their businesses.

Even if I thought I was done and could cash a big check today, I have a 10 year old, a five year old, and a seven year old. Part of financial success is engraining in them financial savvy, engraining in them a work ethic, engraining in them everything that they need to be successful and independent when they're ready. And frankly, I think it's important that they see me going to work every day, that they see me doing things that I'd rather not do, see me toughing it out and working hard in my business, and working hard on my home, and going through the struggles that everybody needs to go through. It's one thing for us to tell our children that they need to get a good job and work hard, and yet have them look at me and say, "Dad, it's 10 o'clock on a Tuesday! Why are you watching cartoons in your underwear today?" That dog won't hunt.

With whom do you most want to share the successes of your life and how are you planning on doing that?

I plan to share the successes of my life with my family, my employees, and the people that helped me achieve that success. You know, I hope that I'm financially successful and can do things for my parents. My brothers and I bought them their first computer. It wasn't a big sacrifice and it wasn't their birthday—it's just [that] we wanted to do it. We wanted them to learn something new, occupy their time, and get on the Skype webpage to talk to us and their grandkids more often.

God willing, someday—if there's more financial success than I can share with the people [that helped me]—I would want to reward the community that helped me be successful. I'm a believer in the local economy. The local business community is probably going to make me financially successful, and that financial success should be returned.

Is there any final thing that you'd like to add?

I grew up in a small town and the only thing to do was go to the movie theater. Every Friday, they'd get a new movie, and that was what you did. All your friends went—all the kids in town were in that theater. It was run by a husband and wife.

One Friday, some friends were sitting a row ahead of me. We were probably being rambunctious kids, and I climbed over the seat in front of me to sit with them—*climbed over*. And the owner of the theatre saw me. He grabbed me by the nape of the neck, dragged me out, called my dad, and explained what had happened. You've got to feel sorry for the guy: it was a husband and wife business; he was trying to keep [it] nice and this rotten kid was climbing over the seats. That wasn't acceptable.

My dad said, "I'll be right there." The guy had [not intended that] my dad [would come] to get me, of course. My dad came and I sat there. And my friends all saw me sitting there. This was not, not good. By the time my dad got there, the guy had realized that he'd probably made a little bigger deal out of this than he should have. I didn't destroy any property. I didn't hurt anybody. I just did the wrong [thing] and I got caught.

So he [my dad] took me home, I went up into my room, and the punishment would be laid out the next day. I had a kind of a sleepless night. The punishment, to make a long story short, was that I was not allowed to go out to the movie or basically anywhere. I was grounded until three unsolicited people came to him and said I was doing something good when they saw me. They couldn't be my friends—it had to be an adult in the normal course of life going to him and saying, "Hey, I saw your son doing something good"—an unsolicited good report.

It's the best punishment I have ever heard of before or since—just basically doing a good deed that would finally, in a small town, get back to my dad. I'll never forget that. It was pretty creative and important. And that's the kind of people that they were and are, and I think that's why their kids have turned out pretty decent.

Mark Zipse

March, 2008

He said, "Well, you know, they're your grades and as long as you feel like you did your best, you don't have anything to be ashamed of." And that's something that has stuck with me to this day, because I didn't do my best.

I think we're heading in to a real recession now, because people spend money that they don't have and they don't know the value of sacrifice.

My father tells this story, and he tells it in front of my mother, about a couple who celebrated their hundredth wedding anniversary. So the press was there, and they asked them, "In all those hundred years, did you ever think about divorce?" And a blank look came over this couple and they said, "Well, no, we would never think about divorce. We've thought about murder a couple of times but we'd never think about divorce."

Mark, when you were growing up, what did you think it meant to be professionally successful and what experiences led you to that definition?

When I was growing up, I don't think I had a clue what it meant to be professionally successful. My parents had jobs, the neighbors had jobs, and I went to school, [and] saw teachers, [who] were working. I did think that I wanted to work with kids. I had good, good teachers and I think that made me want to go into the education profession.

I just had, I thought, terrific teachers. I was in the band. I probably had one of the best band directors you can have, named Marion Jacobs, at Grand Junction High School. I watched him work with groups of students. I played the drums and we, at the back of the band, would say, "We are percussionists," and we'd be fooling around back there, and he would say, "You're not percussionists, you are flat head drummers." We would all laugh about that but he just had a way to work with kids and get them to work together to produce just some great music.

I was influenced probably by the people in our church, and I think service was somehow ingrained in me, and so I just kind of moved in that direction.

Bob Moon, my American Government teacher at Grand Junction High School, probably one of the finest teachers in high school or college that I ever had, inspired me to do better than I thought I could, and really inspired an interest in history and American government, which probably is the reason I became a high school history teacher initially—just that inspiration and a desire to peak my curiosity and to learn more than I knew.

My father [was also an influence. He] was not a yeller or a screamer. If there was a problem, he would pull me aside and we would sit down, usually on the front porch swing, and talk about things that I had done and why I did what I did. To me, that was hard. "Do anything but don't make me sit down and talk about things that I did."

I remember my sophomore report card. I was not a terrific student in high school. I tell people I graduated in the upper 95 percent of my class. Well, you do the math—that means there were only 5 percent below me, but maybe it looks good on the resume.

One time, I brought my report card home and it was not the best and Dad said, "Sit down let's talk about it." And he looked at my report card and he said, "Well, you know, they're your grades and as long as you know or as long as you feel like you did your best, you don't have anything to be ashamed of." And that's something that has stuck with me to this day, because I didn't do my best. It was my dad that inspired me from that point on, not just in academics but [to] "do your best," [even] when you're working on your car or when you're out mowing the lawn. I've not forgotten that.

How does your definition of professional success today compare to other people's definitions of professional success?

I think other people might look at status, or money, or professional gains. I guess I look at success as being happy, doing the job that I've done. I look at success as helping others, service, making a difference in someone's life. To me, being successful is doing a job well and having fun while I'm doing it. I've never had a job where I haven't had fun. I think the satisfaction comes in just doing the job well and hearing someone say, "Hey, thanks for what you did for me."

A student that I had when I was principal at Fruita Monument High School came to us as a freshman. She was into drugs and alcohol and prostitution, and who knows what else. We had a situation, somewhere between Thanksgiving and Christmas, where a couple of kids who had transferred in, lit a cherry bomb and flushed it down the toilet and just exploded the toilet. (That was one of the neatest things I ever saw—the biggest piece of porcelain we found was about the size of 50-cent piece. We had chunks of porcelain embedded in the ceiling!)

As a high school principal, though, I was incensed, because our kids just didn't do that. And so I went over the PA system and [explained what had happened, that] we needed information, and that we were going to offer a reward for any information regarding this incident. This little girl [the freshman student] was up in my office five minutes later and said, "How much is the reward?", and I hadn't even thought about it. I said, "It's $20." She said, "If you'll make it $30 I'll find out who did this." And I said, "You've got to be kidding me. That's extortion." She said, "Well, do you want to know or don't you?" This was a pretty streetwise kid, and I said, "Okay I'll make it $30." She said, "I want half of the money now." I said, "Ooookay, but you better get me good information!"

So, I gave her half the money. Probably within an hour, she was back in my office with the names of the kids who did this, where they got the cherry bomb, who was with them—and from that point on we developed a relationship. She was [not a good] student but she became, in effect, my other assistant principal. If I needed some information I'd go to this girl and say, "What do you know about this? Can you [get] me this information?" And it was a kind of a barter system. She would say, "Could you get this teacher to cut me some slack in attendance because I haven't been coming to school very well?"

For some reason, she came to me and asked for help on an algebra test. And that's really scraping the bottom of the barrel if you came to me for help with math. But we worked on the books, we worked on the answers, reviewed questions, and she passed that algebra test. To me, that was just one of the most tremendous things that I ever did to help this girl.

She didn't graduate with her class. It took her five years to get through high school, but eventually she went to college, got a degree in accounting, and is now a CPA over in Denver. She sent me the greatest letter, which I framed and it's on the wall in my office, saying, "Hey, you really helped me. You made an influence in my life." That's, I think, how a person should determine success.

By your own definition, in what ways are you already a professional success?

I've been a substitute teacher; I've been a high school history teacher; I've been a high school assistant principal; I've been a middle school principal; I've been a high school principal for about ten years; and I've been executive director of human resources for our school district.

I guess I determine success by the challenges and the responsibilities that you're given, and how well you handle those; how well you learn from the challenges and also from mistakes. It's okay to make mistakes as long as you learn from them. I think that's how I would measure success.

Has there been an unexpected cost to achieving success?

There has been. There's that old adage [that] you never want printed on your tombstone, "Gee, I wish I'd spent more time at the office." But I did spend, I thought, an inordinate amount of time in my jobs and I think the time that I spent with my family suffered. I wish I had spent more time with my family, although when you ask them, they'd say, "No, it was okay." But I think I missed a lot by not being home as much as I would want.

What remains unfinished for you in the area of professional success?

I have retired! I've been retired about six months, and I'm still learning how to retire. And I'm starting to do small things: I can go to the bathroom when I want to; I'm learning how to chew my food, and that's been a good thing.

But there's still that little seed or that passion in me that wants to give back, that wants to serve other people, to help other people, and so on. I guess as long as I still have that, I'll be looking for something—something like that to do.

Mark, when you were a youngster, what constituted success in learning and education, and who taught you that?

Grades constituted success in learning but in the beginning I don't think I was challenged. I probably wasn't challenged until I got into college. And, again, those words of my dad came back, "Always do your best."

My first year in college was not really successful and so I took about four years off and went to work for the railroad. I grew up a little bit, not completely—I don't think I've ever grown up. But I came back to college and made the Dean's List the first semester. I'm sure I just flabbergasted my parents when that happened. But then again it's that recording in my mind from my dad, "Always do your best."

What are some keys to achieving success in learning and education that you could pass on to other people?

You need to have fun, do something that interests you, something that peaks your curiosity, that makes you want to learn more. Staying focused, don't give up, always persevere, stay after it, set goals that you think are attainable. But always push the envelope, see if you can do more, just to see if you can do it. But I think that curiosity piece is key. Always have that desire to know more than you know, always want to do more.

How would you say that to a high school student that you observed was not doing what they could?

I think I would say, "find your passion. What is it that really interests you? What is it that excites you? Go in that direction whether it's being an auto mechanic, working with your hands, or figuring out problems. Find your passion, find out what you're really good at, what you like to do, and then pursue that from every direction.

We had a student who was just a whiz at math, came to us from one of our middle schools and I said, "Well, let's do this. You're so good at math. What I'll do is give you the math exam on all of our courses. Let's do the midterm, the final in Algebra, Geometry and on up to Calculus. If you can pass those, we'll give you the credit, send you on to Mesa State [College] and you can do something else while you're still earning credit in high school." He did! He passed all of our math classes and passed them flawlessly. I think there was one mistake on the Calculus test but he said, "That's the wrong answer in the answer key. " We got the teacher and he said, "No, that can't be." So the teacher worked the problem and, "yes," it was the wrong answer in the answer key. We just let him take his passion and run with it and he did well.

Have you experienced kids responding to your remarks about finding their passion with "I don't know" or "I don't know what it would be"?

Sure, we have. [High school] gives you a broad range of areas. You've got English, Math, Science, and Social Studies, but there are other things that you can do with languages, or working with your hands, or working with computers. I think kids just may not know at that point where their passion lies. I think you have to really encourage kids as well. Let them know that they're smart, they're not dumb, they can achieve, they can do things beyond their wildest dreams. They just don't know it yet.

Is there anything remaining unfinished for you in the area of learning and education?

Always. There are always things I would love to learn about. I want to learn a little more about politics. I want to learn about motorcycle mechanics, I've recently purchased and learned to ride a Harley Davidson motorcycle. I want to know a little more about astronomy. I certainly want to learn more about computers. There are a lot of things –probably enough to keep me going until I'm about 97.

> ### *What did financial success mean to you when you were a youngster growing up? And what personal experiences contributed to that understanding?*

That's a good question. I think financial success to me meant sacrifice. I don't know that we were poor, and we certainly weren't rich. I was provided everything I needed; but anything I wanted, I had to earn. That started off with an allowance. My job was to empty the trash and make sure my room was cleaned up. I was encouraged to save but I could spend a little bit.

As I got older, I learned that I needed to work if I wanted to have things. I got jobs mowing lawns so I could earn money for a season pass at the Lincoln Park pool, mowed more lawns and saved money, made that sacrifice and bought my first set of wheels—a Schwinn bicycle.

Then I learned that if I wanted a car, I had to earn it. And so I got a job after school, a paper route. In high school I worked for the Daily Sentinel in the press room as an after-school job and earned the money.

And I think you also have to set priorities. What I mean is set reasonable parameters. My first car was a '63 Volkswagen. It wasn't a '63 Mercedes Benz. It was basic transportation. I learned the value of saving money, the value of managing money and how to sacrifice to get the things you want.

> ### *What do you think it means, today, to be financially successful? And do you think most other people share that view?*

To me, being financially successful means having no debt. I'm financially successful. The home we live in is paid for, our kids have gone through college, I pay off my credit cards every month.

Steve Gammill

But in terms of other people's perception of financial success, I'd say mine probably differs. I think we're heading in to a real recession now because people spend money that they don't have and don't know the value of sacrifice. Work hard and save your money, don't waste it, be fairly conservative and don't spend money that you don't have. Learn the value of sacrifice. You can do that with your finances and you can do it with your time.

We've talked about this [retirement] with our children because they all have told us Social Security is not going to be there when they're ready to retire and I think they're right.

We've told our kids to do research,—really do your homework—talk to people and not necessarily stock brokers or financial people, talk to people who aren't out to make money but who you feel are really there to help you. Learn about interest bearing bonds and stocks and other investments that will carry you through. Don't put all of your eggs in one basket. Don't go out and spend all your money on gold stocks. Gold is great right now but it'll decline. Spread things around and take responsibility for your own investments and learn from your mistakes.

What are some examples of successful relationships that you've known?

My parents were married for 54 years. I think that's a pretty solid example. I have been married to my wife for almost 30. Relationships are important. Everyone in my extended family, grandparents, aunts, uncles all [stayed] married to [their original spouse]. My parents gave us a great example how to love each other, how to get through tough times.

My father tells this story, and he tells it in front of my mother, about a couple who celebrated their 100th wedding anniversary. So the press was there, and they asked him, "In all those hundred years, did you ever think about divorce?" And a blank look came over this couple and they said, "Well, no, we would never think about divorce. We've thought about *murder* a couple of times but we'd never think about divorce." But I've had great examples about how to maintain a relationship and hopefully we've passed that on to our children as well.

Can you recall an example of when you passed some of that on to your children?

There's a quote that says, "The greatest gift a man can give his children is to love their mother." We've tried to hold to that standard for our kids and, hopefully, they'll pass that on to their children.

Our faith is important to us. It's probably the glue that holds the marriage together, a pretty solid relationship with God. That means that prayer is important, it means always asking for guidance, asking for help.

This actually goes back to my father and I didn't realize how important it was until just now. During that first year in college, that tough year, I had a conversation with my dad. "I'm struggling with this class, I'm struggling with tests." I was kind of struggling with life. I think everybody goes through a period like that. I said, "I wonder if there's really a God?," and my dad said, "That's a good question," and he said, "you need to keep questioning your faith and as you do that, you'll find that the answers will come." And he was so right about that. It's just been a real strong central point in our marriage and in our family.

Tell me about your relationship with your children.

My wife brought two children into the marriage when they were young. Then we had another one. We've tried to treat them all the same, recognizing that they each have individual talents.

When they're small, they're just fun and loving. Then they cross over to the dark side when they turn 13 and it's like living with a 13 or 14 year-old insane person.

But then along about the end of the senior year, things smooth out a little bit and you're okay. We hit a couple of speed bumps with our son, who was the middle child. But I've never met a kid who didn't eventually figure it out and turn out to be okay. He's now a tech for Harley-Davidson in Dallas. He loves what he's doing. He's good at it, very successful. We've talked about that a lot with him. We have a daughter who is Personnel Director for a company in Washington, D.C. Our youngest daughter is a graduate of Colorado State University.

She's back in Washington, D.C., loves to travel. She's also very curious. They're all pretty curious. They all want to learn more.

Tell me something that you most admire or respect or love about each of your individual children.

Amy, our oldest, is a workaholic, takes on more than she probably should. She's a great mother, a great wife. She is very smart—they're all very smart—but she is just a go-getter. She wants to do her job well. She's taken on a full professorship in a college, in addition her other job and [being] a mother as well. I don't know how she does that but she does.

Kirk loves to work with his hands. He has a passion for motorcycles, has loved motorcycles since he was little. Loves to work on them and he is so good at it.. That's what I really love and respect about Kirk: he has found what he's passionate about. That's just been a rewarding experience.

Buzzy, our youngest, Elizabeth— you teach your kids to be independent and I'll be darned if they don't turn out just the way you taught them. She is the independent one. She had a job in Washington, D.C. and decided that she wanted to learn Spanish. So, she quit her job, and on her own, she went to Peru to find a foreign language school, spent her own money. Lived there for four months and learned Spanish.

I got a call from her, must have been 2 o' clock one morning. She said, "Dad, I just got into an argument in Spanish with a cab driver and I won." I said, "Well, there you are. You've come of age."

She's backpacked through Bolivia and Chile. She's been on five of the seven continents and I expect her to travel to the other two. I got a call from her. I was home for lunch and she was going to school in Spain. She called and said, "Guess where I am?" I said, "Where are you?" she said, "Africa." "What are you doing in Africa?" "Get your map out, Dad. Morocco is just across the street from Portugal. So, I'm in Africa."

She's our traveler. She's creative with her hands. She's our artist. I don't think she's found her niche yet, and maybe she never will but, she has that curiosity. They all have.

Amy takes classes. She has two masters degrees, a Ph. D. and wants to learn more. Kirk, our motorcycle mechanic, has gone to Arizona and different places around the Country to learn more about motorcycle mechanics. I think they've found their passions and they're curious.

Mark, when you were growing up, what did you learn to regard as personal success, and how do you think you came up with that definition?

I think personal successes is doing something that rewards you or gives you personal satisfaction. Certainly, in my career and also as a parent and a husband, I've enjoyed every minute of it. There are no manuals that they give you when you leave the hospital with your children. You just kind of learn by trial and error. I've been successful in the career area and in the relationships with my children and my wife.

As you think about your own personal success, what remains unfinished?

Just that spark in me that wants to serve other people. I haven't been retired that long so I don't know what direction that's going to go. But I've always had a career where I felt like I've made a difference in other people's lives, helped lift them up, helped make them better than they were or better than they thought they were. To me that just gives me the greatest satisfaction.

Looking at your life as a whole, what areas of accomplishment give you the greatest satisfaction?

Probably in this order: marriage, children, and career. My wife and I are each other's best friends. I have just been blessed with the incredible gift of this woman who just accepts me for who I am and for what I am. It's just been a phenomenal marriage. If there was a perfect marriage I would point to mine.

Children obviously come after the marriage. Just to see them be successful and try to help them as much as we can.

And the career. I've been blessed to be around some wonderful people. I've had some great kids in all the schools where I've been a principal, and [then] the last job I had in education, being a human resources director, was to help teachers feel valued, and to provide the best quality teachers we could find to educate our children.

I didn't realize when I became a principal or an HR director how much counseling you do with people and how much listening you have to do. I feel good about the contacts that I've made with people.

How do you think one goes about empowering teachers and making them feel valued?

Teaching is a profession that for some reason has not been as valued as it should be. I tell kids who are coming into the profession to "think back to when you went to school, who's the best teacher you've ever had? That's the person you want to model. That's the person that you want to emulate."

We have so many good teachers. In my experience at both schools [where] I was principal, at West Middle School and at Fruita Monument High School, I saw just some fantastic, dedicated teachers who really cared about students. The problem is we don't tell those people enough what a terrific job they're doing. But people want [to hear], and I certainly wanted to have a conversation with of all my teachers and say, "You know I watch you in the classroom, you are on top of it. You know what you're doing. You are really good at what you do. You're a master teacher." Some principals don't tell that to their staff.

Time is a valuable part of what we do. Teachers would really appreciate having more time to learn something in their field. So, I did what I could to send teachers to conferences and bring their knowledge back and share it with us.

I have been at the births of many teachers' children. I've been at their weddings, I've been at the funerals of their parents. I've been in the hospital when they've had illnesses. I've helped teachers move out of their classrooms. That relationship is critical and not only with teachers but also with kids. I tell teachers that 90% of education is the relationship you have with that kid in that classroom. If you don't have a good relationship with them, they won't learn from you. I feel the same way with staff. If they don't have a good relationship with me, it's going to be rocky. I've had employees [situations] where we didn't necessarily see eye to eye, but the door was always open and they could always come to me and say, "Why did you do this? What were you thinking?" They need to know that it is okay to come in and say that.

I'd [go and] help the cooks make cinnamon rolls and we'd just talk and have fun. I'd shovel the sidewalks and mop the halls with my custodians. It's important that they see that we're all in this together. We're here to help kids and I think it's the relationship that's so important. It was my goal to have a personal, quality relationship with every staff member that I've worked with. And, of course, you need humor to be successful in any relationship.

I had just become principal at West Middle School. At that time, the superintendent had meetings. We were divided into areas and so we'd have meetings with a group of principals at a school. Once, in October, it was my turn to host a meeting. I was just kind of making a tour of the school, making sure everything was just right. I was a brand new principal, and wanted everything to look really good. I came back to my office about 10 minutes before the meeting and somebody had just trashed my office.

They'd taken this little can of spaghetti string and just squirted it all—I mean it had string hanging from the ceiling and my bookshelves. I backed my secretary up against the wall and I said, "I want to know who did this." She said, "Well, it's Tom Lisco."

Tom Lisco was probably the best sixth grade teacher I have ever seen but he's a practical joker. So we took care of it. I found another place for the meeting and I didn't say anything to Tom.

I went down to the newspaper and took out a classified ad on Thursday to run that weekend. I put his three-bedroom house up for sale for $50,000 and put his phone number in it. It was just great. Of course, his phone just rang off the hook. He took the phone off the hook and then the realtors were coming by and knocking on his door, wanting to see the house.

And you know what, I never had another problem with Tom for the rest of that year.

Herb Bacon

July 28, 2008

Right at the time of the big bust, Dad started this bank. Three banks in the little town had all gone broke. He told how [his bank] would take the currency—the money and silver, a lot of silver—and pile it on a table out in the open, behind the tellers. The farmers would come in. They had a pot bellied stove in the lobby and they'd come in. In the winter, you know, it's cold. They've got to get warm. But, the [real] reason they were coming in was to make sure there was money in the bank.

I remember people going, from particularly Oklahoma, across Kansas on their way to California, coming to the backdoor— knocking on the door, needing food. And my mother making sandwiches and things for them to carry on their trip. That makes an impression that you don't forget.

The estate tax, if you're not careful, will eat up your estate. ... in many cases by setting up a charitable or a remainder uni- trust, (for example: [a part]to charity and [a part] to the estate) we could end up paying a [smaller] estate tax. Because otherwise all you do is just give the money to the federal government to spend—which they don't have any difficulty in doing. This way, the family has some control over where the money is going

> **Herb, when you were growing up, what did you think it meant to be professionally successful and what experiences led you to think that?**

Well, I think, Steve, basically being able to take care of a family and be able to participate in the community in some kind of a responsible

- 29 -

position. I thought that was a part of success. I thought that because that was the way my father operated, and I think he was a good role model. That's where I got the idea—didn't read that in a book.

At an early age, he helped [me] find something to do for neighbors— yard work and things like that, for example. I grew up during the Depression, in the 1930s. It was a tough period. People were having a hard time making a living, and with that example and following what he was telling me, it seemed like the thing to do—get in and do something.

What is your definition of professional success as you look at the world today?

To be able to have a responsible job and to respond to the needs of others that you're working with. I was working at a bank, as you know, for a good many years. People came to me for guidance and help and I took it seriously. In most cases, it worked out. I never made a bad loan—some went bad after I made them, but most people are honest, trustworthy, and hardworking. Some are maybe a little slick but that's the way it is. That's how I related to the community and helping people.

My definition of success today is being able to work with the community. I worked in the bank: that's part of it, but that's not your whole life. You need to spread yourself out and deal with different agencies and groups of people. A lot of those things you can't put in terms of dollars and cents. It's a matter of the welfare of people and helping them to get ahead and take care of their needs.

Given that definition, in what ways are you a professional success?

The way I have performed has been to be a friend to people [so they will] feel comfortable that they can trust me, that they can rely on me to try and help them. That, I think, is a professional requirement. Just as I mentioned earlier, life isn't just a matter of making money: it's a matter of serving other people. Life is a two-way street. With customers, you hopefully will benefit and, by the same token, they'll benefit. When you look at the community at large, there are people out there that need help, and if you're able financially to do something, you should step up and do what you can to help others.

What remains unfinished for you in achieving professional success, if anything?

Well, I look at the many projects that I've been involved in in the community, and none of them are ever really finally finished. If it's a building, there's something else that has to be done for it; if it's a service, the needs may change. It's in flux all the time. I don't envision [that] anything that I have done or will do is ever going to be completely finished. Life isn't that cut and dried. You need to kind of ride with the tide. Conditions change. Economics are a big factor in our way of life. We've been through booms and busts here, and we've seen people come and go. Some have really suffered, and we try to help the best we can. Right now, we're in a very strong economy. How long it'll last? Nobody knows.

When we moved here in '48, the uranium thing was still going, of course, and on through the '50s. And then that quit and our economy went down. Oil shale came in 1980 and we were flying [high], and two years later, it quit and the bottom fell out. It took us 10 years, in our business, to recover from that. That was devastating, as well you know. Many individual people and businesses went broke. That's just the way it is.

Now, we're in a different cycle with the oil and gas thing. The economy is moving way up, and we both know that the energy thing can go up and down. I think that's for sure.

Why do you think you were able to successfully weather the bust that you were just talking about?

A great deal of it was the fact that my father had been through the Great Depression back in the '30s in business. He knew enough to be very cautious all along, even when things were booming. Also, at that point, we had become part of a major holding company and had some [financial] backing from that area. The combination [of my Dad's stories and that financial support] helped us through that period. I think it points out that nobody can survive by themselves,

31

no matter what business they're in. You've got to have customers, and in many cases, you need associates. But I think that the success of our operation, in that difficult period, was good, sound planning and cautious business practices going back a long ways. Those are things you don't read about in a book.

You mentioned that many projects aren't really completed. Can you give us an example of something like that?

St. Mary's Hospital, as we both know, is a very major institution in Grand Junction. It started in 1896. We weren't here then, of course. My first project for them was in 1959, and since then, I bet they've had at least seven or eight major projects. They'd had three or four before 1959. The project that is going on now will be finished in about 18 months [and] will almost double the size of the hospital—and that's not the end of it. If you look at a diagram of the various additions on that hospital, it's just like looking at a puzzle. I mean, there are just pieces all over. We have a building, a 507,000 square-foot building, and we're adding a twelve storey addition that will be almost 500,000 square feet. But when they get through, they will tear down a portion of the old hospital. It won't be immediate, but eventually, that'll happen. It just keeps evolving. Needs change. Medicine has changed.

I look at it as a project from my own personal standpoint. I've been on the foundation board and I've been on the operating board, off and on, for all these years. I've been helping them with their projects, raising money— which is a never-ending process—for almost 50 years, so I'll use that as an example.

It's much, much more than just a building. The Sisters of Charity, of course, are the main operators of all this. My family has been Methodists for years, but I work closely with the Sisters, a Catholic organization, and it's worked perfectly well. It makes you realize that although we may have different beliefs, there's one central source in this, and that's God Himself. And the Sisters fit that bill, and our Methodist background ties in with it. The services that we each conduct in our respective churches is probably different and yet very much the same.

The board probably has a half a dozen religions represented on it and has people from all walks of life. It's been that combined with a strong belief and guidance from the Sisters—and it's worked. It's been an honor to work on it.

That group [the Sisters] is something else. They've got, I think, eight hospitals that they own and operate. Yet, the local board has, I would say, 90% control of what they're doing. [Some] things, in fairness, have to be overseen by the Sisters, but they pretty much let us [operate it].

When you were a young child or a young man, what constituted success in learning and education? And who taught you that?

Well, I was born and raised in the small town of Bird City, Kansas. There were 98 kids in the school—14 in my graduating class. The teachers were very, very dedicated. They probably didn't have all of the background training that today they would have. But they were dedicated to teaching.

My family—and this was true with all of the students—wanted to make sure that you learned how to read and write and math and history and [had] the basics. It was very important.

My father had an eighth-grade education. He became a school teacher. In the early days, they would go to a vocational—or "normal"— school for teachers. My father taught in a one-room schoolhouse for a number of years. I had an aunt who did the same thing, and so did my mother. They were very eager to get any kind of education.

I went on from Bird City to the University of Colorado. I got out of high school in early June and went to CU to summer school. It was in 1947, right after the second World War.

The veterans that were coming in put real pressure on enrollment. So they [the school] said they'd let me in, providing I could cut it. I could go to summer school and if I could pass, I could go to school. And I did. But it was touch and go.

As I look around, anybody that's been a success has to have a certain amount of education. It doesn't just happen.

Today, what do you think that it means to be successful in learning and education?

Well, you have to stay abreast of what's coming in the computer field in many ways. I'm computer illiterate—I've just never really gotten into that. But I can see that, for a young person, it's vital. They can't operate without it.

I do think that [people are] overlooking a lot of basics that they really need. But I don't have the answer to how you crank all that into the system. I think they get so carried away with the magic of the computer that they overlook some of the basic things of math and science.

The Math Center—you're familiar with John McConnell. [editor's note: see John's chapter in this book] John has been very concerned that the schools aren't teaching math and science. And they aren't. They've put it into the computer and there's more to it than that.

If I had to go back to school now, I'd have to start from scratch. But it's pretty important. That's what's made our country what it is today—education.

In what ways are you a success in learning and education?

I don't know how successful I have been, but I have used my knowledge and my training to move ahead in the banking field for 39 years. And I've tried to extend that into the various groups and agencies that I work with in the community.

I can tell you from experience what works and what doesn't work. I think that's a degree of success in itself. A lot of people are very intelligent, but they're not very practical. You've got to have a happy medium: you need to be astute, but you also have to have good judgment. I don't pretend that I'm always right, but I try to be careful in making decisions. I have to rely on what I've learned and what I've experienced.

Can you think of some keys to achieving success in learning and education that you might pass on?

Well, it's not just going to come to you out of the air. You've got to go to class, you've got to read, you've got to do assignments and you've got to pay attention. It means you've got to make an effort and be sincere and work on it, and realize that you don't have all the answers.

I see that when I'm working with different businesses, for example. You can judge their success sometimes in what they're telling you or what they're doing. And sometimes, you can sense that they're not really going in the right direction. I think that you need to be honest and tell people, "Now, wait a minute. Maybe that isn't the best way to do that." Or, "Here is…" and then make a suggestion. Some people are not going to listen and sometimes, of course, I'm not right and they are.

Is there anything left in the area of learning and education that you feel is unfinished for you?

We travel quite a bit. It's one thing to read about something in a book. But to actually go in to a completely foreign country and spend some time and see the people and see how they live, I'll never get enough of that.

We were in Botswana most recently, in Africa, and our group, the company that we were with, had arranged with the Sans tribe. They pretty much control the Kalahari, which is the big desert area of Botswana. The government [to a large extent] turns this area over to the local people. And they had 15 of these people from one group staying with us for about four days. We were in tents, a mobile tent camp. They put their camp up. We were in regular tents. We had cots. We weren't sleeping on the ground, but it was pretty basic. They fixed their own huts with limbs and grass and slept on the ground.

They are gatherers and hunters. They don't farm. They go out everyday and find what they're going to eat. They still hunt with bow and arrow; they use poison arrows and the women don't wear any tops. The men don't wear much either. Most of them were barefoot. Some wore sandals.

We went out with them everyday [just] to see what they were doing. They would find plants. They knew what they were. They'd dig them up. What they wanted was the root, the tuber. They ate nuts and berries, but porcupine was the thing they really liked.

They didn't speak English and were very friendly. There was one young man that wasn't with their tribe but could interpret for them. They were just living the way they lived. There are no fat ones in there—if they don't find anything that day, they don't eat. It's as simple as that.

There was one man in the group that they said was 92 years old —and he may well have been. He was pretty excellent. There was a wide range.

One night, they built this big bonfire and put on a dance for us. They danced and they sang. Those people were living like they have for a thousand years—happy and relatively healthy, as far as I [could] tell.

The one bad habit that they really had was smoking (and we see that as we travel around the world.) There were some berries that they would grind up and use to smoke. There were two guys with us that worked for the Company. They had regular cigarettes. All they had to do was to give [the locals] a pack of cigarettes and they were just in heaven. The Cancer Society hadn't been there yet but, despite that, they really were pretty healthy and very friendly. It was an experience I will never forget.

We went to Uganda a few years ago to see the mountain gorillas. They are very endangered. There's only about 600 of them left in the world. We saw them.

And we were in Bhutan a few years ago, before the king turned things over. It's this tiny, tiny country—not as big as Mesa County— between India and China. The only reason it exists is as a buffer. Either India or China could walk through there in one day and take it over, but they don't.

I had read about the king, King Wangchuck [Jigme Singye Wangchuck]. Of his grandfather, his father, and him, he's the one that decided that they needed to do something other than having a monarchy. He pushed for a regular government and the vote. He had a hard time selling it, but he was very revered and it worked [so far].

Southeast Asia is extremely interesting. We were in Vietnam and little was mentioned about the war. When it was, it wasn't the *Vietnam* War: it was the *American* War. And of course, they came out on top. It's amazing how that country has moved.

We've visited Cambodia, Thailand, Laos. A lot of people think you're crazy going to places like that, but we never had any problems with it.

These are things you can't get out of a book. You can see it on a screen, but being there and walking on the streets with them or out with the Sans tribe makes a real impression.

The one really special thing about travel is that it makes you appreciate Grand Junction. When you get home, you realize how lucky we are. That's been my way of improving or extending my education.

Tell us more about your travel experiences.

In Bhutan, their big sport is archery. So this one day, they took us to a big meet. There were around 3,000 people there lining this field. When we drove in, I saw this white Toyota Land Cruiser sitting there. On the license, it just said, "Bhutan." And I thought, "Yeah, the king's here."

I looked over at a distance of 150 yards, and there was this guy in this white robe. The king tells the people what they're going to wear. The men wore a kind of pantaloon-type thing and blouse-like deal, and the women wore a long dress. Here they were out there in this field, shooting these arrows. And they had these gals out there—the cheerleaders, I guess. They all had these dresses that almost went to the ground, and they're doing this dance. The guys would shoot the arrow and there would be guys at the other end. If it was a good shot, they'd all jump and yell; if it wasn't, they'd all turn their back. It was just an experience to be in the middle of all this stuff.

One place [where] we were was behind this hotel. I walked around [it] and there was a group of people sitting on the grass, a family. And I was taking pictures, and all at once, this young boy walked up to me and kept pointing at my camera. Finally, I realized, he wanted me to take a picture of them. So I got all of them together, like you're taking a picture at Christmas. There were little kids and old people, and I took their picture. I was using film, not digital. I took the picture and then I realized he wanted a copy. He came over and I said, "How many do you need?" He said, "Eleven." When I got home, I sent him 11 copies.

One day, I was going down this street in one of these towns and there was a woman sitting on the curb with four or five kids. She kept pointing at my camera. I realized she wanted me to take her picture. So I took a picture of her with all these kids. I never could get her name straight. But I did take a picture of the store she was sitting in front of. I sent the pictures back to that [store]. I guess she got them—I don't know.

In Bhutan, they do everything in open markets. They're selling everything under the sun: meat, vegetables, skin, dogs—you know, whatever. We came in from India to get into Bhutan. There was only one road in. We came in the early evening and it was raining. There was a big gateway that said, "India" and "Bhutan."

Early the next morning, it dawned on me that I didn't get a picture of that gate. So I got up that morning and went out and it was still raining. And it wasn't more than 100 yards from [that gate to] where we were staying across into India. So I went into India and there were people, cows wandering around, and it was a great sight—and I took a bunch of pictures of the gate and all, and I started back through. [Suddenly], four Bhutanese soldiers walked around me and pointed and took me into this building. I didn't have my passport and nobody knew where I was. I had gotten up that morning and just left. These guys didn't speak English, of course. I kept pointing at the hotel; finally, they just told me to go! But I thought I was going to be stuck there forever. It was a little spooky, because nobody knew where I was and nobody around spoke any English.

There were only three of us in the group, and we realized that this was monsoon time, and the roads, with the rockslides and all, were really bad. And we started to leave that morning. This was also a time that India and Pakistan were threatening each other with nuclear bombs. Well, everybody in our group canceled except a lady from Omaha, who would always travel with this Company. She still wanted to go, and they called us: "Well, she wants to go. Do you want to go?" I know that they wished that I'd say we didn't want to go, but I talked to Laura [my wife] and we said, "You know, it's pretty remote that they're going to do that bomb. If they do, they do." So we said, "Sure, we'll go."

They had two small cars made in India. It didn't look like they had enough power, but they did. [We were] held up early that morning because of the slide, so we waited, I guess, about an hour and a half or two hours, but finally, we started up. It was like going over Douglas Pass, only this is wet and it's slick and it's sliding. So anyway, we went around, got up to where we needed to go across—and we're not going. Vehicles from each way are stopped. There's a slide in-between.

This Namgay [a Bhutanese owned tour company employee] was the guide that we had. He was a Bhutanese and a nice guy. He said, "Come with me and I'll show you what we're looking at." Not quite that clearly, but he spoke reasonably good English. We went over and looked, and I'm telling you—I mean, there were rocks a lot bigger than this table [where I am sitting with you] just all over the road. And he said, "This is the only way you're going to get in. The only way we can do it is if you'll walk across. We'll carry your bags and I'll get a car. I'll come from the other side and we can go on."

Well, we pondered that for a while, and this gal from Omaha and Laura and I said, "Okay." So we climbed over all these rocks. We just got across, and it slid again. Our Namgay and an American guy that was also with us were on the other side with the luggage. I had no idea where they were, except they were in-between. Fortunately, they hadn't started to cross when that happened. But I tell you it got pretty quiet, and then we realized nobody got hurt. But these rocks came cascading down. I got pictures of that deal—these cars sliding around in that mud and those rocks. Anyway, we made it.

When we left, we flew out of a place called "Paro," the only airport in the country. At that time, they flew twice a week and used a small British jet. They flew from there to Delhi in India.

I had 40 rolls of film and had read that their x-ray equipment was the worst in the world. It absolutely would destroy your negatives. I told this to Namgay. "I got all this film, and I've got to get it through there and I can't run it through that machine." "Don't worry," he said. "Don't worry. I'll take care of it."

So, okay, we get through the airport. We're in line and I'm next and he disappeared. He was no place to be seen. I had two film bags and the guy took them and just dumped the film on the conveyor. He pointed as it was going through—he didn't speak English. I was just distraught—we spent all this time and all that film is ruined and gone. On the other side there was a guy standing there laughing. He spoke a little English and had heard all this commotion. I said, "What's so funny?" He said, "There's no machine in there."

And all it was was this conveyor belt and all these lights blinking on and off. Our Namgay guy told me not to worry about it, but he forgot to tell me *why* not to worry about it. And that's part of my education, give or take.

What are some examples of successful relationships that you've known?

Relationship is what it's all about. Again, as I mentioned earlier, we don't live by ourselves. Family relationship is extremely important, very basic. I had a strong family background and I try to convey the same thing to our own kids.

Relationships in business are [extremely important], too. If you don't have a good rapport with your employees, you can tell them what you want to tell them but they're not going to get a lot done. I think that goes all the way through your life: if you can relate to people and make them comfortable and you can be friends, life goes a lot better for everybody. When you deal with a customer, they're not just a number: they're a person. They've got a family. They've got needs. You need to kind of feel a part of that and have an understanding of what makes them tick, what's important to them.

I watched my father. He was good at that. But family relationship is number one, and then you go from there to the business, to working with community organizations. When you get into a community organization of some type, you find a different assortment of people and relationships are different, but still important. The more you try to relate to people and become involved with them and understanding them, things go better.

What examples have you seen in your travels, in other cultures, that stand out to you?

I think we could sense that as we traveled in almost any place. There's a father and a mother and the kids, and they hang together, so to speak. Relationship is a natural phenomenon. People tend to relate.

What are some keys or some tips that you might give to your grandchildren, or even your children

at their ages, about how to be successful in relationships?

I would try to convey to them to be considerate of people; to be respectful, patient; don't be too "jump-in" on everything. Don't be critical. Try to play ball with them. Everybody is not the same, and family backgrounds are different.

When you were a youngster growing up in Kansas, what did financial success mean to you and what personal experiences contributed to that understanding?

I think I mentioned my father giving me every opportunity to work for the neighbors, to cut the lawn and get a little money. I was urged to save a little of that. The big thing that we had when I was growing up in Kansas was the farms. And so—when I got big enough that I could work for a farmer and drive a tractor, work in the harvest—it was a good experience. I knew one thing: I didn't want to spend the rest of my life on a tractor. But we made pretty good money for the times and learned to use it wisely and save a little now and then.

I think I was paid $5 a day for regular farming operations, and in harvest, I got $10 a day which then was pretty good money. I liked to convert some of my earnings in those days to silver dollars. I wish I had kept some of those. Working on a wheat farm was a good experience.

We'd go to work at sun-up and we'd quit when the sun went down. It was hard work,—really was—and hot. Harvest was really brutal. I always drove a tractor and they didn't have any cover. I didn't wear a shirt. I didn't wear a hat—bad deal. I've paid for it since.

The guy I worked for, for a number of years, worked inside the steering house on the combine—that was right behind me—and where he was [was] above me. And of course, there was no radio, so when he needed to get my attention, he just reached in the bin and got a handful of wheat and threw it and hit me in the back of the head to get me to turn around.

People laugh at Bird City. It was a small town with 750 people. Everybody knew everybody. The switchboard for the town was in Mrs. Warfield's living room, which was about two blocks from our house. So you'd crank the phone and she'd come on and you'd tell her who you wanted and she'd plug it in, or she'd say, "Well, they're in so-and-so's house," or she'd say, "Well, your mother's looking for you." It didn't hurt me any. I think it was an advantage in many respects, because you had a whole community that you felt a part of and you were known. I think I was lucky in that respect.

What do you think it means today to be financially successful?

So much of it is related to material things, which bothers me to say—you know, the big cars and the big house. Somehow, "success" has to be modified to give real meaning to "success." I think, as I pointed out, trying to relate to community needs is what I look to. If I can help people do a little better, feel a little better [through] health, [and] education and if I can help improve the lives of people in general, that's success as far as I'm concerned. Being able to say you've got a lot of money just doesn't cut it. But a lot of people feel [otherwise].

In a lot of these fund drives that I work on, I see people that I know have got a lot of money. Getting money out of them is just like pulling teeth. But somebody that has really had a tough time will come through and give a pretty substantial gift. That's people. People will come up [to the Christmas bell ringers] and give a dollar or 50 cents. You look at them and know that it wasn't easy. And then, somebody else walks by, they can give $100, and looks the other way.

How have your travels over your life and the experiences of other cultures impacted your definition of financial success?

You can just see it in these other countries. Take India, for example. A very few people are extremely wealthy and a zillion people are dirt poor. You can tell that the extremely wealthy people don't really relate to [the poor] well. They could help a lot, but I don't think they do. The poverty across the world—it's tough—Africa particularly.

But India—I don't know. We've been in India, I guess, three different times. It's not a fun trip, but it's a fascinating trip. You really see the extremely wealthy and the extremely poor right there.

China has a few really wealthy people now and they've got a lot that aren't. I just think the day is coming when they're going to have a real donnybrook. And I think they realize that and they're trying to think how to avoid it.

The health [care issues are] pretty tough. That's why we should appreciate things like St. Mary's Community Hospital and Family Health West. We should be very thankful for that. Most of the world doesn't have that.

What advice can you share about how to achieve financial success?

Keep your nose clean, work hard, and do the best you can. I don't know what else to tell you. Don't take advantage of people and play it fair and square.

One of the ways that I'm hearing that you've achieved financial success is by giving it away.

I think that's true.

Looking at your life as a whole, what areas of accomplishment give you the greatest satisfaction?

There's a certain degree of success in my working in the bank. But I think I get more satisfaction out of seeing something come about [from] working with a community project. There's just something about it. You can't—you just can't relate to dollars and cents on everything. There's more to it. The people factor is so important.

What do you still want to achieve or accomplish in the time you have left?

I just want to be able to keep doing what I can as long as I can. I don't see dropping out of sight as long as I'm able. If somebody wants me to help and it makes sense, I would want to try and do it.

But there is a limit and I'm starting to run into that. I don't have as much energy as I used to have. It's more difficult to do some of these things. And the travel is great, but we're reaching a point where we can't keep doing that much longer. On our Botswana trip, we were the oldest couple. I can remember when we were the youngest. Reality is there and you have to face up to that. You pick up the paper and you read about some old person and you realize you're five, ten years older than they are. It's just the way it is.

With whom do you most want to share the successes of your life?

With my family. That's kind of what it's all about. My daughter is on the board of the Western Colorado Community Foundation. She's getting the message—understanding about doing that sort of thing and she's enjoying it.

We both [Laura and I] went to the University of Colorado. [She's really] my life partner—and a good one. I was a year ahead of her. Her family is interesting. They were from North Park. Her father was farming a big ranch up there. They moved to Denver and he ran a small hotel. She went to East High in Denver and then went to Boulder [University of Colorado], and we got acquainted.

As an interesting aside, from a family standpoint and hard times, my father started the bank in Bird City in 1929—opened it November 1st of '29. I wasn't on the scene then. I came along in January of 1930. Right at the time of the big bust, Dad started this bank. Three banks in the little town had all gone broke. He told how [his bank] would take the currency—the money and silver, a lot of silver—and pile it on a table out in the open, behind the tellers. The farmers would come in. They had a pot-bellied stove in the lobby and they'd come in. In the winter, you know, it's cold. They've got to get warm. But, the [real] reason they were coming in was to make sure there was money in the bank.

And he made it. Most of the banks around him went broke, but he set a pretty good pattern to follow on how he judged people and how he operated. I've never forgotten that story.

He was a good judge of people—a better judge than I am. He could figure out a weak link in some people that I didn't always see. But he was always pushing me as far as school is concerned, because he didn't have an opportunity like I did. I don't know what he could've done if he really had a chance. But time marches on.

What remains unfinished for you in your life?

[Let me begin by tying] in my family background a little more.

My parents died in 1981 and, prior to that, we did a lot of estate planning. And they decided it was okay to take part of their estate and establish a family foundation to continue charitable giving indefinitely. So in 1981, we established the E.L. & Oma Bacon Foundation.

We had five children at that time and had all of them as members of the board. Since then, one son is deceased, but four members of that group are still on the board. I had an older brother, LeRoy, who died in 1983 and when his widow, Wilma, died in 1990, we established another family foundation, the LeRoy & Wilma Bacon Foundation, and we put all of our kids on that board. My wife and I stepped aside and thought this would give them more of a chance to do their thing.

We [later] realized that both foundations basically were doing the same thing, and since it was a family situation, we decided in 1994 that we would merge the two foundations. Well, life just isn't that simple, and the IRS had to approve the merger. They apparently had not dealt with this particular type of situation and it dragged on and on.

And finally Dan Vogel, a local CPA who had worked with both foundations, worked with the IRS, and they finally allowed him to draft what he thought would work for the merger. Believe it or not, they approved what he came up with. So in 1996, the two foundations were merged and became the Bacon Family Foundation.

The four children remained on that board [along with] my wife, Laura May, and I. We have an outside director to give a little diversification. That is Pat Gormley, a close personal friend who has lived in Grand Junction his whole life. So that's the make up of the foundation.

It's geared for philanthropy. We donate monies primarily to Mesa County, but we go outside of that throughout the Western Slope and, on occasion, we've made donations on the Eastern Slope of Colorado in conjunction with foundations that are established over there; and they, in turn, have tended to come back and help us on this side. So it's been a good arrangement.

This gives us an indefinite period of charitable giving. We've established what we think is a lasting thing that is effective and productive, helpful to others for years to come. My wife and I have it set up in our own estates so that a major portion will go to the Bacon Family Foundation. And I hope that our children will do somewhat the same thing when their time comes.

What are some of the causes that the foundation has contributed to and how do you decide those?

Well, we're pretty broad on that. We've supported St. Mary's Hospital, The Hospice Hilltop, Mesa State College, and other schools. We've worked with indigent people. We've worked with Partners which works with disadvantaged or problem youngsters. There's no end to the needs but hopefully we've helped some.

Can you remember an experience early on that led your family to want to do this?

Well, I was on the board at The Hilltop and, as you know, it's very much oriented to the welfare and health of the people. They had a man who was hired to help in fundraising. We got acquainted with him and got the basic ideas about foundations and charitable giving.

The estate tax, if you're not careful, will eat up your estate. And we determined, with counsel, that in many cases by setting up a charitable or a remainder uni- trust—for example: [a part] to charity and [a part] to the estate—we could end up paying a [smaller] estate tax. Because all you do [otherwise] is just give the money to the federal government to spend—which they don't have any difficulty in doing. This way, the family has some control over where the money is going and the family itself can end up with approximately the same amount of money than if you didn't do that. If it's carefully done and divided properly, the family does just as well and you've got a foundation that goes on helping other people and the government isn't deciding where it's going to go.

What suggestions or advice would you give to people who are doing some estate planning and express to you a reluctance to make gifts to charities?

Get involved with some of these charities and find out how it's handled. I've been on a number of boards; my wife has, too. You find firsthand what they're doing with the money. In most cases, it's well taken care of. If they've got a good board, a good attorney, and a good CPA looking after that agency, you're probably going to have a pretty good agency—or you can give it to the government, and heaven knows where it's going to end up.

Do you think a person has to have a heart for charitable gifting in this arena?

Well, in our own family's case, I grew up in the Depression, the '30s. My family was not wealthy, but we were well taken care of. And I watched my parents give money to the church and to people in need during that very difficult period. They didn't have to do that and that made an impression on me. I remember people [who were] going from, particularly, Oklahoma across Kansas on their way to California, coming to the back door—knocking on the door, needing food. And my mother making sandwiches and things for them to carry on their trip. That makes an impression that you don't forget.

Then you look around in Grand Junction, business has been good but we've got a large number of homeless, destitute people. It just goes on and on. We have always felt that we have a responsibility to help other people. We've been blessed and we shouldn't take that for granted.

Is there anything else that you'd like to add about your Foundation or its philosophies?

Satisfaction: for example, if it is a building project, seeing the building become a reality; to have young people doing certain things and [then to] see that happen. We get a lot of satisfaction in giving monies to the hospitals and then to see what they do to take care of people needing that care, and knowing that the money that we gave helped that come about.

St. Mary's has been probably the number one [charity] that we have given to. The amount of equipment it takes, the cost of operations, and the high number of people who do not have insurance—the need is there to help them.

Another part of St. Mary's—a lot of people don't realize this—is Marillac Clinic. Marillac Clinic is under the auspices of St. Mary's. And

Steve Gammill

St. Mary's is the main supporter of Marillac. Marillac takes care of the uninsured, and there are many, many of them in our county. It's a win-win situation. Marillac, if it can provide basic care to people, keeps them out of the emergency room at the hospital. They're better taken care of. When they need to go to the emergency room, it's a true emergency.

Deanna Strand

December 20, 2007

I really see myself as an educator more than anything. I like to be able to make a difference, whether it's teaching someone how to land an airplane or helping them to understand anything else in life.

... he likes to teach. He's chosen it from the beginning.... "I want to be here because I want to be a teacher. And on top of that, I know how to fly an airplane, so show me how to put all that together."

...I think our human nature is kind of fear-based. We are afraid to let other people move past us because we might lose ground, or we might not be seen to be as great anymore.... I think I've done a pretty good job over the years of encouraging people around me, and I hope I have not been too caught up in the fear of letting somebody else become a better pilot than me.....

Deanna, when you were growing up, what did you think it meant to be professionally successful? And what experiences led you to think that?

Well, I guess the impression I have of success [has] got to come from my parents, in watching them run their own business, as a kid. When I was about eight years old, they settled in Kalispell, Montana, and started the airport operation there. And I think it was through those years of my hanging out at the airport, pumping gas—you know, cleaning the bellies of the airplanes—that I really started watching to see "how does a person do this?"

I had no interest, no clue that I would be interested in having a business of my own or pursuing aviation, either one. But I think as a child, having a certain level of respect for and enrichment from my parents, I probably watched a little bit, saw what was going on.

My mom was not actually working in the business day to day but she did the bookkeeping for the company. So she was there oftentimes, kind of coming and going, taking care of the books and helping the office gals. And then my dad, of course, was the overall manager. It was a small family business, you might say.

I've actually been told many times that I am a lot like my dad. I act like my dad. I look like my dad. I'm sure I watched him a lot. I started my little business in '83, not really knowing what I was getting into. I remember I'd set up my little desk, thinking, "Okay, now what am I supposed to do?" I was about twenty-sevenish or so at that point.

I even remember one evening thinking [about] my dad. I had walked by—passed by—my dad's door down the hallway at the airport at Kalispell, and oftentimes I'd see him kind of sitting back in his chair like this, with his feet setting on the edge of the desk. So one night when I was getting done, and everybody had probably gone home, I was sitting there by my desk and thinking, "Well, maybe I'll try this thing," you know. So I leaned back in my chair and set my feet up there, just like I used to see Dad do.

In my mind, my parents had been very successful in their raising of the five children and the business operations that they ran for something short of 40 years before they sold the airport there. I've felt privileged to have such wonderful family support behind me. There have always been tough years in this family, but I think I really was very fortunate to have the four siblings and my mom and dad—and the continuity of my parents: they've been married for 54 years now, and that's been great for me.

A few years ago, they started including women in the Rotary Clubs. And Dad's Rotary was also including women in Kalispell, Montana. So he said, "Oh, they're letting women into Rotary now. You ought to think about joining down there in Grand Junction." So, probably 10 years ago, I joined the Rotary.

A few years after that, I was up in Kalispell and I went to Dad's Rotary Club. And they, oftentimes, will ask if someone can do a little five-minute talk on something So they came over and asked Dad, if he had something he wanted to say.

And my dad was one of those people that would jump up and go to the microphone and talk. He was the senior class president in college. That day, he just said, "You know, I don't really have anything specific." And I said, "I'll talk." They said, "Oh, that'll be wonderful. Mike Strand's daughter, she'll get up and talk."

And so I went up to the microphone that day and I because I just had this kind of inspiration that I wanted to tell that community what it meant to me to have grown up in Kalispell; and to see all these faces that I, as a kid, [had seen] around town.

It was a privilege for me to be able to go back and see that same group of people. You know, people kind of get settled into a community and raise their families there. It's just really nice for kids, being able to recognize the continuity and the solid environment; not just of my family, but also the extended community. When you're a kid, you don't think about that and realize how wonderful [it] is to have that.

In my earlier years, Dad was in the army. I went to school so many different places up until I was eight years old, I didn't feel like I had that continuity of friends in the classroom and the school. You know, I'm sure Jan [Jan Gammill, compiler's wife] understands that— the importance [to] the kids that feel like they're constantly being transplanted to different towns, and they've got a whole new group of children they've got to become friends with, and new teachers—that [is] really tough on kids.

So I got up to the microphone and told those guys and gals at the Rotary how wonderful [all of that] was—to be raised in a community like that.

There's a really funny story about the guy that owns the sailboat shop. I was a typical kind of snotty, kid-type adolescent with an attitude during my high school years, and I remember going into the sailboat/bicycle shop one day. And I was going to buy something for my bicycle. I had gotten a bicycle and I was buying pieces, parts, for it. I must've been kind of, you know, rude, or whatever, because he was filling out the invoice and selling me this bicycle part and at the top, instead of my name, he just wrote: "B.P.A." under the "name". And I was looking at that, thinking, "Well, I guess he just thinks I'm a big pain in the ass."

And so, years later, I'm at Rotary, and I went over to talk to Jim. He only knew me as Mike Strand's daughter and probably never had a clue I was in his bicycle shop. I said, "Now, I'm just curious: on that invoice that day, what—do you have any clue what that [meant]?"

He simply said, "Yeah. It's 'bicycle parts and accessories.'" He said, "We put 'sailboat parts and accessories' and 'bicycle parts and accessories.'" In his mind, it was nothing unusual.

How does your definition of professional success today compare to other people's definition?

Well, first of all, I was pleased when you asked me to be involved in this, because I think in all reality I do feel like I've been a success in life. And I think that's a really wonderful thing. It's by God's grace that I am where I am. When I moved here at the age of 22, I was this shy, quiet little kid who really hadn't a clue. It is interesting to see how things have evolved.

At that point, I didn't want to fly for a living. I [had] just gotten my degree in linguistics at the University of Montana and had no clue what I was going to do with myself. I was going to go with a job at the bakery; I was going to go become a waitress; whatever, because I didn't know what to do. I ended up back at the airport because I'd grown up around the airport.

In my mind, success means to be able to acquire a level of recognition and expertise that I can then pass on to others. It's just been in the last few years that I've realized how much ability I have and also [realized] a desire in my heart to be able to mentor other people and help them to become better at whatever. ...[I have an] office manager who has an eight-year-old daughter and a flight instructor, a woman, that has a four-year-old daughter. I feel like I am able to help them with rearing their children. There are many different ways that I can be an influence in the world around me. That's what success is to me: to be able to help the world around me, in whatever capacity I've been called to help people.

A lot of people think success is acquiring a lot of money—having money in the bank, getting a lot of properties. I think our society, unfortunately, is really geared towards success [as] being financial. Oftentimes we stop at that. What's that T-shirt say? "Whoever dies with the most toys wins." I think that's unfortunate, but our society does believe that, and sometimes I have bought into it as much as the next guy.

You know, back when I was a kid, we didn't have a lot, but Mom and Dad never led us to believe that we had to scramble to try to get things. If we wanted new skis for Christmas, they would figure out how to help us buy that. So they taught us to think about our financial situation to be able to know that we could afford things. And that has carried through into my adult life.

If I would've thought I needed money, I wouldn't have gotten into [the] flight school business. I've had many people over the years tell me that it's not the place to make a bunch of money. I've basically proved that. This April of 2008, I'll have been in business for 25 years, and in that 25 years, I really haven't made a lot of money. But I feel like I'm comfortable with what I've done. And that's because my dad taught me to make wise decisions, and he taught me how to invest in real estate. I've been careful with the little that God's given me.

Years ago, when I'd had the business probably 10 years or so, I went down to Bob Johnson at the Bank of Grand Junction, because Bob was my banker. And I said, "Now, I'm just not sure about this. Am I just kind of wasting my time here? Or would you say that I am actually a successful business? I really don't know if I've been successful because every month a few dollars come into the bank account, a few dollars go back out and there is never really a lot of money."

And Bob—I thought it was pretty interesting insight—says, "You know, Deanna," he says, "you're kind of like a farmer. You're not really going to ever have a lot of money. Your business is not going to make a bunch of money. But, he says, "you're gradually investing in your airplanes just like a farmer would invest in his combine and his property." He says, "You'll acquire assets in that regard that [you] might not have if you had just [chosen another line of work] or hadn't chosen to figure out how to acquire some assets."

At that point, I recognized that success wasn't having it all or being able to always look at my bank account and see it increasing a lot each year, but just to be able to get by, to make sure I was taking care of myself, paying the bills, not adding a bunch of things on the credit cards, and making more responsible financial decisions as opposed to acquiring a lot of things.

In what ways do you consider that you are already a professional success?

Being able to achieve a level of recognition and present a level of integrity to our community, or even nationally.

I've had this school long enough now and I've been teaching and mentoring pilots, both our local instructors and those that have gone elsewhere—I've got pilots that are flying in Alaska and all over the country—that I've trained, taught, and employed for all these years. One of my instructors was in Denver last week getting his flight instructor renewal done, and he came back, saying, "Wow, everybody knows you. When I say I work for Strand, 'Oh, you work for Deanna Strand.'"

I think that has given me the ability to be that mentor that I'd like to be. And, of course, I was on the Discovery Channel's "Women in Aviation" program, and they've been replaying that for years. That kind of brings it all together.

I really see myself as an educator more than anything. I like to make a difference in people's lives, whether it's teaching someone how to land an airplane or helping them to understand something else in life. I love to teach, and that's something I recognized when I was kid. My younger brother and sister are 10 and 12 years younger than I am. I remember wanting to teach them how to ride horses and wanting to teach them how to ski. I've just always wanted to be able to help somebody understand a motor skill or an insight into something; and I, almost to a fault, like to tell people what to do—if you get in the car with me, I'll probably tell you how to drive out of your driveway.

I'm an FAA pilot examiner. That started in 1986 when they asked me to become a designee for the FAA. That really [gave] me a level of recognition nationwide.

And then I've done other unique things, like teaching for the FBI pilots and teaching for the AOPA, which is Aircraft Owners and Pilots Association; [and there are some other] national organizations that I've gotten to be involved in as an educator. Those sorts of things, I think, have been really fun for me, and I have been able to see that I was recognized and had something to contribute on a national level.

The FBI, for example, only chose six instructors nationwide. Mountain flying is specialized and unique. The Colorado-Montana Rockies is where I [have] done all of my flying—about 10- or 12,000 -flying hours. So, I was one of the six that was chosen. They wanted the FBI pilots to take mountain flying training and they wanted people that were exceptional mountain pilot instructors. They sent all the FBI pilots in from Newark and O'Hare and different places. They would come in, bring their airplanes, and learn how to fly with us.

As pilots accumulate time and hours, I assume that a major risk factor is that they might become complacent and that might be more dangerous than it would be in just operating an automobile. Do you include counseling, advice, and teaching in that area?

Actually, just as when a schoolteacher goes through the education training in order to become a grade school teacher, we are required to go through what they call the "Fundamentals of Instructing." It's the teaching and learning process of how to work with people in education. When I was in [the] University of Montana, I actually thought at one point [that] maybe I should be a teacher and started pursuing education classes. I dropped out of those when I realized I didn't want to teach in that regard

We have to go through the same process of learning the Fundamentals of Instruction, the learning and the teaching process. And so, part of that whole thing is learning how to be what the Fundamentals of Instruction calls a "practical psychologist". The whole idea behind it is [that] you don't just learn how to teach [the] motor skills of flying an airplane: we're also trying to teach a person the knowledge and the confidence. They have to have more than just the motor skills.

I like the interpersonal part of it. I could've chosen, years ago, to go to work for United Airlines and, at that point, with a couple of thousand hours in my log book, I thought maybe I should. But I don't really want to be sitting up in front in a cockpit with 250 people in the back, not getting to interact with those people—just driving the machine, you know. [I like] the idea of being able to work with an individual—he and I and the airplane, or she and I and the airplane, just working one-on-one and watching them accomplish their dreams and acquire this skill.

People sometimes would give up, and you'd have to encourage them or help them to see that they really have developed some abilities. Maybe they're slower [than] another person who's taking classes with them. But they're going to get there, just like the other guy does. Everyone learns at different speeds. [People have] different backgrounds, abilities, and experiences, obviously.

Training the Teachers

As we're getting trained to become instructors, and as we continue on through our career of instructing—which, of course, has been my main focus:the teacher aspect of it—we learn how to work with people and to help them move forward in acquir[ing] their dreams and accomplish[ing] their skills.

And as I [have] trained instructors over the years and then employed them, I've found that's oftentimes difficult. If you get a guy that just really wants to fly airplanes, he doesn't really want to be a teacher and he'll get frustrated. And if he's not willing to take the time to learn how to become a good teacher, he really can't be a good flight instructor either. That guy will eventually become an airline pilot or fly crop dusting or something else because he wants to fly airplanes, but he doesn't want to teach.

The Vince Story—Choosing

Most of my instructors are more the 40 and 50 year old guys that have *chosen*. I've actually got a guy right now who's going through the program with us. He's a retired schoolteacher who, along with his wife, just moved down here from Wyoming. He's got most of his flight training done but he's not a flight instructor yet. So we're helping Vince, even though he's already a teacher, to become a pilot teacher.

He likes to teach. He's *chosen* it from the beginning.[He says things like,] "I want to be here because I want to be a teacher. And on top of that, I know how to fly an airplane, so show me how to put all that together." We know Vince will be one of those guys. I don't know how old he is, [but] he'll be around for years to come, because he's *choosing* this.

What remains unfinished for you, if anything, in this area?

Well, you know that in the last few years I've gotten more involved with John Hendricks from the Discovery Channel. I taught John how to fly in 1998 and he started buying airplanes in 1999. Then in 2004, he asked me to become a pilot for their family and I now manage his airplanes and take care of the family.

So, I've kind of expanded into a different area, separate from the school. But it's also quite interesting to see myself getting involved in more of a private—you know—flying for a private family.

I didn't plan on doing this, so, it really is a whole new adventure for me and has been really rewarding. We've got a wonderful airplane, the Cessna Caravan, that we bought, new off the factory floor in September '04, and I got to fly it home. And I've now got about 550 hours in it. It's a big turbine engine, 675 horsepower—it's just the most fun airplane to fly. I couldn't have dreamed that I would have this opportunity, learning to fly this airplane and being able to take care of the Hendricks family.

Some Hendricks Family Stories and Adventures

We went to Alaska last summer with the Caravan. Actually, they [the family] went up on a cruise ship and I met them up there with the airplane. We toured Mount McKinley, the Misty Fjords, and saw Talkeetna. We actually got the airplane all the way up to the Arctic Ocean on Point Beryl. They were really looking forward to being able to do these amazing adventures in their own private airplane, and with the added safety of a pilot that they knew and trusted.

There was a really rewarding experience while we were up there. In the plane were the mother and father and the two children, who are college-aged kids. The kids had each brought a friend along. We were flying over the Misty Fjords, kind of chasing the whales. We saw some and so we were back tracking to see if we could get some pictures— there was a pod of them and they kept surfacing. At one point, John's son said, "Dad! This airplane is the best investment you've ever made." And that made me feel like I was an important part of the family's being able to enjoy their vacation that summer.

And then, later on, we were flying up to the Arctic Ocean, and Maureen—Mrs. Hendricks—told me that John had told her that maybe they would take a trip to Alaska that summer and go fly around the backcountry and check out some of Alaska. And she said, "Oh, no way. That's too dangerous! All those bush pilots—there's no way you're going to take the family up there, to that dangerous environment." He says [to her], "Oh no, no. You don't understand. We're taking our airplane and Deanna's going to fly us." And she said, "Okay, that's great then. That sounds perfect, let's go." So it was fun for me to hear her relate that story and to know that they had that much confidence in me.

When John asked me if I wanted the job, of course I wanted to be able to offer him what he was asking for, but I really didn't think I was the person for the job. I had owned a flight school all these years. That's really where my focus had been, and I thought [of all the] many pilots in the country that can fly turbine-engine airplanes that have always aspired to be a family pilot.

And then, as I started getting involved in the project and learning to fly the airplane, I realized that who he had hired was somebody with 10,000 hours of Rocky Mountain flight experience. And John is so wise in that way. He really knows how to scope out the people that will do the job, that [have] the background and abilities that he's looking for.

Seriously, I am exactly the right person for the job, because I know how to keep them safe in flying in that airplane, in and out of their little grass strip at Gateway, and around the western United States and up to Alaska. He knew that I would be able to make sure that they weren't [at] any risk. So it was a good decision on his part, too.

But that's a whole new avenue of success that I'm aspiring to. I'm looking forward to seeing what the future will bring there. John's a visionary. [He's thinking about my setting] up an operation in Gateway with some helicopters to do scenic tours out of Gateway. He's talked about the possibility of even flying helicopter skiing off to the La Salle Mountains, over by Moab, [and] taking people down to the San Juan

Mountains and dropping them off for an overnight camping adventure. You know, just drop them off in a meadow, have it all prearranged with the BLM, and then have them do a couple nights backpacking or overnight camping.

What are some examples of successful relationships that you have known?

I see that as the people in my life that have been the most important to me, that have been the best mentors for me. I've got to start with my mom and dad and specifically, my dad. He's just been a really good mentor for me in the way he's handled his life, the integrity he's exuded in his life. That's been something really important [for] me to see.

Jean's Story

There's a Michael [who] was the guy that introduced me to Jesus when I was 17 years old, and it was his mother [Jean] who, I think, kind of prayed me into the Kingdom, you might say. She was one of those people that was just a prayer warrior and spent a lot of time considering the people in her life. I lost Jean this last year. I had kind of adopted her as my second mom—even my mom and dad know that Jean was my second mom—and she became one of my best friends through the years I was growing up. And I just feel like she was such a wonderful person—she just exuded the love of God in her life.

So she became my second mom and I took trips out to Minnesota after she moved there. She was in Kalispell all the years I was growing up, so I would see her on my trips back to Kalispell. And then, she and her husband retired to Minnesota. She meant a lot to me.

And a little of Michael's Story

And her son had such a big impact on my life when I was a senior in high school. He and I dated a little bit through college and both ended up marrying other people, but he was an important person in my life. He became a pilot and started educating missionary pilots in the Seattle area. He had an airplane accident a couple of years ago and he's gone now, too. But I know those people are in a very good place, and it's good for me to realize that someday, I'll see them again.

My sister is also real important in my life. I've got siblings that are just really great—you know, support systems for me, being there for me, understand me, and have watched me through all these years.

The Gail Story

I have another girlfriend who I've known since sixth grade. She and I were horseback buddies through the junior and high school years.

We met on the playground in sixth grade. She knew I had a horse and that whole idea—she was just so excited about that. She actually tells me today that she set out to be my friend because I had a horse.

So we started hanging out together and spending time on my horse. Then later, our parents both bought us horses, bigger horses that we could actually ride together. And we spent a lot years just enjoying getting back into the backcountry taking trail rides. We'd fill our little saddlebags with beef jerky. We'd take our allowance and go buy beef jerky and put [it] in our saddlebags. And we'd ride up the trails and talk, and laugh, and just have—you know—really kid days.

There [were] a few years during college where we kind of lost connection, you might say. But then as we got into the young married years, we reconnected and became good buddies. Now, today, we'll almost every summer take a backpacking trip together. I'll go to Montana and we'll spend three or four nights out in the wilderness or up in Glacier National Park, just backpacking and sitting up on the hillside, watching all the wildflowers and talking about life.

You know, Gail is one of those wise women. And her mom was like this, too. I remember, even as a kid, watching her mom: this quiet-natured, thoughtful, considerate person that was always there for the people in her life. And so, it's not surprising that Gail has grown up to be a lot like her mom. But she just is really one of those very thoughtful, considerate people who is soft spoken, has time to listen—really, truly listen to your questions, and who takes the time to contemplatively answer—not just rushing forth with a barrel full of advice.

What are the downsides you have experienced in achieving success?

I want to say that there are none. But I think in all reality that I did sacrifice relationships in my life for the business success. I went through a number of relationships over my adult years—and I'm talking about "significant others"—and I think there [were] cases where I was more interested in my business and less interested in taking time for my personal life. I think I've sacrificed some personal relationships when I should've put a little more energy there. Instead of doing the hard work there, I did all the hard work at the airport.

I've had a very successful group of employees. My office manager, for example, has been there for nine years, and she and I have developed a great working relationship together. That's a relationship I mentored and worked at.

How does your view of what it means to be successful in relationships compare to what other people consider success in relationships?

I feel like the relationships that I've got today are great relationships. I feel really good about the relationships I have with my friends and my family. But I also feel like, well, I was the one kid of all five of us children that everybody thought would grow up and have children. I was the mothering person [out] of my two brothers and two sisters. Even to this day, I wonder why in the world the Lord did not give me children.

And yet I know. The stories in the Old Testament tell how God gave us choices, and how people move forward into their choices and make wrong ones—not honoring His direction. I chose wrong in many cases. And now we have consequences from our life choices.

I think I didn't really realize that there were life choices. I thought that somehow there was this [plan],—you know—God's will. I was supposed to be on this spot and I was supposed to be living out this plan. There was this perfect person for me to marry and I had to find that person and marry that person.

And of course, that's what I did. Right out of college, age 22, I married the first guy that was there. And then I started looking at the relationship and saying, "Well, this isn't what I want." I should've realized then that this was the relationship that I had. This is the marriage that God had chosen or that I had chosen and I should've stayed committed.

I've had lots of years of struggling [with my school], years I didn't like being a flight school owner, and years I was ecstatic to be there. The same thing happens in marriage relationships, and if I would've chosen wisely there, like I [did] with my school, I think my life would've been a whole [lot] different. I probably would have children and I still could've had this school. I don't have any doubt about it.

Not too many years back, I asked God why I didn't have children, and what am I supposed to do now that I don't have children to mentor, to raise, take care of. And He just basically said, "Deanna, your job right now is to be a friend to your friends." And so that's what I've done over the last five or ten years. God's given me some just incredible friends. Linda Evans is a good friend of mine. She and I have a really great friendship. It's easy for us to be there through the tears and the joys and all the different situations we've had to work through in our lives. So I don't have children, but I've got some really, really great friends—some real solid friends—in my life and that is very rewarding to me and hopefully for them, too.

Is there anything else you'd like to say in terms of your relationships in the future?

I'm hoping I'm making better choices now. And I would suspect that—I, being in my young fifties now—if God would direct me towards getting married again, then it'll probably be with a person that has children of their own. Hopefully, I'll be able to be a good mentor for those children, to be a good positive role model and a good influence in their lives.

I know the whole concept of step-parenting isn't what I would've chosen either. It's not an easy path to follow. I've actually had a couple of relationships where I've been in a pseudo step-parenting role, and I know that it's not an easy road. It's not easy for the children, it's not easy for the biological parents, and it's really difficult for the step-parent, who never is really a part of the family. But I also think that there will be some joy with that, too. Maybe I'll be able to have grandchildren. You know, I think I'd be a great grandma.

When you were a child, what constituted success in learning and education in your mind? And who taught you that?

I never saw myself as a good student and, even to this day, I tell people that I'm a slow learner. I'm easily intimidated by things and my brain doesn't focus as well—it takes me a long time to really get there.

There were a couple of teachers that came into my life. The first one was Mr. Carver. He was a speech teacher. The ability that he had to encourage me, even though I was a very shy, reserved kid, not one that you would've picked out of a class as a good public speaker, was really great. I felt good about being in his class. Also, I had a psychology teacher in high school, and my German teacher, Mr. Laap, who had that extra heart to make the students feel glad to be there.

I did an exchange program through the University of Montana and went to school in Maine for part of the year. There was a teacher there, a creative writing teacher who was so [interested] that he took the effort to make sure I realized that whatever I wrote to him [needed to be] well done, that I could do it better. And, you know, there were lots of red highlighters throughout the pages to say, "Do this, try this. What about this? Why are you...?" He took a personal interest in me and gave me that direction.

So I think it's nice to know that there are people that take that extra energy [and] to have their heart behind their teaching. They're not just filling a position, warming the seat, getting a salary. That's made a big difference for me.

What do others around you think it means to be successful in learning and education? And how does that compare to what you think it means?

In my mind, [the] picture is pretty clear that education means mentoring and helping other people. I think that that's kind of how the world sees it, too. There are a lot of people who think that education is a really important area in society that we're neglecting. You know, we put so much energy into football and movie stars, and the glory that goes with that. The educators, the people that are really making an impact on our children—they're just not considered [of high value].

My family's from Norway, and when I was over [there] visiting years ago—my father's aunt was married to a professor [there]—I became aware that in their country, being an educator is kind of like how we treat doctors or football stars in America.

If you're going to break down the professions into which makes the big difference in our lives and in our future generations, I guess I have to say that the kids are really an important focus, and that we all need to be thinking about how we can make a big difference for the children that are going to be the future leaders in our society. I hope the world sees it that way, too.

Is there anything that remains unfinished for you in the area of learning and education?

Oh, yes. There's so much, in regards to my aviation career, to learn. Every year I'm required now to go to [a] flight safety program, an international operation that teaches pilots who fly Lear jets and all the other different, big airplanes. Last year, I was [in] Wichita [Kansas] for that training and the guy that flies for Jimmy Buffet was there and one of the astronauts going up into space was there in my class. And Harrison Ford goes to classes there. [It's a] bunch of guys that are flying this level of higher-powered, turbine-engine airplanes.

Just look at all the potential training that I could aspire to, and I don't know if I'll ever get there. There's just so much more that I need to know about that airplane. It's fun and it's very rewarding to be able to grow with all that.

And in the business realm, too: I'm an excellent pilot, but I'm also a good business person, having built the flight school 24½ years ago now. I think I'm also good at mentoring employees, helping them move up the ladder, you might say, into certain positions, and to become better at what they do.

[As I mentioned before, we're building an operation down at Gateway.] And I think that's something I'll be able to do well as we put that together. It's called West Creek Air Tours, and as I help establish it, I think I'll be able to be a good asset to that operation. I can imagine multiple helicopters, pilots, and the office staff—it's going to be fun to watch all that happen.

Bernie Buescher used to be the manager over at West Star [Aviation] years ago. I used to watch him and always admired the fact that he had time for people. It didn't matter if it was the janitor or the gal behind the desk, he always had time. I also have watched his employees all these years and thought that they were all allowed to move throughout the [company]. That's a big 300-employee operation, and they were encouraged to move up into management or into supervisory roles or whatever. He encouraged that growth. And I would think that I wanted to be like that. I really wanted to be one of those people that can help people become better at whatever they want to do.

I want to be one of those individuals that can mentor people. I would like to think that I am good at it, but I think our human nature is kind of fear-based. We are afraid to let other people move past us because we might lose ground, or we might not be seen to be as great anymore. So there's kind of a sense of fear that we all bring to our lives. I think I've done a pretty good job over the years of encouraging people around me, [and] I hope I have not been too caught up in the fear of letting somebody else become a better pilot than me or a better businessperson.

I've got a very small little operation, perhaps a dozen employees. But I encourage them to move on to different businesses and even to start their own operations. Actually, we've got three guys flying off the glaciers in Alaska right now and another guy in California. [These are] different individuals that have moved out and started their own aviation careers because we've been able to encourage that.

What do you think it means today to be financially successful? And do you think that most other people share your point of view?

For me, financial success is to be comfortable. What I mean by that is I decided years ago that I needed to have some securit[y]. I couldn't just be living from paycheck to paycheck. I had to know that I had my IRA; I had some money saved that was kind of a safety net. And, there again, I feel like my mom and dad were such great examples in teaching me how to make wise decisions: "Put the money in the bank; don't just spend it all; don't run up credit cards." Since I started having credit cards, which had to have been [during] college, I have never, ever carried a balance on a credit card. I just think that it's important to make wise decisions so that, as the investments start to build a little bit, we have some safety nets—that there's a certain element of financial stability there that we can feel. We can be comfortable moving forward in life and not be worrying about [paying rent and mortgages].

I'll tell you a funny story, too. I had just started my flight school. Mom and Dad, of course, had been in this business all their lives and had never really thought they'd been successful.

My mom watched every nickel [that] flowed through the company and she raised five kids and put us through college. So she didn't think aviation was the place to make any money. When I called her and told her that Steve [my former husband] and I were having trouble and we were going to go our different directions, and I was starting this little school, she said, "Now, tell me again about that business, that flight school you're starting?" She says, "Who's going to pay your salary?" And I said, "Well, mom, you don't understand. It's kind of like I won't be getting a salary. I'll be kind of like what you and Dad did. I'll just be working for myself." "Oh no, no," she says, "I don't think that's a very good idea. I don't think—you need to have a job with somebody."

And of course, I overrode her decision. I thought, "I can [always] go to Denver and sign up for business classes. I would learn about accountants and lawyers and bankers and all the stuff that you learn [about] how to run businesses.

[Then] I thought, "Well, I can just do that right here. I'll learn about business in the bigger picture without having to go off and take education classes. After a while, the people in Grand Junction that wanted to become pilots will all have learned. And then I'll go do something else because, obviously, the people that want to learn eventually will dry up and nobody else will want to learn how to fly." And, of course, five years later and seven years later, there were still people that wanted to learn how to fly.

I took a business class and actually spent $800 for it. I thought that was ridiculous, but I decided it might be of use to me. [Our teacher] made us do projections. We had to do a five-year plan, a 10 year plan, and a 20 year plan. And I just remember thinking how ridiculous it was. I wasn't going to even be in business in 10 years. Why would I want to do a 20 year plan? Well, we had to do it, so I spent all this time putting together my projections.

And it wasn't until now, many years later, that I can see how useful that was. It was just a way for my brain to start thinking ahead as to how I could project into the future. It has all come to pass. I mean the whole idea of handling a hangar and having classrooms and having multiple instructors, and grease boards for presentations to the students. I've got seven airplanes that basically I bought through the bank over the years. It really is that big picture that she helped me design 15 to 17 years ago. It has all come to pass.

By your definition of financially successful, in what ways are you already a financial success?

As I was saying, my mom didn't think that I should have my own business because I wouldn't be able to take care of myself. I think that's one of things I set out to do—to make sure I could take care of myself. I wanted to make sure that I had my securities and my safety nets in place.

Having done that early on has meant that I don't really have to worry about things. So I think financial success has come from being wise when I was younger. Now, I can just carry forward with the calling that God has me doing day- to- day, and not have to sit here worrying about whether I can pay the utility bill.

I have more than I ever thought I would have. But I also know that God has given me more than I need because He knows that I'll give it away. I've given to a lot of people over the years, and that was a lesson I learned in the mid-nineties, through Curt—my former husband, actually.

Curt taught me that tithing was a very important thing. I remember he had a farm up in South Dakota. One year, he was writing a tithing check to the church. It was a huge check. It was like a couple thousand dollars. It turns out his nephew [had] farmed the land that summer. They weren't supposed to make any money. It wasn't supposed to be successful and so he basically told God, you know, if there was any extra aside from the cost of the property and seed and whatever else the expenses were in raising that crop, that he would give it all to God. And sure enough, the crop was successful that summer, and Curt was true to his prayer and gave all the money to God.

At that point, I really didn't understand tithing. I never had thought the whole thing through, but [I realized] that it was something I wanted to consistently do—faithfully, and above and beyond.

I went to Women of Faith [a conference] a few years ago, and Lucy Swindoll [one of the speakers] had a really funny story about how God had told her that every year, instead of just 10%, the next year it should be 11% [and] the next year, 12%. And she says [that] it's just phenomenal, because as she continued to give a bigger and bigger percent, God just kept showering her with more and more so she could give more and more. And she says to the whole group of 17,000 women, she says, "I'm not going to tell you guys how many years ago that was." But she's continually added a percent every year. And, as you can imagine, that lady has been very successful financially.

And after the example with Curt and then listening to Lucy Swindoll, you know, that's going to be me. I'm going to keep giving, giving, giving well beyond what I think I can afford to do.

And even just a week ago, I gave [some] money to one of my little gals to take her four-year-old daughter and go to Florida for Christmas. The Holy Spirit basically led me to do that. When I look back at it, I just have to think, "Okay, that was meant to be. It was the right thing to do."

And I feel very fortunate that God has blessed me with financial extras that I can pass on like that.

> **Can you think of a time when one of your students, to whom you may have given financial advice, decided to go off on their own and start their own aviation business?**

Over the years, I've had quite a few individuals from Rifle, Montrose, Telluride and Aspen that have gotten to the point where they're ready to become flight instructors and thinking, "Well, gosh, shouldn't I have an operation? Shouldn't Aspen have a flight school at this stage of the game? Or Telluride?" And I've always been very glad to help. We've designed all the forms for keeping track of things. We've got it all computerized and we'd be glad to share any of it, rather than your starting all over and trying to recreate the wheel.

I remember calling my dad quite often over the years. [And while our businesses were focused very differently,] he did help me know what kind of airplanes to purchase and to make sure I was getting airplanes that were not going to be a big maintenance hog, and things like that. So he gave me some wise counsel that way, but he was also very wise to step back and let me see what worked best for this environment and not try to control it from Montana.

When I actually started this school, I named it—Dad's airport was called, "Strand Aviation," and so I decided I would call mine "Strand Aviation II." So all my letterhead showed up with "Strand Aviation II" on it and, of course, they were just thrilled. My mom called me and she was all excited and teasing me, and she said, "So when are we going to start receiving royalties off of our second company?" And I said, "Okay, Mom—well, as soon as you start investing in your second company down here in Colorado, I'd be glad to send you some royalties."

And, of course, that's what people thought over the years: that somehow my dad had this airport and so probably he [had] invested down here and helped me get started. And he could've, you know.

Looking at your life as a whole, what areas of accomplishment give you the greatest satisfaction?

I think my biggest satisfaction has come from being an educator, being a mentor to the people around me. And I think, in that big picture, that even when I was a young kid, I always knew that God existed. I was raised in a Christian church, and even though it wasn't really in a personal relationship with Jesus, I always knew that it was an important thing for me.

The whole idea of being able to mentor people in my faith is probably the most interesting to me. It *is* the most important thing in life, and I think that we can make a difference for other people in our faith walk, you know, by setting an example. I see people like Anne Tewksbury and Karen Jensen—people that are wise. Barb Jensen was that way too, just really wise. [close Christian friends] I hope someday I can be one of those people that people will look at and go, "Wow, what a wise woman of God she is." Jan Gammill is another good example. It's wonderful to see people [who] have worked so hard in their own lives to become thoughtful, considerate, sharing, giving, loving.

My Auntie Joyce is the first person I saw love unconditionally. And I didn't even know what that was. I used to watch Auntie Joyce. She would have time to listen to every word and would want to know what was going on with me. She wasn't judgmental, she wasn't controlling—she just loved me just like I was. And so I, years later of course, started recognizing what unconditional love was and thinking that I'd like to be like that someday. That's great success, I think.

With whom do you most want to share the successes of your life and how are you planning on doing that?

I don't see myself as really limiting that to a person or even a group of people. I really think that I need to be open to the people that come through my life. And that's what I think I was talking about: people that are so able to be in the moment. For example, to be at the grocery store in a grocery line and to recognize that I am in this line because the person beside [me] might need a little encouragement; or, driving down North Avenue, getting cut off by a driver, and realizing that person might be in a hurry to get to the hospital.

I feel like it's important for me to let the day progress as it's supposed to and not be constantly controlling it. I really want to just be one of those people that can sit back and let God put the right people before me that I can minister and be available to.

I met a really great gal about a year ago over in Provo [Nicki]. She runs part of a pilot [flying] program over there and is a missionary spirit—that's the only way I can describe her. I've never been around someone who had such a missionary spirit. She's only in her mid- to late-thirties, but she's got such a heart for God; and she just knows how to be there in her day-to-day walk, just to be where she's supposed to be.

She has 18 instructors that answer to her. In her program this last September, there were 90 students that showed up. So she's running a huge operation for the Utah Valley State College program. I see Nicki as being one of those people that really knows how to be in the moment but still knows how to step back and say, "What am I supposed to do to help this person right now, to really be here for this person?"; to not be running off on different tracks trying to accomplish a lot, when really the most important thing to accomplish is just a kind word to this individual next to you. It's a mixed-up world we're living in. There's a lot of need out there, and I think if we take time to watch for that need, that's the really important thing to be focusing on.

Don Meyers

February 29, 2008

... in college, I began to learn to think critically... I had always known about logic and syllogisms...[and] in the critical thinking course, I came to believe that reason is a means and not an end...[Some] feel that if something is reasonable and logical, it must be true...[but] truth doesn't entirely depend on logic or reason. It has as much to do with morality as it does reason.

...One of my heroes is Joseph Campbell. And he said... that he always came back to the Roman Catholic Church because that's where his roots are, and you cannot change your roots.

Don, when you were growing up, what did you think it meant to be professionally successful, and what experiences led you to that opinion?

Well, I have to say that I didn't have much of a concept, I think, about success in life growing up. I'm one of those people who had opportunities come to me, and another way of putting that might be to say [that] I went with the stream, wherever the current took me, and so there never was, for me, a five-year plan. I know [that] in some interviews, people are asked, "Where do you intend to be in five years?" I don't think I'd ever imagined where I would be in five years. It was more like next week and what will happen next. So opportunities came to me—that's the way it was all the way through school.

But your question had to do with growing up, and I think that my impression about professional success would come down to: get a job, make a living.

I admired my dad tremendously for his work ethic. He was a guy who would have two jobs sometimes. He was a fireman and he would paint on his days off—a housepainter on his days off . I remember [that] for a while, he worked for Public Service Company. He seemed to be always working.

There was a downside to that, but what I admired was his work ethic, I think. He was a professional—yes, being a fireman is a profession of sorts, I think. I enjoyed my times down there at the fire station with those guys because they were jokers and they had a lot of fun together. And I would go down—when I got a car—and they would all help me with something that the car needed to have done to it on their—what do you call those?—a tunnel kind of a thing, where you can put a car and go down under and work underneath the car. I think they call it a "pit."

But I don't believe that in my family there was anyone with a professional career like medicine, or the law, or teaching. My mother went to college and studied education. She apparently was in training to teach, but she never taught. And so there wasn't really a model there for how you behaved as a professional educator.

So I don't believe that my experiences growing up ever presented me with something called a "ladder" concept: how you get to success, or, how you climb the ladder. This just wasn't something we talked about.

I think that my take on professional growth and development really couldn't have much of a competitive dimension to it. I didn't think much in terms of competition, and that partly goes back to what I said in the beginning, about things [just coming] to me. I got elected to offices in school, for example, [and I had] opportunities to in a play. I don't think I even auditioned for the first play that I was in in high school. Somebody asked me to come to an audition session, so I went and got the part, you know, so there really wasn't much ambition , I suppose, applied to my concept about competition.

Fast forward to college, because that's really where I began to think about that—"What are you going to major in?" I majored in art because I didn't know anything else, and what looked like a lucrative career was advertising design—design in advertising. So I did that for the first year and was going along just fine, but then, I met a faculty person.

He was a first-year design instructor named John Lembach. He became the closest thing to a mentor, I suppose, that I ever had, and I kept in touch with him for a long time after college, too. He was active in the National Art Education Association. In fact, he was the secretary for a while. I became inspired by Dr. Lembach.

He was a terrific guy. He was a thinker. I guess that was what seduced me the most. Here you have an art class, and people are sitting around talking about philosophical and aesthetics issues. They're not just doing "how-to-do-it" exercises—how to manipulate a paintbrush. It probably was my second year in college when I switched to education from commercial art.

Another influence on that score was a longtime friend named Lyle Johnson. He was in an organization called "The Future Teachers of America." So I joined up with that, mostly because of Lyle—he and I still see each other, talk on the phone, and go to the Denver Art Museum together. We went to a baseball game at Coors Field. Lyle is just a great guy. He had a disability that he never seemed to be sure what it was. But I think it was MS. And so he couldn't walk, what I would [call] normally, but he sure got around. And he was inspiring about teaching. I think that was the only thing he ever wanted to do.

So I'm just going to jump to when we met up again here in Grand Junction. He had graduated a year before I did from the University of Denver and went to California to, I think, Menlo Park. He taught out there for two years and then he came back to Colorado, he and his wife. I don't remember how they landed in Grand Junction, but that's where I had taken a job. And so, lo and behold, there we are together at the same junior high school. Again, he bolstered my hopes of being a decent teacher. He was terrific. We played basketball with the students sometimes. And there's Lyle, you know, hobbling around—an incredible guy—but [his] enthusiasm on the basketball court was as great as the enthusiasm in the classroom.

My student teaching [was] in Denver, where I student taught at East High School. It wasn't a very good student-teaching experience, partly because I really wasn't left alone with a class. Maybe student teaching has improved since those days of the middle '50s. But I learned a lot and I had a very decent supervising teacher at East High School—Edith Niblo.

I remember a practice they had there. When a teacher was absent, they would sometimes call a student teacher to fill in. I did that maybe a couple of times. One that I remember was a physics class. I was called out of the art room to go down and substitute for a physics professor. Now, I don't remember what happened that day, but I'm sure it wasn't physics. We must have had a good philosophical discussion about art and science, or something like that.

Another thing that I remember was that there was a student in the art class who was injured in some way. I don't remember what happened, but Edith told me about him being in the hospital—in Denver General Hospital—and so I thought, "I'm going to go see him," which I did. A small black kid, but for some reason—to me—that was a moment of success, because here was somebody I didn't know other than in the classroom, and I just decided to go and see him. I don't remember any of the conversation; he didn't have much to say. I think he probably was feeling lousy, but just the notion that you can do that had probably never struck me before.

In what ways do you consider yourself a professional success today?

I guess probably I'd measure success in terms of some of the leadership positions that I've had in my lifetime. One of the first ones I'll mention is the Art Center Board, which I served on for 25 years, off and on—mostly on. Probably because of me, they decided they needed a limitation on the terms a board member could serve. But I was sure a part of that organization for a long time. I was the secretary and I was the gallery manager at the Art Center for a number of shows. It was hard work, but I felt good about [it]. I said something earlier about not being assertive, but I did seek out that position. It was early in the years that I was here, probably in the late '50s.

The Faculty Senate at the college, [Mesa State] was an elected position. Actually, we'd had the Faculty Council before that, and when we became a four-year college, it turned into a Faculty Senate. I served as secretary of the senate for a couple of years. It seems like it was more than one year—maybe that's because it was so tedious.

Because I've served as secretary of a committee running a Presbyterian church recently, I wanted to mention one little incident [that happened while I was serving] as Faculty Senate secretary. I guess my impulse to insert [in the minutes] caustic comments about what went on at senate meetings got me into a little hot water, and I was censured by the senate and asked if I would please try to limit my remarks to what happened at the meeting—the facts, please, and nothing else. That was fun.

I was in the art department at the college and became department head in 1975 when my predecessor, Alvie Redden, retired. I served as department head for 15 years. That was an interesting leadership opportunity also.

Department head at the college came [about] more because of Alvie's retirement [than my seeking it]. I should imagine nobody else wanted to do it—sometimes department heads get their jobs that way.

It was mostly a maintenance job. I did try to keep the faculty and the art department—which was very small—working together. Besides trying to keep the faculty more or less on the same page in what we were trying to do, there were times when I had to deal with personnel. The least desirable of those [jobs] were evaluations of the faculty in the department, but that was something I had to do as chairman.

There were a couple of incidents where I had to deal with conflicts. I remember one particular time when a faculty member and a student were really close to blows. I mediated that incident in my office, separately at first, and then with both of them there. They were mad at each other, I'm telling you! But I'm proud of the way that turned out. I was not trained in mediation, but what came of it is that I learned how to listen, and I listened to each of them and got their point of view separately and then brought them together. No bones were broken.

Another time, we had a faculty member who was a very talented guy and a veteran of Vietnam. He turned out to be what I call "charismatic." The problem with that in a small department like ours is that, if you begin to attract a little following, first thing you know, you've divided a little group that was cohesive, and some students become loyal only to this one person.

I found that troublesome, but I never figured out how to deal with it. He went on finally to another job in Wisconsin. I think it's—and this is just my own judgment about it—insecurity that makes you think you've gained something if you can get students particularly loyal to you.

Another leadership position was the Monument Presbyterian Church Session [governing body], which I was proud to serve on. I have to say that that job was, again, mostly maintenance. We spent an awful lot of time figuring out how to balance the budget. But there was one issue that I'm rather proud of, and that was [all] about [a] flag in the sanctuary. [Editor's note: the issue referenced was the question of placing the American flag in a position of prominence within the worship area of the church.]

The decision [by] the Session was a unanimous one, though not lacking in discussion, and I was right in the thick of it. I felt like it was a real cause—one of those big issues that I enjoy being a part of. Now, I've noticed that a couple of other churches, one [right] here in the Valley, have taken up this issue, and I believe they have had to compromise on having a flag in the church.

It came down to confusing the nation with the church, from my point of view, and I think other members of the Session felt the same way. Really, a church and a nation are not one. This is not a state church. There are feelings that some people have about our country being chosen by God and [our] success [being] attributed to divine intervention. That may or may not be the case, but I don't think we're blameless in any way in this country in our history. The issue of the flag was a moment of truth for me, and one that I enjoyed thoroughly.

Another organization that I wanted to mention is the Grand Junction Commission on Arts and Culture that I have been on for about a year now. That's a positive organization, because it seems like everything we do is about enhancing the atmosphere of the arts in the Grand Valley. We've got a great leader—her name is Allison Sarmo. I just have tremendous admiration for her leadership and her inspiration. She is also the director of the Art on the Corner project, which is the downtown sculpture project that Dave Davis inspired 23 years ago.

My wife, Joan, was on that commission before I was. When they change the sculptures every year in May, there is a certain amount of cleaning that takes place. Some people even wax the bronzes so they retain their luster. Yours truly and Joan got the job of cleaning and painting the pedestals. We've done that now for probably four years. We'll go down with our little green wagon and our paint roller, and we'll come along and repaint the pedestals so they're nice looking for the new sculptures.

Sometimes, when I'm talking to people at an exhibition and they don't know what to say about a painting, they will often make the remark, "That's a beautiful frame, isn't it?" And I clench my teeth and try to divert the conversation to something about the work of art. But now that we've done the pedestals for Art on the Corner for so long, I have to confess that when we walk down Main Street and look at the sculpture exhibit, we generally check out the pedestals first before we look at the art.

Don, when you were a youngster, what constituted success in learning and education to you? And who taught you that?

I would probably have to say that school success was measured by grades. I won't say [that was] easy [for me]—I studied—but my grades were always pretty high and I enjoyed school. Enjoyed? Is that the right word? I think I was one of those kids that was always scared in school, and maybe that was the motivation more than anything for working hard and learning.

The other thing about education would be the awards. That was something else that just seemed to come. I never could quite figure out why I would get a scholarship award, for example, in grade school and junior high [and] high school. But I did apply for a scholarship after high school to the University of Denver and got it—one of six for the year. I had chosen DU because of an uncle, Roger McDougal, who had gone to DU. I never knew him, but I knew about his attending the university. He was killed in a lightning strike in the mountains west of Denver before I was born. I [had] read the family stories about Roger, and so I thought DU must be good, because everybody seemed to admire Roger. I was never sorry I chose that university to go to school for art.

How and when I learned about success in education may have come [as late as] in college, I think. That's probably when I learned how to learn—or even thought about learning—conceptually. I began to learn to think critically. High school didn't deal with that very much. I took a course later in critical thinking, which was valuable. I had always known about logic and syllogisms and so forth, but when we studied that in the critical thinking course, I came to believe that reason is a means and not an end. That's not to say I didn't appreciate what we studied, because you know you have a better sense if you've actually written a syllogism and talked about the procedure. I have some friends who seem to feel that if something is reasonable and logical, it must be true. And I guess someplace along the way in college, I began to realize that truth doesn't entirely depend on logic or reason. It has as much to do with morality as it does reason. And so there's a little conflict there, I think, but I certainly think that analysis is important in deciding what is true.

Oh, incidentally, yesterday I heard a recorded interview with Bill Buckley [William F. Buckley]. He was defending his position on a test for voting that he justified in terms of the Founding Fathers intending that voters—the electorate—be educated. [That is] something I really would have trouble defending morally—[the question of] who should vote and who should not.

I want to say a little more about truth being moral and not just logical. Somewhere along that path, I discovered Albert Schweitzer and the notion about reverence for life that he held so dearly. And I remember a film. I can remember him walking down a street or a path along some trees in Africa, where his hospital was. He was talking about the trees with great love, and with appreciation and reverence for all forms of life. And so that's been a notion that I've tried to equate with truth.

Curiosity is something important in how to learn; so also is not being defensive. That would mean, not picking an ideology and clinging to it for dear life. Defensiveness seems to me to cut off curiosity and the search for truth.

My advice about learning would be to read challenging stuff. While I do read some leisurely books from time to time, I try to do that. [I read] mostly things like *A Biography of The Koran.* It's really a history of thinkers within Islam. Read challenging stuff and question your beliefs.

One thing I wanted to add to that was a little bit about my own history in the church. I married Joan in 1961. She was then director of Christian education at the First Presbyterian Church at Sixth and White. I did not join the church. People don't say much to your face, but I think there was talk behind the scenes about, "Why doesn't Don join the Church?" So for 40 years, I participated. My wife worked in the church for a while, then [we] had a family, and then she went on to teach in public schools. But nevertheless, there was a certain amount of wondering why I refused to become a member. My explanation for that, frankly, was from my experience in education. I knew that I would get elected or chosen to be on committees or student councils or church sessions or whatever. I didn't really want to do that; somewhere along in this story, a light began to go on that maybe there was a calling in this—something I could do and do well and be proud of—and that was art. So I always looked at some of these "distractions," I guess I was calling them, as reasons for not joining the church. I did a lot of things [in the church] besides just the art. I went to conferences at Ghost Ranch and over there at Estes Park and [others], probably because I was married to Joan, but also because I have a big mouth and wanted to comment on things and talk about stuff.

But finally, coming to Monument Presbyterian, I think it began to dawn on me that maybe membership had something to be said for it in the sense of being critical. That is to say, maybe criticism from the inside is more credible than criticism from the outside.

I guess I will conclude this section on education with a remark about regrets. I don't have an advanced degree. I have a master's degree, but I don't have a PhD. I don't even have the terminal degree in art, which is the Master of Fine Arts.

The way I see it is that there would have been depth gained by doing the terminal degree or the PhD, either one. My son, Mike, has done the MFA in sculpture at Mills College in California, and I think what he gained from that was invaluable to his becoming an artist himself. So, I will refer to myself as a habitual dilettante who dabbles in this and that and likes one-liners and reactions rather than in-depth study.

What remains unfinished for you in the area of education and learning?

Well, a specific thing that I would mention is study of the Bible. I mentioned earlier that I was reading a book about the Koran. But one of my heroes is Joseph Campbell. And he said, one time, about the Church—and this is what struck me—that he always came back to the Roman Catholic Church because that's where his roots are, and you cannot change your roots.

His background was in Roman Catholicism, and a lot of people have read—or heard Joseph Campbell, when he was alive—talk. His career was mostly in anthropology and the study of other religions, world religions, wherever and whatever they might be.

Now, in listening to his lectures on television and tapes, and reading, he was as critical of the Roman Catholic Church as anyone, but that comes back to that point about being critical from the inside, doesn't it?

But regardless of the criticism, it seemed like he acknowledged the fact that that's where he started. I remember the session where he was at Chartres Cathedral, and he was talking about Chartres Cathedral with the most devotion and reverence and spiritual intensity that I ever heard him speak—about that place, particularly—and it was the Catholic church. It wasn't then, but it would have become the Roman Catholic Church.

So, Bible study has become interesting to me, because there is so much to know. In fact, I'm not sure you could ever know enough about that great book. And so that's one thing I will continue to do. I suppose I have to say at the same time that my interest in comparative religion remains, and I'll probably go on studying more of that.

Another unfinished dimension in education would be art history. Though I'm not teaching art history anymore, there are certainly times like [that which is] coming up this month at Monument Presbyterian with Ben Lawrence [a staff member]. Ben has asked me to provide some visual material for his sermons. We've done the first one for this coming Sunday and they look pretty good, I think. They are a variety of images from a number of—a full range of—periods in Christian art. I hope they'll be interesting to people and challenging at the same time.

Don, today, at this stage of your life, what do you think it means to be financially successful? And do you think most people share that view?

There's sort of an assumption, I think, in our culture. Maybe it's more [in] the American culture, Western culture, that the accumulation of wealth is desirable, is a measure of success. And I have to say that I never quite understood that. I mean, as I said before, earning money seemed to be one of the things that you ought to do. At some point, I decided I wanted to own a home—Joan and I decided we did.

In grade school, which was during World War II, I learned something about saving money. I mean, we were buying saving stamps and pasting them in little books, which eventually became savings bonds during the war. But the impression, I think, that I had as a child—which would probably be in junior high years—was that there was a certain amount of pressure from the family to earn some money. And I didn't really want to. I didn't care much about doing that. I had friends who had paper routes and various things, and I guess the first job I had was caddying at the golf course.

Well, it was nice to earn some money, but for the most part, I thought it was kind of a distraction from what I liked or wanted to do most, and that was [to] make things. It wasn't just painting and drawings, but making three-dimensional things. I remember my brother and I made a little farm out of mud buildings in our backyard, and we must have spent hours on that. Now that was really enjoyable, and [it] seemed worthwhile to make this little model farm out of sun-dried mud.

When it came time for [my son Mike] to go to kindergarten, he did not want to go because he was too busy. Now that I think about that, it almost sounds like a repetition of my record of not wanting to get a job because I had too many things to do. But after the first day in kindergarten, he came home and his comment was, "School is good." So that took care of that.

I would say success, financial success, is being able to do the things you want to do. Joan and I have enjoyed travel a great deal and have saved up for it, and probably spent more than we should. I don't know how you measure that, but I think travel is part of learning, and maybe it's pleasurable, too. I guess I can't speak for Joan, but I think she just has a hankering to go places and see new things. And so it is pleasurable, in that sense.

I like to have enough money to afford art materials so I can make things. I actually inherited the money from my mother to build the studio that I have, so I didn't have to work very hard for that, either.

One time, a colleague of Joan's who was working on one of those—I call them "pyramid schemes,"—wanted to get me into that. I was not interested. I know he made the remark to Joan, "Doesn't Don like money?" And I guess my sense of that is, "Only for what it can do that I really need or want to do."

There is another question that comes up, though—and it's not about success and financial success—and that's your kids. A multimillionaire recently said that he does not believe in leaving money to his kids. I thought about that a lot. There is that sort of nagging thing about helping them, especially when they're starving artists. Jeff is a stage manager in New York, and he is almost making ends meet in his "profession." So we are helping. But that's another one of those questions about financial success.

I think, for me, it's important to have enough to give to worthy causes, as well. And I count the church as the one that we do the most charitable donations to. But there are other charities—such as Catholic Outreach, Amnesty International, the ACLU—to count a few of the organizations that we believe are important. The Southern Poverty Law Center—we contribute to that too.

"Buy what you can afford," I guess, is my motto. Credit cards are just a convenience.

Something else is taxes. It seems like that's the bane of so many people's existence. But I heard a guy on the radio say he enjoyed paying taxes, because if you live in a civilized culture, there are certain dues to be paid. "If I drive down a road and it's well maintained and I can get from here to there safely and in good time, I'm proud to pay my taxes," he said. I guess that's another way I look at financial success.

Don, what are some examples of successful relationships that you've known?

Well, I would want to start with my marriage. If you say 47 years is a sign of success, then I'll accept that. I think that there's always a ways to go in relationships, because people are individuals, and they don't always agree on everything. But the reason I would say our marriage has been successful is that we help each other. I remember reading a book one time about the different forms of marriage, and one of them that struck me—and I guess I have some friends that are like that—[claimed that] it's like two people who live together because of the economic advantages, but they each have their separate lives.

Well, that's not true with us. We do a lot of things together, not the least of which is travel. Another thing we enjoy doing is the theater. That's been a great pleasure for both of us. One of the places that we'd like to go back to—we've been several times, actually—is the Royal National Theatre in London, where we've seen some marvelous productions. One I'll mention here is the American musical, *Oklahoma!*, staged beautifully there. I'll never forget that performance because of the magnificent stage and the British actors [who] did a terrific job with it.

I always ask Joan to read things I've written. I wrote a number of progress reports when I was doing the cross for Monument Church. She read those reports and had helpful things to say about wording and vagueness and saying it plainly.

Another way that we work together is in her teaching at Taylor Elementary in Palisade. I have taught the children a few times, but more often I go out and help her hang up the exhibits of children's work and/or take down the works.

Another thing that I've told other people is that we pretty much forget each other's mistakes. Joan says, "You tend to forget painful things, don't you?", and I do. But that's part of it; you don't have a list of mistakes that your partner makes.

Humor. We try to make humor a part of our lives. It's either our own crude humor or the humor that comes from theater or radio or whatever.

Relationships with our sons have been, I think, a source of pride. They are both moral and considerate young men. They have turned out to be more social, at least more social than I am. Mike has a great gift, I think, for entertaining. Now, he's single in Oakland, California, but he will have parties at his apartment for his friends, and I think that probably goes a long way to keeping friends. He seems to have a social gene in him that works.

Both Mike and Jeff are hard working, and they have done what Joseph Campbell called "following their bliss." Jeff worked in New York for several different financial organizations [wire houses and banks]. At his last one, he was a kind of a go-between [for] the bankers on the one hand and, on the other hand, the publishers. They did in-house publishing at the bank, and Jeff was more or less taking the jobs and feeding them to the people who did the publishing. So he was on the hot seat there. I remember when he worked at Guyton's Fun Park, one of them said that he was a "cool head" and never got rattled. That probably [helped] him well at the bank when he was dealing with these two [factions]—bankers always want it yesterday, and publishers always want to have it perfect.

So there was a certain amount of refereeing that he had to do there. But then came 9/11. The [bank] people decided to lay off 800 employees, and Jeff was one of them.

He had been working in the theater after hours and had done a few plays, and when he got laid off, he said, "Well, you know, I've saved up some money"—he was hoping to buy some property—"[but] I think I'm going to try this theater thing."

And so that's what I mean by "following his bliss." He said to me one time, "You've always been disappointed in me, haven't you, because I'm not in the arts?" And so I think when that happened to him in New York, he saw [it] as his chance. Now he's doing okay—not making a lot of money, but he does the summer in Maine in the repertory theater there. This will be the fourth year. He did a play in Red Bank, New Jersey, that we went to see last May. So it's become a career for Jeff. He works hard at it, and I think that ability to stay cool is probably good for a stage manager—there's a certain amount of watching the clock and things like calling actors when they're late to rehearsal.

I heard something the other day that was troubling in its way, but a truth that I think is important. There was this man who was very sick.

I'm not sure what actually had happened to him, but in the hospital, he was worried about his son who was having difficulty with drugs—in fact, [he was] seriously addicted to some drugs. When he thought he might die of his own injuries—the father—his greatest worry was he wouldn't be able to help his son. In the process of his recovery, he said, "I realized [my] son's life is separate from mine. I can only do so much and I cannot live his life for him." Well, that may well be one of the most painful [of] insights, but I think there's something to that. In relationships, you can't own someone or do everything for them.

Successful relationships, I think, have to do with being civil to everyone. I'd like to think that I am able to ignore status. I remember one faculty colleague I had at the college who didn't seem to want to talk to custodians. That seemed strange to me, I guess. I enjoyed talking to anybody on the staff. Lazarino [for example], who was one of our custodians—I forgot what his first name is—was a pleasure to know and to work with. He just loved to go in and fix the tools in our wood shop. He was a great guy.

I found it hard to reconcile how you can be in a position of teaching and still have that sort of status attitude about someone in a position lower than yours. "Lower" is a term that bothers me anyway.

Looking at your life as a whole, what areas of accomplishment give you the greatest satisfaction?

Well, there are several things that I would point to. But I believe that, ultimately, my family is at the top of the list, and I've already talked about Jeff's career at some length.

Mike's an artist in California, and I'm proud of that. He has done more in the short time since graduate school than I could ever imagine having done. He's a sculptor and has done two pieces in Grand Junction: one at the Art Center and one at the college. But most of the work that he's done has been out there in the Bay Area of Oakland and further south. So the lives of our sons and our life together as a family—that's probably the top of the list.

I wanted to mention four things that I've always felt were accomplishments that I take great pride in. The first one is the scholarship to the University of Denver. I mentioned that earlier actually, but it wasn't just that it was worth a lot of money. It seemed like a sort of affirmation of [my] schoolwork in high school and some indication of a promise of what could come. I'm very proud of the scholarship.

The second one would be the faculty award that I got at Mesa State. I was the third one to receive that. It was called the "Outstanding Faculty Award," and it's a peer award—selected by your peers. While it's something that gets passed around and you take your turn, I always felt that being [only] the third [person] to receive it was something important. I almost missed it. I knew I'd been nominated, but there we were at commencement—when they announce these things—and I had no idea that I would get it. I was sitting there, kind of dozing, when it was announced. Somebody nudged me and said, "Get up there, you fool!" And so I did.

The third one on my list is the Colorado Governor's Award for Excellence in Art that I received in 2002. We went to Denver for the presentation, and George Rivera was one of the other recipients. There were three of us that day, and I met [George] for the first time. I was the last one ever to receive [that award, probably because of] the economic downturn in the state after 2002.

The fourth thing that I want to mention specifically is the piece at the First Presbyterian Church called "Reconciliation." It is the largest piece that I've ever done and is a relief sculpture with stained glass in it. That was a long-term project—three years, I think. I got a one-semester sabbatical leave to do that piece. That was the only time in my career—when I was teaching, at least—[that] I worked full-time on my art.

Mesa State is a state institution with tax funds, and so I think there was a little bit of controversy about doing a project for a church. Fortunately, the administration didn't challenge the [issue] of church-state separation, and I was certainly glad to have the chance to do the project.

In summarizing about my successes, I would have to list the artwork and the teaching probably about equally. I used to refer to myself as a "teacher-artist," and the reason I put it that way is that I earned my money from teaching. I've sold some art but not very much, and certainly not enough to earn a living. The art that I've done for the church turns out to be something that has a little more tangible purpose. It's done for a particular place, for people that are tied to that place, and you'd like to think that the art has something to say to them. So, for me that's been a great opportunity, and I have to give credit to Joan for that—for getting me involved with the church.

The piece at First Presbyterian called "The Servant" was published in *Crossroads Magazine*. I would guess it was probably sometime in the late '60s [that] *Crossroads* published that piece.

I did some portraits of my faculty colleagues at the college—I think five pieces. I've enjoyed those because they are not portraits in the sense of what these people looked like: they're portraits of them as personalities. I chose people that I admired as teachers, for the most part, but I also found them to be flawed individuals. And so in my portraits of them, those flaws are evident.

One example is an English and German instructor who had also attended West Point. He was a very acerbic personality and loved to needle his students. So I did him as a horse whose head was a pistol. That has seemed sensible to me, just for formal reasons. The shape of a horse's head is kind of like the barrel of a gun. I went to the museum and researched how to do Peacemakers [a brand of pistol] from the frontier days. That became the head of the horse. The horse also was mounted on a very small circular track and it had train wheels. And so you can picture this thing going around and around on this very small track. Those were the kinds of symbols that I would use in these portraits.

I think I was a good teacher and I've enjoyed the challenge of it—more in later years, I guess, as I began to learn more. Alvie Redden [a teacher at the college] and I had become acquainted when I was in the school district here and he was at the college. He needed some help and asked me if I'd like to teach in the college. I had a lot of catching up to do, both in the studio and in art history, when we decided to share that job. But I grew to love art history and art appreciation.

I really enjoyed teaching art appreciation as a general education course. These were students from the sciences, from business, from all areas. I thought that was really a great challenge and opportunity. Some of those students had never been in an art gallery, and they didn't know the first thing about how that can affect your life—a concert, or a play in a theater, or an art exhibit.

> **Can you think of a student you taught that course to who really thought it was beneath him, perhaps not manly, but was turned around as a result of your coursework?**

The key word you used was manly. [There] was a young man who was in high school—just graduating. I had actually known him for some time, so he was confident in talking to me about going to Mesa State. One day he called and asked me if he could come over and talk about the art department at Mesa. "Sure,…. Come on over." I explained the program, the classes that he would be taking, and so forth, and finally it got around to the real reason why he wanted to talk. And that was that, apparently, in his family, there had been some aspersions cast about artists and their manliness. And so he wanted some assurance, I guess, that it was okay for him to study art.

Regarding unfinished things, there are some unfinished sculptures in my studio that keep staring at me and saying, "Come on, let's get this done." There are also a couple of unstarted ideas and the always-nagging problem of what to do with the art, since I haven't managed to be commercially successful. How am I going to dispose of the art? That's a great burden, I think. We're talking about legacies here, and there could be some tangible burdens in the form of the art that's left over.

But I'm going to conclude by saying that [my] successes in art are probably the most for God and not for me. One of my inspirations has been Paul Tillich, as far as theology is concerned. He's the one who I remember talking about the Divine Being inside of you—if you can find it. The task is to reveal the Divine within yourself. I don't know if that's a contradiction or not: saying that success in art, or life, is for God, when you regard God as within yourself. That's something you have to discover.

> **Would you add a piece about the philosophy of art?**

I came to believe that I—that we, as a teacher and also as an artist—should have a philosophy to base what you teach on, as well as the work that you do as an artist.

So, number one would be, art isn't easy. That comes from years of being self-conscious about other disciplines and the way they regard the arts as touchy-feely. Art isn't easy.

Number two, art is not just decoration. [While] I certainly believe that there's an element of it that should please the senses—the sensory experience that you have in the colors and the lines—it's not just sensory pleasure.

Number three, art should say something. It should challenge you to think about what it means. Art should demand interpretation. It's a sort of dialogue between artist and viewer, and the viewer has some responsibility in coming to the work.

Number four, art is not just a commodity—and that comes from [someone] who is a complete failure at selling artwork. In some circles, it is regarded as just another thing to be bought and sold—that often times what you're buying is the name of the person who did it. That's the aspect of commodity that probably is the most troublesome—the buyer wants something that will increase in value [rather than just] love for the piece.

And I guess number five, in my philosophy, is that art can provide a sort of tangible dimension to faith. I'm moving this into the [area of] "art should say something, and it *can* say something about religious faith."

But visual art, because of its permanence—as opposed to performing arts, which are ethereal—provides something lasting, something that you can get ahold of.

So, that's the philosophy.

Jamie Hamilton

March 12, 2008

Chris said, "I have two rules: be on time and play hard. Everything else takes care of itself. Because, if you are not on time, you won't catch the bus, and you won't be with me...."

About a month later and I was over at the old Albertson store...with my daughter who's three, or three and a half, at that time. We're looking for cards...and my daughter comes up, looks at one of the cards, and goes, "I know him."...It was one of the three stooges...I used to watch that show [when I'd get up to give Dane his nighttime bottle]. And she goes, "Flllloooorrrbbb" [sound] like Curly used to do on The Three Stooges show. And I said, "Why do you know that?" And she said, "Every time you got up with Dane..."—she came up and looked right over my shoulder from the top of the stairs... and when I got up she ran back to bed. She watched The Three Stooges with me.

I'd like to think that I'm fairly simplistic. I think if you stay true to your values and your judgments, success will follow, whatever that definition is. The material things... are not why I do any of this stuff. It's being able to influence and improve the community that we're in. That's my definition of success.

That would be a legacy [keeping Home Loan intact and locally owned from within] that I think would give recognition and credibility back to all the people that went before me. There have only been five presidents in the history of our organization.

Jamie, when you were growing up, what did you think it meant to be professionally successful, and what experiences led you to that definition?

I did read that question and the word "success" didn't come to mind, but the word "professional" did. I [had] the idea, at least in the '70s when I [was] growing up—late' 60s or early '70s—that "professional" meant a professional athlete, professional football player—I tried to play a little basketball, professional basketball—or, in my case, what I really focused on [was] baseball.

And so when I heard the word "professional," it meant professional baseball, and with that, "success" [meant] being at the top of the game as a professional baseball player.

I never truly equated success with any monetary riches. I grew up in Denver—I was born here, but I grew up in Denver—and we had two stations. I watched the Cincinnati Reds and the Pittsburgh Pirates, sometimes the St. Louis Cardinals. I was watching Johnny Bench, Pete Rose and Concepcion. That was my idea of professional success, playing baseball Saturday afternoon on *The Game of the Week*.

I guess I assumed that there was monetary riches to go with that, but [as] you may be aware, in the '70s, there wasn't anybody making big money playing professional baseball. There wasn't a million dollar contract until 1981 after the first strike.

Obviously, Mom and Dad instilled the idea of making sure you do things right, and that involved all sorts of different things, from chores to school to church and, in our case, to family night, which was *every* night, sitting around the table and just talking about your day's efforts.

How does your definition of professional success today compare with that?

I think society makes professional success—equates it with—monetary riches. And that's still something that doesn't drive me now. I enjoy it, I've had some financial success, but I think professional success is consistent effort—tenure—and I think that's [tenure] something that's kind of got away from young people now. My idea was that if I wasn't playing professional baseball for my entire life, then I was going to get a good job, like my dad, and work 30 years with the same company. A long tenure was professional success to me. To jump from one job to the next—it was just like you couldn't make up your mind on something.

And so today, I think that the biggest part of the test is an integrity that goes with it. If you're going to say you're going to do it, then you do it. If you can't do it, that's okay, but tell people that you can't do it. Don't lead them on. So going back to what Mom and Dad talked to us about, if you're going to say you'll mow that lawn by three o' clock, then mow that lawn by three o'clock.

So I see professional success today as consistency, tenure, and integrity.

In light of your definition today of professional success, in what ways are you already a professional success?

Well, believe it or not, I measure that [by] those definitions. I measure [it] by 25 years now at Home Loan and Investment Company. I've been out of professional baseball four times as long as I was in it—thinking [it] was going to be the career for me when I graduated from Mesa State College.

So I think that my success started, and I mean this in all due respect, as a clerk in the insurance division; I worked [up to being] an agent, [then] to what was called a producer, [then] to a sales manager, moved up to vice president, moved to president, and then had the opportunity to buy it ten years ago. We now employ 63 people.

When I played professional ball, the best manager I had was a guy by the name of Chris Cannazzaro. And Chris managed in the big leagues. He was the first All Star with the San Diego Padres. He moved from the Mets to the Padres—first All Star for the Padres—and then it was the Atlanta Braves, the year that Ted Turner fired everybody and told the press that he was going to be the manager. Chris was the only guy to be retained. And Chris said, "If you do that, I'll quit", because of the integrity of the game. So they named Chris interim manager. After that season was done, he quit and came back, all the way down from the big leagues to A-ball [Class A baseball leagues].

[He was the] best guy I ever learned baseball from and the best guy I ever learned life's lessons from. He set us down [with] these packets of rules of what we could do, how we could dress/couldn't dress, from the California Angels Organization—what we could do as far as mustaches and long hair, and whether we could drink beer when we were on the road. Just a bunch of different rules.

Chris told us, "I have two rules: be on time and play hard. Everything else takes care of itself. Because, if you are not on time, you won't catch the bus, and you won't be with me. And if you don't give me your best effort, then I'll recognize that. You won't be here then."

So, I will tell you that [that] story is what I used from the day that I took over this insurance and banking operation. We've got two rules: be on time and work hard—the synonym for playing hard. And, when I took over the athletic director's position [at Mesa State College] two-and-a-half years ago, that's the only two rules I mentioned to our staff. "If you're on time to meetings and at your games and I see good effort, everything else takes care of itself."

Now, I will tell you, I have learned [that] in the bureaucracy of higher education, there's a lot more rules that are written down and I have to be within those parameters. But to me they're just common sense, and our coaches understand that as well.

So, I think 25 years' tenure of being in a business, being in the same community, giving back to that community, and being based in integrity, tenure and consistency is the definition of professional success. I'm not there yet.

And have there been any unexpected costs for achieving that success?

I guess it's never really hit me until these last couple of years. The answer is "yes," and right now the example on the top of my mind is that it has cost me [both] financially and in [my] time because of my intent to help a cause, whether it's Mesa State College or Partners or Junior College World Series.

I've had to ask people for assistance. But then they ask me to return that favor later on. That's the unexpected cost: I'll ask for donations to Mesa State for our athletic department and scholarship program. Some will say "you bet" and then two weeks later, I'll get a letter from their favorite charity, asking me to help.

Now, that's money that's going to kids, which I appreciate. But in my case, it's my personal dollars. Like I said, I never thought about it as a cost until someone asked me just a couple of weeks ago, "You raised $300,000. What has it cost you?" And then I realized [that] there's a couple of guys here [for whom] I had to turn around and give a hundred bucks for Kiwanis tickets, or a thousand bucks for a Partner's Auction.

I'd like to think that there hasn't been an emotional or relationship cost in it with my family. I've been married 27 years and I think we have a great relationship. My kids—my daughter is 24, working in the insurance business in Denver; my son is 21, playing baseball at the University of New Mexico. We just got back from watching him for a week of playing baseball in Arizona and Minnesota.

Because my wife, Debbie, is such a great mom and has been such a great mom, I'm sure there were times that I was making a presentation to the the Elk's Club or doing something on JUCO's behalf and it cost me some relationship time with my family. We made [it] a point that, while we'd miss some little games or dance recitals and those types of things, my insurance career allowed me some time flexibility. But in retrospect, I've probably missed some relationship time there. So that's a cost, and to me, that's a more valued cost than any financial cost.

But other than that, I can tell you that I enjoy the community service aspect of things. Some people play golf, or work out, or ride a bike, or run for stress management. I can honestly look you in the eye and tell you that when I serve on the United Way Board, or work at the Chamber Board, and help the RSVP, [Retired Senior Volunteer Program] and hear the issues that they're trying to face and the problems they're trying to solve,—it takes me out of my world and the stress of my day-to-day operation, and puts me over there trying to solve a problem. Whatever experiences I can lend to help solve those problems is neat. And it's a cleansing for me to be able to do that.

What do you think remains unfinished for you in the area of professional success?

Well, I'd like to think, at the age of 51, that it's a longer tenure. I heard a guy speak when I was in my first year in insurance. I went to a St. Paul, Minnesota, class; this guy [the speaker] was intriguing to me because he was a CPCU, which is—in insurance terminology—a Chartered Property and Casualty Underwriter. That is basically a master's [degree] in insurance, and in the same breath, [he] went [on] and got his JD [essentially a doctorate in law]. And I've always thought that was intriguing.

A lot of times [when] I offer professional advice, what people really want is legal advice. And I say, "I'm not your attorney but this is what we have. You need to speak to your attorney." But it would have been also cool to be able to say, "Okay, I do have my CPCU [and] here's the insurance aspect of it. But from a legal standpoint, this is something else you can look at." His [the class speaker's] comment was, "I think it's always healthy to have two careers," which I believe.

I think my community service has been one career—and, of course, my family is there—and the business has been the other career. My choice to help out after I was asked [to be] the athletic director has been a good one for me. I love being around the young people—having the empty-nest issue with our kids going off to college and not being in the house. And so the last three years have been fun: just go work with young people.

I think I still have a good 10 to 15 more years of being able to give back to the community and [leave]—I think the word "legacy" is what you use—and that's a little bit further out there than I want to admit.

Jamie, when you were a youngster, what constituted success in learning and education for you and who taught you that?

Grades were important to my parents and they instilled that to be important in us. I say it from that standpoint only because I watch my children now, and learning is more important to me than the grade aspect. I think part of that is just the different times, but I also think, regarding my folks, [that] it's much like baseball: a 300-hitter is considered an above-average hitter. A B or A student was considered an above-average student. That's how we measured it. So we measured everything by statistics. With grades, you get good grades, or you get good test scores.

And so it is important to get those homework assignments done. My brother went to CU on a football scholarship—he actually went there on a baseball scholarship as a freshman, but they dropped baseball, so he walked on and got a football scholarship. My sister is actually the best athlete in the family. She was All-State in three sports in high school and then ended up going to Idaho State on a volleyball scholarship.

At the dinner table, very rarely did we not have all three of us sitting down to eat, even though we all three were in different sports. I still regard those as the greatest times in my life—all three of us. Mom worked it out that in-between one practice time or another, we all ate [together] and talked about what happened in Dad's office, what my mom did as a volunteer at school, and what all three of us did. That's something I still try to do today with our children—at least we tried to do it when they were here in high school.

So, going back to your question, the measurement issue was great. That was important to us. What really instilled it in me was when my mom and dad suggested that I go to Regis High School in Denver, which was a parochial high school.

In the Jesuit program, you are measured. They weekly ranked our class on where [we] were from one to 175, and our Jesuit priest told us at the end of the week that "You're number five this week" or "You're number 90 this week." There was just a competition in an all-boys school that probably, because of my competitive nature, just said, "By God, I want to be number one."

The Jesuits also believed in what we call the "blue-book mentality." For example, in a history class, they'd give you a blue book of white paper and say, "Tell me about the War of 1812." Then my job, in one hour, was to write as much as I could on the War of 1812, and grammatically correct. If I didn't punctuate right, I was [marked] off on that. And I used to think, "God, that's terrible." But I will tell you that today, when I read some of the emails that I get from some of my associates and some of my competitors, I am going, "How do they ever write a letter?"

To this day, when someone's going to be hired by me, after I do an interview, I ask them to write a letter on why they want to work at Home Loan and Investment Company. I want to see if they have the ability to put their thoughts down and do it in paragraph form and be able to communicate. The service business involves quite a bit of communication.

Has your concept of success in learning and education changed over the years?

Yeah, very much so. What really got me into that is when I was serving as a board member for U-Tech—I think it's now the Western Colorado Community College.

It was amazing to me. I learned from Kerry Youngblood, who I think is an exceptional educator, that basically everything in our United States or the world has changed on how we deliver a product—from vending machines, to banking services, to insurance services, to technology services. Everything has changed except how we deliver education: it's still the three R's, so to speak. Yet, people don't learn that way. I mean I truly believe in the technical aspect of things; [for example, consider] a young mind that's bright but can't do any algebra stuff, [yet] can turn around and do a design on a new house someplace and put it together. Why do we think that that's worse [less desirable] than being able to get a good grade on an algebra project?

That's why with my kids now, we never put a big deal on their grades. I have said, "Tell me what you're learning, how you're doing it—are you getting [the] job done on time and working hard? Are those things happening?" And they communicate with me. So we sit at dinnertime: "Tell me what happened and what you learned, and what does that mean to you?"

Last week when I was with [my son] and 10 other players in New Mexico, we were talking politics for a couple of hours. [It was] an interesting insight on the 21-or 20-year-old mind that's looking at the three candidates for United States President, what's going to get them to vote and why they think they will vote the way they're going to vote. I'm amazed to hear what influenced them and how they learned about it and how they learned about things. So I am all about the learning *process*. I don't know that I measure it with grades as I did when I was growing up. I think people learn differently and can still be successful, whatever trade they decide to do, without having a GPA behind their names. And that's helped me as we hire young people, as well. I don't ask about GPAs. Some will put their transcript right there and I [say],

"That's fine, but what did you learn?" Grades are measurement, but I don't know that I put a lot of credence in them anymore.

From your observations and experiences, what are some keys to achieving success in learning and education?

Well, there's the ability to write. I enjoy speaking to groups; I try to practice that and to give a message that is succinct and comes to the point. But I think we're all lacking in the ability to write a good letter. [We do] text messaging or [we have] email systems. We've learned how to do that quick and easy. But I think the written letter does say something about your integrity and your professionalism. So, I do like to measure that. Again, I have my applicants write me a letter on why they want to work for our organization or what they can glean from it.

But I think the other aspect of it is [that] I look at the accountability of things. Do they go to the classes they say they're going to? Are they on time? Were they involved in extracurricular things?

I think that's a measurement because when they come to our organization, we want them to be involved with the community. We think that's healthy for them and their family, mentally and emotionally. We also think, ultimately, business comes through that, because my simple mind says if you do good work, people recognize that, and they'll come to you for advice.

What did financial success mean to you when you were a youngster growing up, and what personal experiences contributed to what you understood financial success to mean?

It's interesting [that] when I read through your questions, I really glossed over financial success. I think I can honestly say I've never done anything for the dollars. Whether I'm selling widgets or selling insurance, money comes with that, and maybe sometimes more money than other times. I guess at the end of the day, it's more of a perception [coming] from somebody else that I might be financially successful, or that "they" seem to be financially successful.

Steve Gammill

I can tell you that, as I wanted to downsize my house, we ended up building twice the house. The kids had left and Mom is looking forward to grandkids. I wanted to take it from where we were and downsize, because I wanted to be able to invest those dollars in, maybe, a second home someplace, or to be able to travel and do some things.

Growing up, I guess what I would consider financially successful was having my own house. When Deb and I were first married, we rented for eight months—maybe six months—and then did the proverbial closing on Black Monday in 1981,—timing being what it is. I borrowed $5,000 from my wife's folks for the down payment and we bought a place in the Vineyards. It was a balloon interest rate. [It was at] 9.5% on a $60,000 house that was ballooning to 16.5% in three years. And within four months, the place appraised at $19,500.

I was making $500 a month and my wife was making $650 as a teller. And it never affected us because [that] was more dollars than we'd ever had before. Did we go without some things? I would imagine, but we sure didn't know that we didn't have them.

I was looking at other people, our neighbors, closing up and having to go back to the bank. But my father-in-law and my dad always said, "Whatever bad times you're going through, get that house paid off, because at least you've always got a place to stay."

Growing up, financial success was strictly a house to live in. Now I guess it's the luxury of being able to jump on a plane and go and watch my son play [ball] without thinking about what it costs to do that. I mean, I'm conscious of it, but it's not like I have to save for it. I can write a check or put it on the credit card and, at the end of the month, get it paid off. I guess that drives me to make sure that I can continue to do that as the economy nationwide goes down.

I can remember at Regis [College] having to take my lunch because it didn't have a hot lunch [program] that time, unless you wanted to buy a hamburger. And honest to God, exchanging pennies for quarters so I could buy a Pepsi—that was a treat for me. A quarter for a Pepsi seemed like a lot of dollars. Before, I had to sneak nickels from my brother, and now I drink two or three Pepsi's in the morning for breakfast—I don't drink coffee. I made my goal: I can have Pepsi anytime I want it.

Let's talk about relationships. What are some examples of successful relationships that you've known

Well obviously, I've been married 27 years. My wife has put up with my idiosyncrasies, and she has been so good at taking care of our children while I was out trying to help the community or make a living—that is really a good relationship. We're really working hard now on even improving that relationship from a communication standpoint. Interestingly enough, you talk about me reliving these stories—we're trying to each do that right now. Once a week we're talking about some childhood memories, just to bring up some things as we help each other. We shared a wish list of the things that we want—not necessarily materially, but emotionally—so that we can help each other obtain those goals. So, that's been a good relationship for us.

I have two stories from my kids. First of all, I'll do my daughter. When we lived in the Vineyards, my daughter [Sarah] was three years old and my son [Dane] was just one. I'll never forget [when] we won the "Shoppers Hotline." That was a card that you could take to the store: they would registered it [so they could] see buying trends and things like that. I'll never forget when I signed up for it, I asked, "What is this going to cost me?" [And they replied that it was] nothing, [that they] were going to give rewards out based on the number of people who signed up.

Lo and behold, we won! That was in 1986—we won a microwave. I didn't have money to go buy a microwave. My wife could not breast-feed, so with Sarah, I always had to get up in the middle of the night and heat up the old bottle. [After] Dane was born, I said, "With this microwave, I can now get in there and heat up the bottle and get them ready to go."

So, there was about three or four weeks there where my son was getting up like clockwork at 3:10 in the morning. We had just gotten cable in our house and TBS was coming on, which I loved because they showed all the Braves' baseball games, and they'd show highlights in the morning. A lot of guys that I played with were now making it to the big leagues. And another thing they did at three o'clock to 3:30 was [to show] *The Three Stooges*. And so, I get there at 3:10 a.m., I grab my son, I get a bottle warmed, I sit down, turn on the TV, put the bottle in his mouth, and I sit there. I watch TV and [then] it's like 3:32. He's burped and ready to go, so I get up and go back to bed.

About a month later I was over at the old Albertson store, 12th [Street] and Orchard [Avenue], with my daughter, who's three or three and a half at that time. We were looking for cards for Mother's Day, or a birthday, or something, and my daughter comes up, right next to me, looks at one of the cards, and goes, "I know him." And I looked over and said, "What are you talking about?" It was one of the Three Stooges. Remember, I used to watch the show. And she goes, "Flllloooorrrbbb" [sound] like Curly used to do on *The Three Stooges* show. And I said, "Why do you know that?" She said, "Every time you got up with Dane..."—she came up and looked right over my shoulder from the top of the stairs and watched, and when I got up she ran back to bed. She watched *The Three Stooges* with me.

[And about] my son—this is a relationship [story] that I still tell. My dad is a mentor, my father-in-law is a mentor and—to be quite honest—Sam Suplizio was a mentor to me from a baseball and business aspect. Unfortunately, later on in his life, we grew apart. One of the things I saw in Sam, and other people that were successful in their business or professional careers, was that they tried to force the business, or the baseball or football, on their kids. As a result, it kind of pushed them away.

When I saw that happening in a number of different peoples' lives—guys that I've played with, friends of mine—it was like [the] dad was wanting to control what the kids did and the kids really wanted to do something else. So I made a real point that Dane—when he was old enough to play soccer or flag football, or baseball—I said, "That's fine."

I'll never forget [when] we went up to see my sister in Seattle and went to a Seattle Mariner's game. It was just neat to be in the ballpark again—I was only about five years removed from playing professionally, maybe a little longer than that—[and we were] sitting there, having a good day, with cotton candy, sodas, and just all the things going on in a major league baseball game. So when we got in the car [to leave] and my son was in my lap—he was probably three or four years old—he was talking by then, and I said, "Dane, did you have fun?" "Yes, Dad, that was the best."

So I tried to use that, as an avenue at least, to talk to him about him playing baseball. I said, "Dane, that's so good, because—you know, I work hard, trying to instill what's been instilled in me—if you work hard, one day you could grow up and be a star." My son, *three or four years old*, said, "Dad, you be the star. I'll be the moon."

And I realized right then that he had no ambition to be the star. I was thinking "baseball star" but it [had a different meaning] to him. So, it really proved to me that he was going to be his own man—and he still is today.

[It makes] me feel good [that] he is playing collegiate-level baseball, but he does it because he *wants* to do it, and he does it his way. He had options for golf and for other sports. I learned early in our [family] relationships that I don't force things. I think I have really good relationships with our kids and my wife.

There are other special relationships that I've seen that have worked. I have a good business partner in Craig Springer. We know each other's needs and wants from a business, professional standpoint. He makes me look good and I try to make him look good. It goes back again to an old baseball [adage]: "Don't show me up and I wont show you up." And that's just baseball—just getting down to the basics of playing the game of ball. We try to take that same thing to everything else that we do, from the JUCO World Series committees, to Mesa State athletics, to our business.

What else would you like to achieve in the area of relationships?

I would say that it's important to be able to have that really close friend. I'd like to be my wife's best friend. I don't know that we're at that level, because I don't know that I would share business issues with her that are bothering me. I hate to put any stress on her. I think I'd like to get better at communicating that [with her]. Other than that, I just enjoy people and the idea that if you need help, you can talk to me and I'll help you out—and just to be able to be a guy with other guys and a good friend if other people need it.

Jamie, what did you learn to regard as personal success when you were growing up, and how do you think you came up with that definition?

Again, we'll go back to my parochial education. We learned, as I told you before, about the blue-book presentation, and I learned how to communicate. We also learned—one of my Jesuit professors taught me how to learn by the use of acronyms. For example, in learning how the digestive system works, we used to take the word "digestive" and then each letter would stand for a part of it. Then spell the word all the way out and at the end of the day—at the blue book—I could write all this down and have a very nice presentation of 500 words on how the digestive tract works. I try to do that when I'm [preparing] speaking engagements. It makes it simple for me to take a word that is apropos to [the group I'm speaking to].

But what I've learned and what I still try to express to all our people, besides being on time and working hard, is that attitude drives everything. And so, when I'm doing these presentations, I always get a word that has an "A" in it because "A" is for attitude. Attitude stories are what make the day go right or not. If I walk into a room of 63 employees with a frown on my face and [I'm] not upbeat, they'll feel that in a heartbeat. I may or may not have a bad day going already but, for the most part, they shouldn't see that. You'll find there may be very little difference in people. But you'll find that that little difference can make a big difference. That little difference is attitude and the big difference is whether it's positive or negative. So, I challenge every one of you to make sure you maintain a positive attitude, because that's the big difference between people.

I also learned very early on that if I did struggle on a test, Mom was there saying, "You'll do better the next time"—very encouraging, and making sure I felt confident about myself. Sometimes you're going to fail and you've got to live with that failure. That's [one of the things] I liked about baseball. I think part of my success in the business world is realizing that there were many nights that I didn't get a hit. But that next night, I got back up at the plate and tried it again, and had some successes.

So the analogy, in insurance terms, is [that] I try to get a hit every day. I try to sell a policy every day of my life. And sometimes you hit big home runs and sometimes you sell a little motorcycle policy that gets you $5 in commission. But, everyday, if you're consistent, that consistency [brings] the financial rewards, the attitude rewards.

As you think about your own personal success, what remains unfinished?

Well, I do have to pay off my house. We built a monstrous house here four years ago and that's driving me to pay that off as quick as possible. What's now changed over the past couple of years is that both of my children have shown an interest in getting into the insurance business. As I earlier mentioned, my daughter is an underwriter for an insurance company in Denver, and now she's thinking [about] coming back to Grand Junction and working in Home Loan and Investment Company [his business].

The uniqueness of Home Loan, even though we're a 110 year [old company], is that it's never really been a family-run organization. There's been a family history with the Daniels, but Sam [Suplizio] bought it from Harold Daniels and Sam sold it to me. I have people in line in our organization who may be able to buy it from me because—again, my quick [baseball] analogy—I don't want to be the person that broke up the Yankees. I want to keep it a locally owned, non-family owned business and continue to grow.

So, I'd like to have the opportunity for my son and daughter to come and work here. Whether they would buy me out or not, they would have the ability come in, work hard, and earn some [opportunities].

I would think right now that it would be a measure of success to be able to continue the tradition of what I think Home Loan is all about: giving to the community and being an icon. That's a hard word, but we've been recognized over the last 110 years. It would be nice to make sure that [it] would be continued, either by my children or other good young people that we have in our organization.

That would be a legacy that I think would give recognition and credibility back to all the people that went before me. There have only been five presidents in the history of our organization.

Looking at your life as a whole, what areas of accomplishment give you the greatest satisfaction?

Well, a strong marriage and two great kids—I'm very blessed—and being healthy is very rewarding, and I thank God for that. In my business, in the insurance business, you see a lot of disasters. You see a

lot of traumatic issues that happen, from car accidents, to devastating fires, to death, to health problems. I've been very blessed that [that] hasn't happened to me or our immediate family on both sides of the family.

I'm very proud of the fact that I played professional baseball, and the more years I've been out of it, I realize how difficult it is to get into it. My son is 10 times the athlete that I am. Now, whether he gets a chance to play professional baseball [or not], I don't know. Number one1, does he want to? Number two, is he going to get that opportunity?

I'm proud of starting out as a clerk in the insurance operation and now owning a company that has 63 people. And I'm proud of the fact that I'm concerned about those 63 people and their families. Every night when I go to bed, I think about what can make us better as an organization.

I'm extremely proud of what I think—and again, trying not to sound boastful—I've done, stability-wise, for the athletic department of Mesa State College. In the last seven years, there've been five athletic directors. When you get five different personalities trying to run a department—the coaches, the people that are working there—heads are spinning because there are just different ways to implement programs. We've balanced the budget now for the third straight year, which hadn't happened for five previous years. We're going to have this Athletic Director Scholarship [a fund made up of his salary, some savings money in the College and some other financial commitments.], which is going to be close to half a million dollars by the end of 2008. We're going to be able to make a transition to a young man that's been there the last seven years who's really been doing the work...—by the name of Butch Miller—as Associate AD, and to be able to take those student athletes to the next level.

[Being Athletic Director has] been fun for me. It hasn't been stressful and I actually think that I'm a better manager, or leader, there than I am in my own organization. I don't have as many emotional ties there as I do with people that I've worked with for 20-plus years. I can go over there, get the facts, say yes or no, and not [need to] know the politics behind it.

I'm proud of being able to give back to my alma mater. Because of what Tim Foster's [the current college president] done, I've been able to help put Mesa State on the map in Colorado. It's a well-kept secret here: we've got 6,200 students now, projected to go to 10,000 in the next five to seven years. Grand Junction is growing, and we're seeing the different faces that are happening on the campus with the [new] facilities. That's been fun.

I'm proud to be, basically, the fourth chair [person] in the history of the Junior College World Series. I'm proud that Sam [Suplizio] believed that I was the guy that could take it after he had created it and made it what it is—that he felt comfortable that I had enough business and baseball savvy to be able to continue that tradition.

And that's fun for me, because it puts Grand Junction on the map. It's a community event and it's still affordable, it's still family oriented, and we're going to continue to do that. For example, this year, we're fortunate enough to be able to drive the bus on getting turf at Stoker Field for the high schools and the college. When the college was getting the soccer field put together, I approached the general contractor and said, "What kind of discount can you give us if we do two fields at once?" It saved money for the college, it saved money for the JUCO committee, and JUCO guaranteed a hundred thousand [dollars] of it. Instead of going through a bid process, we got a contract turnaround time in less than 45 days and got it installed in less than 60 days. That just doesn't happen in the bureaucracy of municipal government. That was fun, because the assets of a non-profit had driven the bus, and I helped steer it.

Besides family, the things that I'm proud of are being able to give back to the community and being involved with those types of things. I very rarely say "I." It's always been "we" that have done it but those are things that I am proud of.

I'd like to think that I'm fairly simplistic. I think if you stay true to your values and your judgments, success will follow, whatever that definition is. The material things that come with whatever success I've had financially are not why I do any of this stuff. It's being able to influence and improve the community that we're in. That's my definition of success.

Dennis and Patti Hill

December 18, 2007

One day, I waited for everybody else to leave the class and I walked up to my teacher and said, "You know, I'm not really going to need this stuff, because I'm going to be an entertainer." And she didn't laugh in my face, which I thought took a great deal of self-control on her part

—Patti Hill

And I want to open my hand and not hold on to this life so tightly. I want to live radically for Jesus. I want to be in a place where I say it doesn't matter what I have to wear, what I have to sit on, what I have to eat—I will follow Jesus anywhere. That is what I want. That's where I want to be headed.

—Patti Hill

I have no aspirations of passing the business on, you know. I don't see that as my legacy. The people I've impacted are my legacy…If I was able to show them perhaps a glimpse of the face of Christ in some way or another, that's the legacy that I want [to leave].

—Dennis Hill

When you were growing up, what did you think it meant to be professionally successful and what experiences led you to that conclusion?

Patti:

I don't think I had a notion of what a professional anything really was. I did a lot of dreaming. I admired success from afar—usually, you know, movie stars or ice skaters. I did not consider that [as] something for myself. I think that came from being brought up in a home where we were mostly just trying to survive. And real success for us was to survive and not look like we were poor.

Can you think of an event or an experience that exemplifies that?

Patti:

Well, my father passed away when I was three and my mother was the sole breadwinner. But she was in a dilemma. She did not want to leave us alone. So she worked mostly part-time and we collected veterans' and social security death benefits—or *survivor* benefits, because we weren't dead. We were surviving. And so that's what we lived off of.

I think of a time—it was kind of early on—and we lived in a housing project. Things were very difficult. My mother bought me a dress at a rummage sale and she made me a promise not to tell anyone that had happened. There were times when we had macaroni with butter and salt and pepper for dinner. Our furniture was lawn furniture, the kind with the webbing. That was our living room furniture. I remember our mother battling the cockroaches constantly. And she got pretty good at whipping her shoe off and slapping them right across or against, you know, the wall. She was a meticulous housecleaner and it was really difficult for her to be dealing with that. We didn't stay there too terribly long. I was there for first grade and the start of second grade. And then we moved to California.

Dennis:

For me, I think it got wrapped up in the making of a good salary, making a lot of money. Not huge, you know, but it was always kind of a goal to make a good, solid middle-class living. That's what my family did, and we were a pretty typical family. "Do it now." That's my dad's favorite phrase.

Tell me about a time that you heard him say that.

Oh my gosh, it was just a constant thing. It was always, "Do it now. You're no typical kid." I remember my brother found him a wall plaque [done] in metal scrollwork that says, "Do it now." In fact, Dad still has it up on the wall in their house. It was just perfect. That was his motto.

What experiences can you remember that influence what you meant by "a lot of money"?

Dennis:

I remember we did a project when I was in junior high school where we had to research different professions. It was kind of a life skills class. I remember studying about becoming a dentist. And "Dennis the dentist"—I got that a lot. And I remember you needed to find out what kind of education or training or experience you needed and what they got paid. I remember they got paid $30,000 a year. And that was so much money.

Frankly, I had no idea what my dad made because he never talked about that. That was [between] him and Mom. They were the ones running the house. And I remember asking him once, "Well, Dad, how much do you make?" He made up some stupid figure and I learned right there not to ask that—it's not something that you tell other people."

You know, I never thought of myself as a hard worker. It just was what it was. When I was in high school, my first real job, the summer after my senior year, was around an insurance company. I worked for the building superintendent. The reason I got the job was because my grandfather was doing a little project right there. He was pouring concrete. We were mixing the concrete, shoveling gravel and sand and cement into the mixer, and wheelbarrowing it around in the backyard. The big boss, his name was Jim, and my grandfather were friends, and a week or so later, he offered me a job just because of how I had worked. I remember being surprised at the time because I wasn't working hard—I was just working. I was just doing it. That's how you did things.

I got into trouble when I first started working because I wouldn't take a long-enough lunch. I had to take 30 minutes. I would sit down, have a sandwich, and cookies, and apples, and stuff. It would be 15 or 20 minutes and I'd go back to work. They had a time clock, so I had to clock in and out. He [the boss] came to me one day and said, "You can't do that. You have to sit there for half an hour."

How does your definition of professional success today compare to other people's definition of professional success?

Patti:

I would only be guessing at what other people perceive to be success, but I know that there are folks that really chase after the almighty dollar, and that collecting things is what's important.

I'm a writer now and my professional success is two-tiered—maybe even three. On one tier, I need to be satisfied with what I produce—that I create something satisfying to me artistically and that I feel good about [what] other people [see in it].

The second tier of that is honoring God, because I feel my profession is also my ministry. With any story I write, I want to reveal a truth about God or a relationship with Him that the reader may not have considered otherwise. That is what good literature should do. The author should take you to someplace you've never been before or shift where you're standing so that you can see a belief or a situation from a different angle. I want my work to resonate with people and to be a blessing for the Lord's sake.

Then thirdly, and this is where [some] tension comes in, I want to have some financial success for a couple of reasons. First, because it makes life a lot easier. But more than that, I feel like I owe it to my publisher, because they really gamble on my producing a product that is going to be saleable. They give me advance money before they have seen the whole manuscript. They've just seen the first few chapters. They've seen a synopsis and maybe an outline, and that's all. [They invest in] the production of the book, and the designers, and the covers, and readers, and editors' salaries.

Do you think that your publishers consider you professionally successful?

Patti:

That's what's so odd. Yes, they do. And I don't really understand it. Maybe it's because [Dennis and I] have a retail business and, while we're not all about the bottom line, we sure keep a close eye on it. We know it's important. Yet [the publishers] can indulge in these little things that I put out that don't have a really big following yet.

Dennis:

I think they see you as a large part of the future of that genre of writing.

Patti, by your own definition of professional success today, in what ways are you already a professional success?

I have fulfilled my contracts. Because of my personal injuries, I couldn't even touch my keyboard. Being able to [have] produced four novels is huge for me. Just the physical, creative energy that goes into that, I feel like that's a success—part miracle, part just dog-headedness. I feel like I've taken the opportunity given me to honor God and to share with people the good news of His love, His total acceptance and salvation. So in that respect, I think that's the part of my career that has been the most satisfying.

You know, the word "success" just seems so—I don't know—arbitrary.

You commented on how your injuries made it difficult. Can you tell us about that experience—of not being able to physically touch the keyboard?

I injured my neck in 2000. I ruptured a disk in my neck and it was impinging [on] my spinal cord for 15 months without a clear diagnosis. I was in so much pain that even petting the dog or typing was just impossible—it was just too painful. I could go for a little while, but then it would just creep up my arms, and by the end of the day, I was in very, very bad shape. There were days when I would look at the clock. It'd be 9 a.m., and I would say, "How am I gonna make it until I can take my sleeping pills tonight?" For one period of time, it was so bad that all I really could do was lay on the floor and just try not to move too much. I even thought I was dying and made funeral notes. I told one friend, who I felt would understand, where I put those notes. I did not want to tell Dennis I had done it.

And then, when my weakness got to be bad enough that it was showing up on tests, they finally sent me to a surgeon who asked me, "Well, how much of your life is impacted by this injury?" And I said, "All of it." And he said, "Well, then it's time to do it."—do the surgery. I thought it was a little tardy, myself. So we did the surgery.

I was not completely well right away, and I have some residual things, but they're not enough to keep me from doing almost anything I want to do—except for a triple salchow [a skating jump] on ice. I haven't really felt like I should risk that! But other than that, I'm doing everything I want to do, like swimming with dolphins and climbing down into caves and writing stories.

It was five years. It was a long time.

Dennis, how does your definition of professional success today compare to other people's definitions

I think most folks measure it by dollars and cents. How profitable are you? How big is the house; how many cars, toys, trips? That is not a huge motivating factor for us or for me.

We talked a little bit about that. We struggle sometimes a little bit with the things we have but, you know, we're not climbing the property ladder to the ever-bigger and newer and grander houses. To me—and this is going to bleed over into a lot of things—our faith drives [success]. You know what Jesus taught about money. Hey, God provides for the sparrows and the lilies of the field—and how much more worthy are we of his attention and care and concern? [People tend] to horde and accumulate the things that will rust and fade, that we can't take with us, rather than [building] up stores and places that will last right here—primarily in relationships with other people.

And so how I judge success professionally is how it impacts other people. With my customers, what kind of job are we doing with them? Are we honest? Do we have integrity? Do we have respect, friendship, welcome, and hospitality?

In the store, are we treating people well or are we just after a fast buck? I keep telling people that I'm really not interested in short-term gains. I'm more interested in long-term thinking when it comes to customers.

For example, I'll sometimes guarantee a plan where maybe I don't have to. I'll pass up that short-term gain to have a customer, basically, for life. I mean, people appreciate that honesty. And it's not a come-on, it's not a crass commercial attempt.

Certainly, money matters. We have to have black numbers on the bottom line when it's all said and done, because if we don't do that, we won't have a business to return to. And it also goes to how we treat our employees, in developing those people and the relationships. We have really long-term folks that have been with us—and I'm proud of that. I think that says something for the culture and the atmosphere that we've created. My job, when it comes to employee relations, is [in] the kind of a workplace I provide for them. I'm kind of a facilitator, providing the opportunity for them to maybe step out and risk it or try it—at least [I] want [them] to get up [in the morning] and enjoy their job.

Patti:

He brings that philosophy home and practices it on me. And it works. That's why I went back to school and why I try to write. He does have an atmosphere around him where he thinks the best about people. [It makes] you want to rise to that expectation.

Can you tell us of an experience that taught you that?

Dennis:

I've been thinking for the past several years that my dad really impacted me in a very subtle way. Dad didn't really do a lot of teaching [or talking about] those sorts of lessons. He just did it. My dad was a salesman who worked his way up to management-type positions. But at heart he's always been a salesperson.

I was never privy to the inner workings of what went on at work with him, but I do know that he's made lifelong friends with coworkers and with customers. We used to go to events that customers would invite him to: dinners, weddings, or parties. Dad was such a relational person and he really applied that into his workplace. In thinking about that, I know that he has really impacted me.

Was there, for either of you, an unexpected cost for achieving professional success?

Dennis:

Not that I can identify. I feel very blessed. Perhaps—and it was really more her cost and the kids' cost—[it] was that I had to work weekends. For me, it was just a busy day at work. But it was fairly isolating for Patti and the boys, especially when the boys were young, because everyone [else] was home on the weekends. There were things to do and outings to go on and this and that; the picnics, the dinners, and movies, and—"Dennis was at work." That impacted their ability to participate in a lot of [things].

Can you think of an instance or experience when you were not there?

Patti:

I can think of a time that was very dramatic. The boys were small. Matt was maybe three and Geoff was six. And the phone just stopped ringing on the weekends because all my friends were, of course, involved with their families. I had gotten home from church and was tired and lonely; I was crying. And I said,—and it kind of came to me—"Jesus, could you meet this need in me? Could you be my husband, today?"

And it wasn't a second after that prayer was out of my mouth, [that] the phone rang and it was a friend. They went to church with us. They invited the boys and me over to their house for lunch and for playtime with their children. And I just was loving Jesus for doing that for us.

The unexpected cost of my career has been the marketing. It's a big world. The publishing world has fixed budgets for promoting their books. Of course, the bigger the book, the bigger their marketing budget is for that book. And so, they rely on the author to contact radio stations and newspapers. We're a little isolated here and I've pretty much saturated the market.

I've done a lot of speaking, which I enjoy very much, but it's all very distracting from the creative process. You're always under a deadline, even though you're marketing. You need to be working and be creative and, you know, have all these little balls in the air.

Once, my idea of being a writer was, "La, la, la, la, la. Well, I just think I'll write today. I have this creative energy. I just can't hold it inside. The words are just flowing off the edges of my fingers."

It's really more like, "Ugh, I've got to go upstairs and write today." It's not always like that, but it's usually an act of sheer willpower and/ or obedience to get to my computer. Once I'm there, I'm okay. But almost anything else is more fun than sitting at your computer looking at a blank screen and thinking, "They're waiting for this."

So there has been a little pressure there but I am pretty disciplined, except for right now around Christmas. It's all out the window. It's time to remodel the bathroom and bake cookies.

What remains unfinished in the area of professional success for each of you?

Patti:

Well, I could be a better writer, and I don't mean that market success would be that. I just want to become a better writer and have it add to God's Kingdom. I may never know that until the Lord says, "Hey, you're a lamb or you're a goat." So for me, that's it.

Dennis:

The first thing [is] to make sure that we open our doors [the business] for the next year. And the longer we do it, in a strange way, the harder it gets. I have had to become more business savvy, which I'm not good at. I'm a pretty good nursery person or plant person. I like to learn and I'm good with people. That works pretty well for the position that I'm in. But I still don't understand what depreciation is. You know, it's been explained to me, and I could probably spout some definition but truly in my heart, it's just one of those things that I wish I didn't have to deal with.

We've [also] been going through some financial upheaval and partnership changes. We bought out a partner earlier this year—[and there is a mounting] debt load over that. To my simplistic little brain, debt is bad. You should have income and owe no one any money. That makes a heck of a lot of sense to me but our accountant tells me over and over that in a business of our size, we cannot exist without debt—that it is not the terrible, evil thing that I think..

And we're consolidating some things. I've felt like we've kind of drifted for the past five years. It's been a very slow [and] gradual thing. So we're trying to focus on what we are doing well, how we can do more of it. "If it's not performing, can we fix it or [shall we] throw it overboard?" Just asking difficult questions sometimes. I have no aspirations of passing the business on, you know. I don't see that as my legacy. The people I've impacted are my legacy—my wife and my kids, our family and the friends we have, our kids' friends, my customers, and people in the community. If I was able to impact them in a positive way, if I was able to show them perhaps a glimpse of the face of Christ in some way or another, that's the legacy that I want [to leave].

If Bookcliff Gardens dies when I die, that's okay. If it dies before I die, that's okay. That used to scare me a number of years ago. I think these difficult times—these worrisome times—have kind of ground that down a little bit to where I realize that those are not the real important things in my life.

I love my job. I've [said] it a hundred times: I think I have the best job in town—and I believe that. But if I lost it tomorrow, that's all right.

When you were younger, what constituted success in learning and education and who taught you that?

I don't have a heritage of high expectations in education. Even going through high school, I wasn't planning on going to college because I was just thinking about the man I was going to marry—somebody [who was] going to take care of me. But all my friends were leaving for college and I think the party girl in me, the same one that didn't want to be left out, said, "Well, you better get on this thing, too, and go."

The nice thing was [that] in the early '70s, when we went off to school, tuitions were very affordable and I could pay my own way out of my social security benefits. And so, off I went to Cal Poli, only because that's where most of my good friends were going. That's where I met Dennis! So it worked out both ways: I got my "MRS" degree and a little education along the way.

But then, when I went back to school, things really changed. I graduated when I was 39, so I started when I was 35. It was like another person came to live in my body, and I was really obsessed with being successful. I'm not really sure where that came from, because that monster had never lived in my body before. I did not think I was a very smart person. But then,—and this is part of Dennis's gift to me—"Of course, you can do it. You're very smart. You'll do a great job." And so I really went after those A's. I didn't get anything but A's and ended up being the class valedictorian.

I was called to the president of the school's office.When I got there, he couldn't see me, so I saw the secretary, who gave me some tickets for my family to sit in a special section because I was an honor student. That's all she said.

That word, "valedictorian," never slipped out of her lips. And so, I said, "Oh, that's really nice." She goes, "They'll want to make some comments, so, what do you say was your greatest success while attending Mesa State College?" I said, "Well, finding a parking space everyday."

So graduation day comes, I'm very excited, and Dr. Gerlock [the leader of the graduation ceremony] is having a terrible time finding the valedictorian. I, in typical Patti fashion, very flippantly said, "Oh, I'll do it." He just gave me a terrible look. And finally, he called out, "Does anybody know who Patricia Ann Hill is?" And I said, "That would be me."

It was just because I never saw myself as being a valedictorian or somebody that would fit into that slot, whatever that slot was. It made it more fun to be a valedictorian not knowing you were one.

Going back to when you were a little girl in your early school years, do you remember what life was like in school?

We moved a lot at first, and I think that had some impact on my performance. Now that I've been a teacher, I understand how that works. I did get tested when I was in third grade after taking [an IQ] test, because my performance on the test was so much higher than they expected it to be. I don't really know the results, but they thought maybe they would advance me in school. I was shocked. I thought maybe I cheated or something. In third grade, you just really don't have an inkling—at first I thought the testing was because they thought I was too dumb to be in school.

Junior high school was the black hole of my educational existence. In math class, I was totally non-attentive to the teacher, because I had no idea what she was talking about. I would mostly daydream in that class. One day, I waited for everybody else to leave the class and I walked up to my teacher and said, "You know, I'm not really going to need this stuff, because I'm going to be an entertainer." And she didn't laugh in my face, which I thought took a great deal of self-control on her part.

Then, in high school, things weren't much better. In Algebra class, I was just involved with thinking which boys around me were cute. I had Algebra right after swimming class. That was just bad, because my hair got wet everyday. It is hard to concentrate on academics with wet hair and not being sure your makeup's on right.

That summer I became a Christian—just out of loneliness. I know that God was courting me even when we still lived in Inglewood, but when we moved down to San Clemente, I was so lonely I even agreed to go to youth group which I never would've done before. And the Lord just captured my heart. I don't know what the dynamic was, but it made me a better student. I wanted to do well for Him.

My GPA went up every year. I was not an honor student [when] I graduated, because that freshman year really plucked my tail feathers. But I *did* take Algebra over on my own accord. My Algebra teacher, when I was a freshman, had given me a sympathy C, and I knew that I didn't know one lick about Algebra. So I took it over in my new school and I got an A.

My mother, bless her heart, graduated from high school the same year my sister did. You know, she had to stop school to take care of her family when she was 16. I can never remember her asking me if I had done my homework or helping me with spelling words. [That's not to] say anything bad about my mother. It was just her reality. She did not know how to cultivate that part of our lives. So, going to college, getting into a new atmosphere of learning, and having success was very important. I think I did so well the second time I went to college because [by then] I knew what I wanted to do—I was already married and I wasn't distracted by all the cute boys.

Dennis, when you were younger, what constituted success in learning and education and who taught you that?

I remember in elementary school, I was just an average student. I skated along. I could do the work, I was smart enough, but it was just never really that impacting for me. And I remember in the first three or four grades, it was all S's. We didn't get A's and B's until in the fifth and sixth grades. You could get an E for excellent or an S for satisfactory or a U for unsatisfactory. I was just S, S, S, S, S.

The teachers liked me and commented about how conscientious I was. I didn't even know what that word was but learned to spell it really early, because it was always on all my report cards.

Going into junior high was a real turning point for me. I remember doing reports in elementary school, [writing] about Ecuador or something else, and it had to be 10 pages long. Oh boy, I made sure it was eight-and-a-half pages of photographs, maps, charts, drawings, graphs, and [with] just a little, tiny bit of writing. I didn't like to write.

But in seventh grade, in my Social Studies class, I had a teacher named Miss Lincoln. We had an assignment to do a report. I think it was on India. She was handing them back and grading them, and I'd done my usual half-assed job—lots of charts, and pictures, and maps. I was artistic and I liked doing that, so they were beautiful.

Towards the end of the class, she handed everyone's report back—except mine. And she said, "Dennis, I want to see you after class." So the bell rang, everyone left, and I went up there. I had no idea what was going on. She handed it back to me and said, "Dennis, I know you can do a better job on this. You have one week."

And it changed my life. It really did. I don't know what she saw, but something that said [I] could do a lot better. This is all about applying yourself; about just digging in and doing the work. And so I did. I got an A—it changed my grades from S's and B's and C's to A's. The next year in Algebra class, I just said to myself, "You know, [you] can do this." And I did. And I never got anything but A's in math after that.

It was about how I viewed myself and how that could affect how I performed. What I could do was what I believed I could do. Obviously, there's limits to that: I'm not going to be a middle linebacker for the Denver Broncos, no matter how positive my attitude might be. But we tend to limit ourselves so much by how we view ourselves.

And I saw [it] in my own life when Miss Lincoln said, "Not good enough, Dennis. There's better than that in you. Give it another try. Take another week and do it." And that's affected, certainly, how I see myself, and also how I interact with other people. You know, we talk about the legacy I [want to] leave in the people that I've interacted with, whether it's Patti or my employees. And it is because, "I know you and I know you can do that." I guess in a way I'm kind of trying to pay that back to Miss Lincoln. It was such a stunning, eye-opening thing for me: "You can do better than this. You have one more week. Just..." She believed that, and so I started believing it.

I remember as a kid, and this was in elementary school before [the] Miss Lincoln's incident, I'd go home and there were days where I just didn't want to go out and play with my friends. And I would sit on the couch and read the encyclopedia. I would just flip through and read articles.

I still like to learn. My mom is an avid birder. She wasn't when I was a kid, but I think that part of her was there [even then]. For me, it is horticulture of plants. Our son, Matthew, is an entomology major. He just loves that stuff and anything to do with biology. [Patti and our other son, Geoff] talk about Hindi films and books [while] Matt and I talk about bug anatomy.

Can you think of an experience with Matt when you first became aware that he loved learning?

Dennis:

Oh, it was right away. He was totally taken with dinosaurs from a very early age. We'd get the *Golden Book of Dinosaurs* and read that to him, and he would just pour over it. And he could pronounce those names at, like, three years old.

Patti:

Well, I have a story about Matt in that area. He was about, maybe, the third grade. And they had the Teranadon Trot. Dennis was home working on a fun household project. But the rest of us, Dennis' mom, myself, and Geoff, did the Teranadon Trot together but we *walked*—we're not running people. We walk places. And we were pretty much towards the back, because the boys had short legs. The staff paleontologist was participating. He was a rather portly gentleman and was in the back of the pack with us. Matt was peppering him with questions about dinosaurs, and this poor man was having a hard time breathing, let alone talking about dinosaurs. The man was amazed at the breadth of [Matt's] understanding and knowledge of dinosaurs. We would hear about that a lot from his teachers—he was considered the classroom genius. If the kids had a question about the natural world, they'd just ask Matt.

Dennis:

Well, that's continued even now. Last year he was going to the University of Idaho, but he took a class at Washington State on aquatic insects. He [didn't] even have his bachelor's degree yet. The professor had known of him from his work there in Moscow, and [when] introducing the class, that teacher—talking about the syllabus and the reading—said, "If any of you have any questions, that young man over there is probably your best resource to talk to."

It's just amazing the stuff he knows. When he's passionate about it, nothing stands in his way. Education was important to [us]. You know, that is one thing that we always pushed—getting a great education was something that [we] really impressed on the boys. Not necessarily a college education, although that certainly was the first choice.

Well, let me ask you both, then, how valuable do you think high grades are in your definition of success in learning and education?

Dennis:

I don't think they're the "end all be all." I think they have importance. Our boys were not straight A students. Geoff was much more driven by grades than Matty was. But if they came [home] with a B, it was not so much about the B—it was more about the effort that they had put into it. And if they had put a good effort into it, then that was okay. If they got a B or a C because they were just goofing around, or not applying themselves, that was worth a sit down and a talk.

Patti:

It didn't take much, because they wanted—they wanted to please us. I don't understand where it came from but they're awfully good kids.

Patti, you mentioned earlier that you have also taught school as a career.

Yes, and what I observed in my classes and in my own learning is that effort was what brought about learning. It wasn't natural ability, it was really the effort that the kiddo was willing to put into a project. Risk taking, I think, is also very much a part of learning.

What are some examples of successful relationships that you have known?

Dennis:

I think that Patti's and my relationship would probably [be] first. And I think my parents, too. They've been married for 50 years now.

We do not operate anywhere at all along the lines of my parents. They bicker and pick and snipe, and we don't do that very much. But I think my parents have impacted me, certainly [in that] you're married and you stay married, and that's just the way it is.

Patti:

Of course, our relationship is the thing that's so satisfying. It's just good and you've [speaking to Dennis] enriched me so much. I think our relationship with our boys is also a source of great satisfaction, although they are just way too far away. Matt called last week when he finished finals, just because he wanted to talk to me and tell me he was done, and how good he felt about it. It meant the world to me that, of all the people he could've called, he called me.

And Geoff, [at] twenty-seven, still calls us every week, sometimes twice a week, just to talk. It means *so much* to me that they value our relationship.

The relationships with our extended family—aunts and uncles—especially on Dennis's side of the family, are precious to us—friendships and people at our church that are like brothers and sisters to us.

I'm really close with my sister and her husband, with my mother and my stepdad.

Dennis:

The relationship between you [speaking to Patti] and your mom has been an eye-opener for me. I never had any sisters; it was just my brother and me. But just to see how you [two] interact. It's different with guys. There's more feeling, more overt feeling that I see between you and your mom. Guys just tend to be even keeled about that, and I think it's because we don't risk going into those sensitive, touchy areas. And you and your mom do. But you love each other and that never varies. Something happens and you get past it. That has been an eye-opener for me.

One thing though [that] I think changed our relationship a lot was a marriage seminar we went to right after we moved to Grand Junction. That was '78, '79. Tim and Bev LaHaye came. They had written a book together about marriage. This was before all the "Left Behind" stuff that he did. That was really what they were about—marriage and the relationship.

They came to Grand Junction and I remember we were gathered at Two Rivers Plaza, listening to them. And they talked about different personalities. You know, there are those personality tests—there are usually four basic personality types. They made the offer that we could pay an extra 10 or 20 bucks and they'd send the test. We could mail it back and they'd tell [us] about [ourselves]. So we both did that. I remember how eerie it was. It was kind of like we were looking over our [own] shoulders going, "They [the LaHaye's] have been hiding in our closet, watching us." They really knew me. And they had me pegged: I was pretty quiet and introverted—not a real outgoer. They talked about personality—your major personality, your secondary personality, your strengths and weaknesses, and some of the vocations that you might consider. I remember reading that over and over and really taking it to heart, especially the weaknesses. And I really purposed in myself to work on shoring up those weaknesses. I really made an effort to do that. It's funny talking to people now, because they [say], "Oh no, you're not. I mean, you were never introverted. You were never quiet."

Now, once you get me started, I just babble: talk, talk, talk, talk. But the reality is that it's true. I like to sit and veg out, whether it's with a book, a TV, or just quiet. That was a real turning point in my life.

Patti:

Listen, you know, we're made by God with strengths and weaknesses. Our weaknesses drive us to God, really. We look to Him for strength and growth. But I think that [LaHaye] class and the information on how to understand people did so much for helping us to accept [weakness], but also to look at the strengths [people] have, how worthwhile they are and how God sees them.

And then to recognize in our boys that, "Oh, look-it: they're a little like you in this, and they're a little like me in that. And they're going to have these kind of struggles because of these weaknesses but, you know, that's not a big deal."

In addition to that story, what lessons has life taught you about how to achieve success in relationships?

Dennis.

I don't have a story or a specific instance. It was kind of a gradual discovery, and I've really tried to pass this on to the boys. I read an article in a newsletter back when I first started Bookcliff Gardens in 1980, and I remember the title of the article was "Hire Only Good-Natured People." I probably still have it tucked away in a file somewhere at work. It just talked about the importance of hiring good-natured folk and all the reasons why. I really applied that to how I looked at hiring retail people for the nursery. I was looking for just the qualities of the person, not their experience, not their knowledge of plants, or retail, or anything like that. I've had some of those people, and they've been pretty uniform disasters for us, whereas the people that were just good-natured, hardworking, pleasant, people-skilled—heck, we can teach them all that other stuff.

You get so much farther in life: "Okay, I [can] go through life unpleasant or I can go through life pleasant." How would I respond to someone if they are outgoing, and friendly, and engaged with me, and interested in me? It just dredges up all these good responses. But if I'm kind of grumpy and standoffish, or suspicious, or terse, or short, [I'll] get a [like] response: you get back what you give to people.

Patti:

You know, I don't think anything shaped me more into the person I am today than just having that encounter with Christ's love. That was the very first thing—just to know that I was loveable, that He had always had me in His hand even though I suffered a great loss at a young age. I wasn't forgotten, it wasn't a mystery to Him. That was so life-altering. I don't even think I could measure the importance of that, and so I've tried to pass that along to our sons and to Dennis.

After Dennis, the people that God used the most to transform me and to teach me how to get along with others are my own children. It really was the first time in my life [that] I had to be completely selfless. From the day I found out we were pregnant with Geoff, God started a new work in me and He used them to refine me. I'm not done yet, but if you could chart learning about how to get along with people or how to treat people, there was just a spurt of growth upward, a steep learning curve when I became a mother. I kind of realized if they needed something, it had to come from me, at least until a certain age.

And then, probably the next hardest thing I had to do was [to] start saying, "Well, I guess that doesn't have to come from me," and start taking that gradual step back. Understanding that weaves into your other relationships. There are going to be times when you're the one—you're the one that's going to make a difference in a person's life. And there are other times when it has to be someone else. And they're both heavy burdens to pick up. And so I credit Matt and Geoff with making me the person I am today.

> *Looking at your life as a whole, what areas of accomplishment give you the greatest satisfaction?*

Patti:

My children and my marriage. To have an ongoing relationship of such intimacy with other human beings over a span of years and have it still be growing, changing, important, of high value—to me, that is tops. That's the cat's meow. I think that is possible because of Jesus Christ—because I have been forgiven, I know how wonderful it feels to be forgiven.

And so, because He did not hold back, I don't want to hold back. Now, I do not love perfectly the way Christ does, but He's my role model. I hope my boys know that I would go to my death for them, as I would for Dennis.

Dennis, looking at your life as a whole, what areas of accomplishment give you the greatest satisfaction?

I'd agree with Patti. For me, it goes back to relationships. Those are the things that'll last. The relationships that I have with Patti, Geoff, and Matt, and also the relationships I have at work with my employees—I 'm proud of those. I've forged productive friendships with these people and I think they've been bettered by that. That's been my goal, to make those around me better, [and that includes] my customers.

You know, Patti and I were taking a walk last night and talking about it. Several years ago, I kind of ran into this verse. In fact, it was at the Jensen's bible study. [Dave and Barb Jensen hosted a bible study for years.] In Ephesians 5:2, in the NIV [New International Version], it says, "So walk in love." And the [translation] I use says, "So live a life of love."

They're such simple words, but they really encompass what Christ would have for us on this earth. What he wants us to do is to live a life of love. You know, Jesus was challenged: "What's the greatest commandment?" And He came up with, "Love the Lord your God with all your heart and soul, mind and strength; and love your neighbor as yourself." I mean it's basic,—you do that, and you fulfill all the law and the prophets.

We forget that so doggone much. And certainly, I'm imperfect in that—and appallingly so, it seems. Yet, I think that's the thing that we need to be doing: live a life of love, Christ's love, not just some nebulous feel-good thing—to live a life of love, to be the face of Christ on this earth.

Each of you has expressed something about your areas of accomplishment that gives you the greatest satisfaction. Have you found any downsides to achieving that success?

Patti:

You know, if you treat people the way Christ wants you to treat them, you're going to have some really weird friends. They're going to be very high maintenance, friends that are hurting, [either] in a physical sense or hurting in an emotional sense. And I've had a lot of friends like that.

Sometimes I [think], "Oh Lord, couldn't I just have a normal friend?" The real truth of it is that none of us is really normal; we're all emotionally wounded, have certain mental deficiencies (like short-term memory—like where-did-I-put-my-glasses issues), and we all have physical issues.

And so I say that God has brought these high-maintenance friends. And if they were interviewed, they'd go, "Oh yes, I have a high-maintenance friend named Patti."

I have a friend that I [talk to] mostly by email, because she lives in Minnesota. I love her so much. You know, I'm often on the receiving end of their grace—these people—and that's a very humbling and good place for me to be.

When you're that invested in somebody, there's going to be pain. But it's a fair trade-off for the relationships you have, for the intimacy that you gain.

Dennis:

You know, when you really devote yourself, when you really let down and love someone, you're risking pain. I remember when Matty was probably about eight years old. It was Halloween. Jeff Mills and Brian Poole lived down on Pheasant Run, and they had called and said they were going to get together later on that evening to go trick or treating. Matt went down there and a few minutes later, here he came [back]. He went running upstairs, jumped up on his bed where we had the little bunk bed, and he was crying. He was just so brokenhearted because they had gone without him.

My God, I remember standing there, you know, rubbing his back and just bleeding for him because he was just looking forward to it so, so much. It still pains my heart to think about it. You bleed, too, you know. That's the price and it's got to be worth it. It's always got to be worth that.

Patti:

When Geoff was going through his hard times in junior high school, he'd come home crying. I was *sure* someone was molesting him at school. He just wouldn't talk about it. We went—we dragged him—to a counselor. We did family counseling and—oh, Geoff was so mad at us for doing that. But we had no idea how to help him feel better about what he was doing. And when we came down to it, Dennis and I were the ones that had to adjust our thinking. It wasn't Geoff.

We had to give him the message that he could handle this situation, that he had all the tools he needed to accomplish dealing with these bully-type people. And so that next Monday, as usual, he woke up with a stomachache and he didn't want to go to school. And I'm being "Little Miss Sunshine,": "Geoff, you can do it. No problem. Hey, babe, have a great day at school," I'm saying. I closed the door, "Oh!!", and I just sobbed. I just sobbed for him. "I'm not so sure he can." It took [about] two days and he was a new person full of confidence. It was us having to believe he could take care of these blankety–blank-blank children who were treating my little baby child in a mean way.

Dennis:

It's like dog training: it's not about training the dog, it's about training us.

What do you still want to achieve or accomplish?

Dennis:

Grandchildren.

Patti:

Grandchildren. And wives. I want to accomplish having a great relationship with my daughters-in-law.

And I want to open my hand and not hold on to this life so tightly. I want to live radically for Jesus. I want to be in a place where I say it doesn't matter what I have to wear, what I have to sit on, what I have to eat—I will follow Jesus anywhere. That is what I want.

Dennis:

I see it as more a continuation, perhaps a deepening, of what we're already doing, or what we're trying to do: impacting people, by being the light of Christ in a dark world, living that life of love but being a positive impact on people around us.

And that's a never-ending thing as long there are people around us. You talk about how ugly you are because you don't want ugly or difficult friends. You, Patti, are an inspiration in that way. We [most people] like to socialize and interact with people that are kind of like us, we *normal* people. You [Patti] don't do that. You see someone that's in need, and you just go for it. And yeah, you get your stomach tied up in knots, but you do that, Patti, and that is an admirable, admirable thing.

Howard Littler

March 7, 2008

...I never saw myself as a boss; I saw myself as a member of a team. If you give people the opportunity to be creative and innovative, and give them permission to make good decisions, most times they make good decisions. I [simply] got out of the way of the talented people and gave them permission to do their thing.

A leader in educational areas shouldn't view what they're doing as a job, but as a mission. Everybody's got a job. I don't know how many people have a mission. But you need to have a mission, have a desire to make a change.

There's a concept that's called "institutional inertia".... Change in a public setting is incredibly difficult. We are seeing that now with our whole political process and the notion is, change, change, change. We ought not to be focused on change for change's sake, but on trying to break loose that institutional inertia. Some of the ways that one can focus to make that change is [not] trying to revamp the whole system. Change comes, I think, in little tiny bits. We used to think "big is beautiful." I think little is beautiful. Minutia—pick away at things that you can change and make a difference.

When you were a youngster, what did you think it meant to be professionally successful and what experiences led you to think that?

It was probably more towards my high school years that I began to give thought to success. I don't know that I necessarily used those kinds of words. I was born in northeastern Colorado on a small farm, and we were not well to do, by any means. We struggled financially.

There were four kids in the family. I was the third and had two older brothers and a younger sister.

During my early, early years, school [was] a little country school, all eight grades in one room, about 15 or 20 kids. It was a little neighborhood school before the massive consolidation of school districts in the state of Colorado. My grandfather had taught there, my dad had gone to school there, and my aunts had taught there.

I started at five years of age and I had a late birthday, in September, so that made me pretty young. I always considered myself valedictorian in first grade, because I was the only first grader there. Then a little girl came in, moved in during the second grade, and I quickly slipped to salutatorian

I spent three years there, my first three years, and then the community consolidated [the schools] in a kind of nasty "neighbor against neighbor" move to "town school." We went to town school. I couldn't imagine that there were 30 kids, all my same age, in a school.

During that same period of time, my dad had some very serious health problems, and so he spent time at home. My mom worked outside of the home to try to make ends meet. I really grew up, in my early time, under the tutelage of my dad, so he and I are very close— not that my mom and I aren't, but I spent a great deal of time in my early formative years with my dad—who is now just getting ready to celebrate his 90th birthday this spring. He is an incredibly wonderful man—taught me a lot of things.

No one in our family had ever gone beyond high school; college really wasn't talked about in those days. Hard work—a work ethic—was incredibly important to my family. So as far back as I can remember, I had some kind of a job; if not at home, such as chores, it was dishwashing in the café, working in an upholstery shop or grocery store, working on a barn—all those kind of things. So to get ahead in life, hard work, perseverance, honesty, and a day's work for a dollar's pay was how I grew up.

My focus in those early years and on into the teenage years kind of centered around working enough to get gas for my car, keeping that thing going, and hanging around with the guys. I really didn't have much interest in school. That was kind of a sideline.

I managed to graduate,—probably 150 out of 160 students—barely, from high school, and I had one of the few epiphanies in my life. I was walking down the aisle at graduation, pretty excited to be done with school, and I got about halfway down and it struck me, "*Now* what are you going to do?" And I had no idea, and I'd never thought about it before—"*Now* what are you going to do?"

At that same time, my best friend was involved with a young lady and got married. I didn't have a wide circle of friends, so I was kind of by myself. I got in with a different group of kids through my working at an upholstery shop, and they were going to college at our little Northeastern Junior College there in Sterling, Colorado. I said, "Well, why not?"

I announced that to my parents, and I'm so pleased because I really expected them to laugh at me. And they didn't. They were most supportive, probably surprised, and wary of this whole adventure.

So I started at Northeastern Junior College. I wasn't able to read very well, I didn't know much about math—didn't know much about anything, quite frankly, relative to studies, and I had no study skills.

The first quarter I got pretty much straight C's and I thought I was the smartest person in the world! My very first experience in academic success! That was fun—that was exciting and I enjoyed it. By the time I finished two years, I was a learner, excited about it, and had pretty much straight A's. I had to work hard for that. I decided to go on to the University of Northern Colorado, which was focused at that point in time as a teacher's college.

I liked to travel—"What's over that next hill?" In fact, a buddy and I went to California two different summers to work, and barely made it out there and back, in terms of money. But it was an adventure and I met new people and we enjoyed that.

How does your definition of professional success today compare to other people's definitions of professional success?

I don't know that I have a sense about other people's [definitions]— it's an individual thing. Professional success, for me, perhaps centers around working through other people to make change. I'll give you an example. I taught for a number of years in the area of special education, working with kids with disabilities. I felt like I had some talents, but that I could have a larger impact on kids' lives working through other people. That led me into the administrative work, program planning and development. I have pretty good organizational skills, and I think that is an important attribute. So my vision was toward getting the best out of others—adults in our world that spend time in education, in teaching kids. I had an impact from that perspective.

Monetarily, I have done quite well, but that wasn't the focus. Certainly if you're going into education, money is not the drawing card. It's an opportunity to make a difference in the lives of other people that may not be as fortunate as we are, and I think a lot of people that get involved with education, whether it is working with kids with disabilities or kids in general, want to have an impact of some kind. So that may be a thread that runs through people. I'm not sure.

By your own definition today, in what ways are you already a professional success? And give me some examples.

One of the things that I had in my mind when I moved to Grand Junction from Colorado Springs: "I don't know how long I'm going to be here, but my goal is to leave things better than I found them." I had a family and it was my first opportunity at a management position.

That was an up-and-down kind of thing: things would improve some, and then there would be setbacks. So as I got close to retirement, two or three years perhaps before my retirement, I realigned that goal—I wasn't sure that I was going to leave things better than I found them. We have this perception in our minds of how we think the world ought to work, how things ought to be. And how long does that last after one leaves? So my notion about success at that point was, if I've helped a kiddo or a family along the way, that would [be] success for me. And so that's how I was able to square that. I don't know that I did leave things better than I found them. I don't think I left them worse, but perhaps along that road, I was able to help some people along with a little bit of guidance.

What are some examples that come to your mind?

Perhaps a notion that's called "People First." I'll use the examples of kids with disabilities.

Freddie has cerebral palsy. That puts Freddie into a category of "he's not first." It's the notion [of the] *cerebral palsy* [that comes first], rather than saying, "Well, here's Freddie."

Freddie has lots of attributes. He also [happens to have] cerebral palsy. We need to think about turning that concept around. "People First." [or, "Kid First."] I think that's an important notion.

There's another issue that has been an incredible guidance for me, and that's called the grief cycle. Apply that to kids and families who are struggling because a child learns differently. We all expect, when a child is born, that we're going to have the Gerber baby. Everything's perfect, and then something goes awry for whatever reason—accidents, birth trauma, or whatever—and things aren't okay.

A natural reaction, at least initially, is what's called "shock and disbelief" by the parents who didn't get their Gerber baby. So they go through this time—and it's different for everyone—and then they hit a stage of anger: "Why did this happen to me? Why did I get picked on? What did I do to deserve this burden?" If we in the schools are involved with the parents, it is at this point, then, that the anger gets focused on the school or on somebody else.

The next stage is blame and the notion of "blame the schools because they can't fix my kid. Why don't you do something about this?"

Lots of parents then go into a searching mode: they're going somewhere else to find out why and to get this thing fixed. They spend a great deal of energy and money and attention searching, and most times they don't find it—but they need to look.

Finally comes acceptance—not everybody gets to that point—and then, [they] continue ahead from there. An interesting thing about the grief cycle, and what I think people miss, is that it is a recurring event.

A good example, I think, is a child with a disability [who has] struggled greatly both academically and socially. The parents have gotten through that and things are going pretty well. All of a sudden, Mom and Dad realize that Daughter's never had a date. They start the grief cycle all over again. They're angry; they blame; they search; then they try to accept.

And so we need to keep that in our heads as we deal with angry parents. Give them the space to be able to go through that grief cycle and work along with them as partners.

Howard, what remains unfinished for you in this area?

Well, I'm retired. However I still do some consulting work, and one of the really fine jobs—and I've not told people this, but I would do it for free—is with the Bureau of Education on their programs for kids with disabilities. I get the wonderful opportunity to travel all over the United States.

One of the great experiences I've had was when I was [attending] a parent meeting up on the Menominee [Indian] Reservation out of Green Bay, Wisconsin. Part of the process was to get input about programs for kids. I had eight or 10 parents show up for this parent meeting—I was just taken aback. Parents came in—Native Americans talking with a Wisconsin brogue. It was just a wonderful experience. The different cultures and the different tribes—180 Indian schools across the nation, and everyone is just a little bit different. It's a wonderful opportunity to let me keep my fingers in the pot a little bit, and perhaps give some advice and direction in terms of what kids do. The kids on Indian reservations have about three times the percentage of disabilities as kids in typical public schools. There are a lot of reasons for that—poverty is probably the biggest [along with] fetal alcohol syndrome. Perhaps as high as 30% of kids on reservations are suffering from one kind of disability or another.

A while ago you were mentioning this hypothetical child named Freddie and telling us about the "People First" idea. Tell us more of the Freddie story.

This takes me way back to Sterling, Colorado, when I was quite young and was involved there in a church that my family attended. It was a mainline church called "Evangelical United Brethren Church." It was a Methodist kind of a church in our community. There was a young pastor there named Bob Persky. He was a really exciting kind of guy. The people just loved him. He was young and innovative and he took the kids on camping trips, played baseball, and all kinds of things that I had not done much before.

Maybe 20 years later, I was reading a journal about kids with disabilities, and here was an article by Bob Persky. I was just amazed and I thought, "This can't be the same guy." I wrote him a letter, and it *was* the same person. He lived in Connecticut and he had gone away from the ministry and focused his efforts on working with kids and families with disabilities. He had written several articles, a novel, and a number of pamphlets. His wife is an incredible artist. She illustrated a lot of his work, and they are very, very famous charcoal sketches.

So I contacted Reverend Persky and brought him here to Grand Junction to attend one of our parent training meetings, what we called "Roundhouse Conferences." He was on the National President's Committee as a consultant for kids with disabilities. He gave input to programs such as Lyndon Johnson's Great Society and some of those kinds of initiatives. And then, later on, Lyndon Johnson was the president who signed our initial legislation—federal legislation that provided programs and services for kids with disabilities. Prior to that, they were served in church basements and homes and the "dumb school." So that's kind of the beginning. Reverend Persky was probably the person that planted that seed for me—the "Kid First" notion. We see it [today] in news stories and articles, but I think it is still "in process."

What is your definition today of success in learning and education?

I have strong feelings about that. I'm incredibly distressed [over] the direction that public education is headed today. I was hopeful that this event, this [current] notion about what creates success in learning, would run its course—it has not. I'm talking specifically now about this notion [that] we're hell-bent to test every kid ad nauseam, and we're [just] not going to deal with issues that someone decided were unimportant, like relationships, learning a second language, drug and alcohol abuse, honesty, work ethic. We're hell-bent to test kids and we're spending so much money, time, and effort trying to get everybody above average. We've decided that the development curve does not exist anymore and we're going to be in Lake Wobegon, where everybody is above average. Well, the fact of the matter is, I think we're doing a massive disservice to society.

Several years ago, about 15 or 20 years ago, Sandia Laboratories in New Mexico—it's a research center that really has nothing to do with education—was commissioned to do a study about why American education was failing. [Incidentally and] quite frankly, I don't think it is, even today—not even close. But they [Sandia] spent a great deal of time and effort and came up with three issues that they said were critical and missing from our educational system.

As surprising as it might seem, it wasn't math, it wasn't reading or science. They were: [1] we're not helping our kids to develop good relationships with one another—how to get along with your fellow man; [2] we're not doing anything about drug and alcohol abuse; and [3] we ought to be teaching kids a second language.

We're missing the boat. I don't know very many people who have lost their jobs because they weren't technically accomplished [enough] to do that job—at least in the world in which I've traveled. People ran aground most often because they couldn't get along with one another or their boss [or their] parents.

Our kids today are smarter and incredibly talented, more so than [kids have] ever been. We simply need to redirect that. And particularly if, in our community, God forbid, we say anything about self-esteem. That's a bad word. But quite frankly, as far as I'm concerned, that's the ball game. When we do our best work is when we feel the best about ourselves.

You are doing consulting work and you have a philosophy of education that you've talked about. Do you feel that you have the opportunity to enhance or pass on that philosophy?

I think I do. One of the things that I did and I would encourage other people to do, particularly if you're interested in a leadership kind of position, is to be able to identify one's own weaknesses, and then surround yourself with people that have those strengths. Lots of people don't do that because their ego gets in the way and they want to be the boss. I don't believe in the boss concept—I believe in a team concept. As a leader, I think you should be one of the people. So look for those folks that can shore up your weaknesses, and then exploit those talents that they have. A leader in educational areas shouldn't view what they're doing as a job, but as a mission. Everybody's got a job. I don't know how many people have a mission. But you need to have a mission, have a desire to make a change.

There's a concept that's called "institutional inertia" that I think is an important one. Change in a public setting is incredibly difficult. We are seeing that now with our whole political process and the notion is, change, change, change. We ought not to be focused on change for change's sake, but on trying to break loose that institutional inertia. Some of the ways that one can focus to make that change is [not] trying to revamp the whole system. Change comes, I think, in little tiny bits. We used to think "big is beautiful." I think little is beautiful. Minutia— pick away at things that you can change and make a difference.

Another thing that has helped me a lot is analyzing the people around me, my supervisors and my colleagues. Pick out the attributes that they have that I like, and then try to implement those. Conversely, [I can] look at folks around me and say, "You know, that doesn't work. I'm not going to do that." I think that if one is observant, [it can go] a long way in terms of managing [one's] own behavior.

I mentioned earlier that there was this federal legislation that, quite frankly, forced public education in public schools to begin to have a place at the table for everyone, regardless of their needs, and to provide public funding from an equitable perspective. Well, what I observed happening is somewhat of the backfire—and it is still going on today. Programs for kids with disabilities are very expensive and there is a lot of competition for our dollars. I see a lot of people and programs fighting for those dollars and saying, "Well, why should we be investing a lot of money on kiddos that are never going to give back to society anyway?"

Early on I decided that I was not going to use that as a club. [I was not going] to say, "Well, we're going to provide these programs because the law says we have to." My notion was to say, "We're going to do this because it's the right thing to do. We're going to provide a place at the table for everyone." I think that helped gain ground rather than beating people into submission. .

[An example of what I am getting at] had to do with the press, quite frankly. I was asked some years back to do an interview about programs and services for kids with disabilities in the school district. I tried to stay away from the press as much as I possibly could, but I kinda got cornered on this one, and so I said, "Well, okay. We'll talk about what we're doing in this district for kids with disabilities." It was a 20-to-30 minute interview. Then I got the article, and what this reporter had done was he had gone down to the administration building and pulled all the financial stuff and made a big issue out of how much we spent per child for kids with disabilities, as opposed to the Gifted and Talented program. That, in my opinion, was a pretty dishonest way of going about the business of reporting—I had no idea [the interview] was headed in that direction. I was pretty upset about that, pitting one program against another.

What are some examples of successful relationships that you have known?

My parents would be a good example. This summer, they're going to celebrate their 70th wedding anniversary. One of the things my dad said is, "I don't believe in—divorce, I believe in a fight to the finish." That's an example of a solid relationship. It needs to be an ongoing process.

A couple of other things that I think are important in relationships is that you need to have fun once a day and you need to have a wonderful sense of humor. Those kinds of things go a long way.

We tend, I think, to say "I" rather than "we." People tend to take their lives too seriously and get hung up on the little issues.

What made you say, "You've got to have fun every day"?

The way I organized the staff is that I had a group of five or six people that I considered among the more talented folks that I had an opportunity to work with. We would have management meetings once a week. The purposes of these meetings was to review the screwups of the week and to plan and develop programs.

Part of the meeting was dedicated to everybody [telling] a joke. A lot of times the agenda would have a little saying on it that I put there that was meant to be humorous. Just an effort to lighten the load a little bit, [because] what we went about was serious and quite important and not without its frustrations.

A particular example has to do with a gentleman who was our state special education director. He now lives here in Grand Junction. We would have meetings two or three times a year. Once, I took my management team with me to one of the state special ed meetings. We flew out of here one early morning. One of my colleagues, just a wonderfully talented lady, was Sally Manahan. I picked her up and, along with two or three others of us, went to the airport. When we got off the airplane, Sally looked down, and she had one blue shoe and one black shoe. Of course, that was pretty funny for most of us. Sally didn't think it was really funny, but she managed it because she was a real trooper and a fun person to be with.

And so I took the opportunity to share that little experience with Fred, the special ed director, prior to his initial address to the group. He then took the opportunity to explain to the rest of the group that there was a person in our midst that had one blue shoe and one black shoe. It got a big laugh.

What was your position before your retirement?

My title was Director of Pupil Services, and my main responsibility was to oversee and manage programs for kids with disabilities. The average numbers of kiddos that had one kind of disability or another, ranging from kiddos with severe profound disabilities to kids with minor speech and language problems, is about 10 to 11% of the population. And so, given that we had 26,000 kids in our school district, we had upwards of 2,000 kids that had disabilities, and a staff of—including instruction assistants and so forth—a couple hundred people. That's a lot of people to manage. Quite frankly, you can't manage that many people.

So you would need to rely on giving people permission to do the right thing, and not overseeing. I think it goes back to my notion that I never saw myself as a boss; I saw myself as a member of a team. If you give people the opportunity to be creative and innovative, and give them permission to make good decisions, most times they make good decisions. I [simply] got out of the way of the talented people and gave them permission to do their thing.

What programs or achievements are you most satisfied with?

Really, two issues come to mind that I think made the difference for kids and families.

The first was probably in 1985 or '86 when we went through a process called "deinstitutionalization." There were three state institutions for kids with disabilities in the state of Colorado: one in Grand Junction, the Regional Center; one was the Ritz Center in Denver; and the center in Pueblo, Colorado. Lots of kiddos were warehoused in institutions rather than being cared for at home, because of the nature and severity of the disability.

We overdid that. We put kids in institutions that should never have been institutionalized. But that was an evolutionary process. And so what happened through legislation is that almost overnight, the law said, "Thou shalt not institutionalize kids any longer." And, "Those that are already there, get ready to [put] them in schools, because you didn't serve them." It was a major, major challenge for us here.

The state tended to send school-age kiddos to the Grand Junction Center. The Ritz Center and Pueblo Center served more adult populations, although they had some kids. But we [in Grand Junction] had, by far, the most kids.

So our challenge was to deinstitutionalize about 125 profoundly handicapped kiddos. There's no facilities, no money, no staff. How do you do that? Well, we struggled incredibly. We went about the business of writing some grants and begging for dollar support and looking for teacher talent.

The major problem we had is that the Regional Center had one school district to integrate kids into. Ritz Center had the whole metropolitan area, for crying out loud, and Pueblo [also had] a much larger area. So we really struggled to try to respond. And the only kiddos that we did not integrate into public schools were those that fit into two categories: medically fragile that couldn't be moved, or kiddos that were dangerous, [that were] a danger to themselves and others. We served them on-site. That was our responsibility as a school district, although we really didn't receive much funding for that effort.

We had a major challenge in trying to convince the school board and schools to provide space and to begin to help us serve these youngsters. Lots of people—and probably I, at first—were somewhat skeptical about this process. I was convinced that some of the kids needed to be integrated and we had done some of that. But I wasn't sure that all of them should be. We saw two things happen immediately.

The staff that had worked with those kids, inside the institution or in an isolated setting, began to dress better, began to feel better about themselves, began to respond differently. The second thing we saw was the same thing for the kids. We saw cleaner clothes; we saw better manners; we saw better behavior; we saw incredible differences within a very short period of time, and we didn't do anything, except move them from one physical setting to a different physical setting. So I knew at that point in time that [this] was *exactly* the right thing to do. It was a major struggle, but it worked.

The other program I think that made a major difference, and is still making a major difference, is that we were one of the first school districts to provide programs for preschoolers. I think early intervention for little tykes who need an extra helping hand is really critical.

Howard, as you were growing up, what did financial success mean to you? And what personal experiences contributed to that understanding?

It was an expectation that we have jobs as soon as we were old enough to kind of make our own way to help the family. We were not well to do. Financial success for me was keeping gas in my 1953 Ford, a quart of beer on Saturday night, and to be able to participate in buying some of my own clothes. I never contributed to the family food bill, certainly, or lodging, or anything like that, but I tried to pay my own expenses to the extent that I could. So for me, financial success was gaining independence—not having to go ask Dad for a buck.

Today, what do you think it means to be financially successful?

Well, that reminds me of a funny little story. I belong to a book club. A bunch of guys get together once a month and we have a book in common. We get together and sometimes we discuss the book. Sometimes we just visit. There is one gentleman who is married to a school administrator. Somebody asked him, "Bill, what do you like best about being married?" And he says, "P-E-R-A," which, of course, is our state retirement plan.

Financial success for me, right now, is the ability to take a $20 bill out of my wallet anytime I want and I don't have to worry about it. I'm not interested in gaining a big bunch of wealth, but I want to be financially independent enough to be able to assist my family if they need help. I want to be able to travel. That's always been an important event for me and my wife—to see what's on the other side of the hill. So I live comfortably now. I don't want my 401K to go in the tank because of the stock market, but that's not something that I could necessarily control. So, I suppose, from a financial perspective, I'm there. I don't have a need to amass anymore things.

What advice would you share about how to achieve financial success?

I don't know for sure. I guess I had luck. It's like waiting your turn—a concept that used to really irritate me when I was a kiddo. But it brings me to a notion of responsibility. This is probably my age speaking more than anything else, but it appears to me that kids today don't have to wait their turn. If they don't have a several thousand dollar stereo or a cell phone that takes pictures—and the list goes on and on—they think they're put upon. Did they earn it, or did they expect it? I don't know that I'm advocating that we should do without, necessarily, but I think we need to prioritize in terms of wants and needs.

My wants appear to be my kids' needs, if that makes any sense, which brings me to a little story about my sister-in-law, whose name is Barbara. My wife, Pat, and Barbara, who was here for [a visit], went shopping. So I gave her this little lecture about wants and needs, and I said, "Now, when you're down there shopping, you ought to really consider whether [it] is a want or a need." I was blabbing along and I didn't feel like she was paying attention. I really didn't expect her to, because I was just having some fun.

They were gone most of the afternoon. [When they] came home, Barbara was just mad as the dickens. She said, "It's all your fault." And I said, "What are you talking about?" She said, "I didn't enjoy the day at all! Every time I picked up something, I said, Is this a want or a need?" So that's been a family joke for us every time Pat's sister has come. I give them the lecture about wants and needs.

What else would you like to achieve in the area of relationships?

One thing that comes to mind. We have a friend that called one day. He called me and one of my colleagues, Mr. Vanderhoofven, and he said, "I'm getting ready to retire. I want to buy you lunch and I want to learn about retirement. What do I need to know?"

We met him for lunch and had a delightful time. And he said, "What are the important things that I need to know about retirement?" We talked about a number of things, but the one thing that struck me the most in the course of the conversation [was] that we said, "You know, you're probably going to be surprised at the people you spend time with in your retirement." *I* certainly have been surprised. Some of the folks that I have the best relationships with now I never dreamed I would be involved with. They were, most of them, colleagues from work that I had previously dealt with on a professional level. I valued them then, as well, but I valued them in a different way. The relationships that I've developed since leaving my "job" have been a surprise and have been incredibly rewarding.

The other thing that was a surprise for me was that there are lots and lots of people out there in the world that didn't think about education every day of their lives. There's another whole world out there that I didn't know anything about. I thought everybody just thought about education all the time. I did. And I'm exploring every piece of that right now, through people I had no intention of being involved with—through people I've met in all kinds of different ways. What an opportunity. What an opportunity to grow and learn.

[Something else] that's made a difference for me [is enjoying reading]. I was never much of a reader. Certainly, [I did] a lot of professional reading, [but] my gosh, I've read several hundred books since my retirement, and what a wonderful way to explore stuff that I had never quite thought about.

One of the adventures I had, which is just so much fun, was that I decided to read a biography of every president. I started with George Washington, made my way through that process, and [had a] wonderful experience. I learned so much history and got a perspective on how people became who they became.

Howard, what do you think it means to be personally successful?

Well, it's probably a combination of several things. I have two great kids and a grandkid. Wow, that's certainly satisfying! It's wonderful to see them grow and develop, and even at their ripe old ages of 30 and 32, they're still kids and they're still *my* kids. I still worry about them. And then there's that opportunity—that little grandchild. Man, that's another whole ball game. And so that's certainly a lot of satisfaction.

I don't know that there have been very many do-overs, but there are a lot of do-agains. I had the wonderful opportunity to teach overseas for five years, and that was early on in my career. I went to Okinawa at the height of the Vietnam scene. What an incredibly wonderful experience. Once again, my notion of wanting to see what's on the other side of the hill. I got to see a lot of Southeast Asia, and then I came home and got married. Pat and I went to Germany. We spent three years there and a year in England, traveling and working. I grew a lot from that experience, I think. The thing that gives a flavor to how you view the world is getting out of "happy valley," wherever your happy valley might be, and realizing that there's another world out there—developing relationships that may last even through today, looking at how other people, perhaps, view the world.

So, that's not a do-over but is [something] I'd like to do again. One of the things that Pat and I really were excited about when we retired—Pat retired from the school district as well—was to join the Peace Corps. We'd talked about that a lot, and really wanted to do that, but Pat's health didn't allow it to happen.

Do-overs relative to my profession: there is an issue that strikes me as important to mention. I should have been less tolerant of mediocrity.

I spend—I think it's fair to say lots of people spend—too much time on the problem person, the problem staff member—the person that is not pulling their weight—rather than nurturing the superstars. And so I would probably be less tolerant of mediocrity and [I'd spend] more effort in helping and supporting the superstars.

> ***Howard, in wrapping this conversation up, I'd like to ask you to tell me one or two things that you most admire or respect about each of your two children.***

Well, this would go for both kids. I really appreciate both Sam [daughter Samantha] and Charlie's sense of humor. They're totally different kids, like most families' kids are.

Sam is the little kiddo that loves school—quite bright and did a great job; not that Charlie isn't bright. But she really excelled academically. She's so talented with language—the use of the English language, if you will. What an incredible vocabulary she had as a three year old or four year old, or five year old. And she is sensitive and caring.

As for Charlie, one of the things that he has that I don't is a really easy-going attitude. He is a really bright kid, as well, and he is a learner through experience. I was like that—I learned more by doing, by practical application, than by reading.

He is on a management job now in the private sector and we talk from time to time. His knowledge and his expertise in dealing with people is so far beyond where I was at that age. I just marvel from time to time, "How did you know that? Where did you learn it? I didn't know that 'til I was 50 or 60." And so, he just astounds me constantly, in terms of his comments about how to solve a problem or how to deal with people.

Finally, let me talk about my wife, Pat. She is a wonderfully talented, bright, creative individual. She has been a major player in my "success" over the years, and I want to recognize that. She probably is in a very unique category. She is one of the most tolerant people that you'll find on the face of the earth—she has tolerated my behavior for almost 38 years. She has helped to ground me and guide me and has been a partner and a major player.

Steve Gammill

Pat and I met in Colorado Springs. I was doing what I refer to as my "stupid teaching," actually my *student* teaching. Then I took a job, my first job, in Colorado Springs as a teacher. Pat was a senior in the high school where I was teaching, although we weren't dating at that time. I met her through a fellow that I was rooming with who was also from my hometown and who married Pat's sister. We dated for a while, and then Pat left and went to work in Washington, D.C., with the FBI. I went to Okinawa, taught for a year, came back, and we got married. We went overseas to Europe and spent four years.

As I look about me and focus on the people that I care about, even those I don't know, what's really important is that there's a smile on your face. If you've got a smile on your face, things can't be too bad. As we bump through life, learning from our mistakes, that will take us a ways.

Merritt Vanderhoofven

March 14, 2008

I came to realize that an awful lot of people are standing around waiting for somebody to say, "Why don't we?" And in turn, because people infrequently say that, we end up not doing much of anything. If somebody has the inclination to say, "I wonder if" or "Why don't we try"....

I have some real mixed feelings about the educational system which we have today, particularly the presumption that accountability is the vehicle with which we're going to find the solutions to educating children. I'm absolutely convinced that [that's] starting in the wrong place. It's not capitalizing on the gifts and talents that our teachers bring to the classroom and it's not capitalizing on the positive aspect of finding a better way. It's building something on a coercive mechanism that has people not only fearful, but unreinforced by what's happening in their profession.

We used an approach that basically said, What we're going to try to do with these conferences is to stimulate discomfort and from that discomfort, give people a foundation of where to look to find another way.

Merritt, when you were growing up, what did you think it meant to be professionally successful, and what experiences led you to that definition?

I was raised in Delta in a household of hardworking people—wonderfully energized, intelligent, well read, articulate. My mother was a hobbyist, relative to words and literature, and it provided a tremendous stimulus for interests later in my life. At the time, I was busily engaged in athletics. And my interest in school was little more than the fact that that was a social event that we participated in. I had no tremendous aspirations to be intellectual, to be a straight A student. I had no sense about being college-bound.

Our family was not, historically, filled with college graduates. My brother, four years older than I am, was the first. My mother had been a junior college graduate during an era when one could become a teacher if one had that level of education. This was in Oklahoma.

I was just a kid that enjoyed every day. Mostly, I worked at the fun side of it. I had been a kid with a heart condition. When I was six years old, I was put in a bed for a year to allow my heart to heal. So from that point forward, my opportunity to participate in athletics was pretty much limited to a support role, except for baseball.

In baseball, I had the opportunity to be involved in a system that was called "Old-timers Baseball." That was the little league baseball [organization] of Western Colorado for lots of years. The beauty of that, which was different from the little league of today, is that it was a system run primarily by the kids participating in it. The entire Old-timers Baseball system in Delta consisted of one supervisor and a collection of probably two dozen teams that were basically run by the kids involved. It required kids to assume responsibility for the organization of their system, the selection of their teammates, the operation of the games, the planning, [and] the practices.

So it was a marvelous kind of program, perhaps among the most significant dimensions of my early childhood. It taught me more about leadership than I learned again until I was out of college.

I want to throw in an aside here. I have told you that I am inclined toward describing the clock [as] if you ask me the time, I will describe the inner workings of a clock. My brother is also a hobbyist of language, and when he was in high school, he memorized this thing: when asked what time it was, he would respond with,

> "I am deeply embarrassed and greatly humiliated
> that due to unforeseen circumstances beyond my
> control, the inner workings and hidden mechanisms
> of my chronometer are in such inaccord with the

great sidereal movement by which time is reckoned
that I cannot, within any degree of accuracy, state the
correct time."

That is a representation of part of the early interest that I began
having in language and a sense of [the] value of vocabulary from this
wonderful family and extended family that had no specific expectations
of higher education.

My father was an employee of Holly Sugar, which was a sugar
production company in Delta, for 30 years of my life. He was the guy
that got out of bed every day of his life, worked, and was driven by his
work. I watched his striving to do everything he could in support of the
economic and the psychological well-being of the family. And then—
supported, on the other side by my mother's enthusiasm for literature
and an extended family—it created a wonderful social environment
just to be a kid, just growing up.

I was not a serious student until a teacher basically persuaded me
that I had much more potential than I was demonstrating. This teacher
did a marvelous job of expecting more of me. During a period of
probably about a year, I moved from being a mediocre student who
really didn't value what we were doing in school to a person to whom
it mattered whether I was making bad grades or better grades.

The impact of that teacher's expectation did a great deal to shape
my career over the years. Our potential needs to be challenged and
needs to be encouraged, and we need to have a sense of expectation.

Frankly, I believe that it is largely true that unless the schools or
the families are making a specific effort to expose kids to a range of
options in their lives, kids [will remain] pretty well focused on whatever
they know. I knew a little bit about teachers—most kids know a little
about teachers, because we all had some. I had a friend whose father
was a sheriff and another whose father ran a co-op. But I never thought
of myself as a retailer [or as being in law enforcement], or as doing
the kind of work that my father did. I simply didn't feel inclined—I
didn't have the gifts that he had for that kind of work. So, my target
was pretty well narrowed down to the thing that I knew, which was
education.

I made my way into college and spent a couple of years [at] Adams
State [College in Alamosa, Colorado], not being a very serious student,

but in the education arena. Probably the greatest highlight of those two years was that I encountered a marvelous teacher by the name of Joseph Daniels. He was teaching general Biology to freshmen. I had had miserable experiences in biology classes in high school. It was so poorly taught and so little engaging that I discarded it. Joseph Daniels taught in a way that was engaging, that captured the learner by showing relevance to every aspect of what he taught. [That] that was possible in the field of biology to this day is still amazing to me. It was a tremendously engaging experience and I ended up as a Biology major because of Joseph Daniels.

Were you satisfied with the progress of your undergraduate college career?

No. I was neither comfortable nor satisfied with the quality of education I acquired as an undergraduate. My sense was that college teachers are really not very good. They have very little sense about the how and the why learners would be engaged with the content that [they] were trying to share, that they were themselves hobbyists in their chosen field, and that they live with the presumption that everyone will be equally driven by the importance of that content. And, the truth be known, I believe that I was not an exception—[I was] a person who really tried, really struggled, to make a connection between what was being offered and what it might mean to me.

In the meantime, I'd transferred from Adams State College to Western State College [in Gunnison, Colorado] where I finished my undergraduate degrees in Biology and Psychology. And I took Physical Education classes continuously all the way through school, [and that] became another area that I could teach.

I graduated and promptly went to work as a lifeguard at the swimming pool in Delta, not knowing quite what I was going to do next, and not knowing very much about how one goes about looking for a teaching job. Suddenly, it was about time for school to start, and I hadn't even made an application for a job anywhere.

The reason why I regard this as particularly important is that it's a manifestation of the extent to which I have had the good fortune of being at the right place at the right time for some tremendously important things to happen in my life. In this particular occasion, about two weeks before school started, I sent out a handful of letters to a handful of school systems that were listed as having vacancies that might be available to me. I got a response from one of them, which happened to be the West End Public School District, which is centered in Nucla, Naturita, Uravan, and Paradox—the west end of Montrose County, [Colorado]. I went over there for an interview. This was at the height of the uranium boom. The West End felt like it was right at the edge of the world, and if you took a little bit of a step backward, you'd fall off. It was halfway to Cortez and tremendously isolated.

Nonetheless, there was a lot of activity. It was a thriving economy at the time and the school system was growing like topsy. The vacancy that they had was for a Science teacher and a Physical Education teacher in a middle school, a combination of sixth, seventh, and eighth grades at Nucla. By the time I was there for my interview, school had started and the interviewer took me to observe the school and look into classrooms. The substitute teacher was already in the classroom. They offered me the job, I accepted it, and went to load my things to be back in class on Monday morning.

Here I found myself in a classroom—a homeroom of sixth graders—but teaching also seventh and eighth grades. I was teaching Science and Physical Education to that range of kids. I stepped into the classroom, realizing that I had learned practically nothing that was supposed to teach me how one goes about teaching children.

I had encountered excellent teachers along the way, and I realized the importance that expectations had to the learner. That was the primary tool I took with me to the classroom. Of course, I took my most recent scientific biological science knowledge into my classroom, but [that] had very little to do with what might otherwise be a typical curriculum for sixth graders, seventh graders, and eighth graders.

We had a textbook that was being used for each of those grades, but the entire collection was 10 years old. So I felt licensed to see what I could do to take the learning experience in a direction that would be useful, that would be enticing, that would be available to the kids. And frankly, I just entered the classroom and went on my instinct. And I loved it! And the kids responded! And their parents responded! I got tremendous feedback as the process moved forward. I struggled with the same kinds of things that every teacher does, in terms of the misbehavior of this student or that student, and sought to find ways to deal with those kinds of issues, but the rest of the story was a wonderful, wonderful learning experience—to just kind of figure it out as I went along.

Within the first month, one of the kids said to me, "Well, do [you] have [your] cow license?" And I said, "I didn't know you shot cattle over here." But the question was relative to the hunting season—*everybody* in the West End in Montrose County went hunting. As a matter of fact, we had a week off to let them go hunting and I didn't even *have* a cow license, for crying out loud.

It became increasingly apparent that the narrow scope of what's out there in the world that I had carried out of Delta was even greater, even narrower, for the kids that we encountered in the West End. There were kids who had never been to Montrose, which was about 70 miles away; who had never been to Grand Junction, which was 90 miles away. These kids' sense of what their world could be was, "I'm either going to be a uranium miner underground, or I'm going to drive a truck," or something that is right in the heart of that industry. I compared that to my sense, when I was that age, that I didn't want to work in the factory with my dad, but I didn't know what else I wanted to do

Children who happened to be farm children, and there were several farms in that vicinity, of course had that as an option. But any option that had anything to do with higher education, any expectation of higher education, was nowhere in their vernacular, with a few exceptions.

And so, [in addition to] just loving teaching and feeling that I saw kids responding to expectations and engaged, that period of time started shaping for me a sense about where education could take kids—if there were just some things we could do to make some things happen, we could have an impact on their sense of self and their sense of their future.

I was loving what I was doing primarily because I was loving what I was seeing happen in the kids. We were using sports, which had been a first love when I was little, and the Physical Education part of our curriculum to engage kids that weren't as easily engaged in academics. We were using sports as a mechanism to energize kids in the academic side of stuff.

Unfortunately, though, I felt like I lacked all of the essential tool skills of teachers who were artists at teaching basic skills. I could address the motivational dimension, but I didn't have the knowledge to teach children reading, writing, arithmetic. I had not been educated in [that], so again, I was feeling my way.

I decided that if I was going to move my career on, I probably was going to have to leave. I decided to take a year's leave and get a master's degree in Counseling. [Leaving the West End] was a very painful and emotional thing, because of the connections we'd made.

We left, my wife Dorothy and I, and settled in Delta. I went to work on Morrow Point Dam for the summer. I got a call one evening from Roy Johnson, my principal in Nucla. He announced that he'd moved from the principalship and, through the federal programs administration, into the superintendency. He offered me a job to administer the federal programs. I had no aspiration toward administration, but he said, "Well, I had to pick it up, just like other people had to pick it up, and I know you can do it." And then he said, "I'll offer you $7,500 if you come over here and take a shot at it."

That was a 50% raise and it felt like all the money in the world. Dorothy and I decided to give it a try, and the [deal] we made [Dorothy and him] was that we would go ahead and start our family if we returned to the West End. So that's what happened. We backed out of the internship, the opportunity to get my master's in Guidance Counseling, went back to the West End, and took over the administration of the federal programs.

The federal programs at the time consisted of Title I and Title III [NDEA—Title III and ESEA—Title I]. One was the support for science programs and encouraging curriculum development in science, and the other was for disadvantaged youth. It was part of the Johnson Administration era of trying to do something about the indigent.

There was a lot of money. Relatively speaking, it had a major impact on the West End area and the whole nation. I believe Title I ESEA became the most significant federal intervention, relative to development of the special education system that Colorado now has, because it simply offered money to do something with kids who have very great needs. With a budget of about $50,000 to $75,000 for the ESEA program, and my need to learn to administer money and to deal with hiring, we began the process and hired remedial teachers—I think three.

But that was the end of our money, and we were not doing enough for the population and the magnitude of the needs represented. I found out that there was another system in Colorado called "Special Education." It didn't exist in the West End, had not existed in Delta when I was there, and had not existed in my experience. It simply was not being addressed. Special Education had to do with the entire population of disabled children. This population, during that era, was largely seen as the population that became identified and eligible for placement in the state home and training school in Grand Junction, or—if they happened to be deaf or blind—they qualified for admission to the Colorado School for the Deaf and Blind in Colorado Springs, or they might have made their way into the program in Wheatridge [Colorado].

There were three institutional components that defined what happened with kids with disabilities. The special education system at the state level in Colorado was trying to come up with a shift in responsibility for those youngsters from institutions to public schools. So, at that time, partial reimbursement for the salaries paid to Special Education teachers was available. We found that if we put the federal money with the state reimbursement money, we essentially doubled the budget that we had available.

In order to do that, we had to have a "director of special education" in our school district—so I declared myself Director of Special Education and set about becoming an administrator of special education, which ultimately became my career direction for the next 25 years.

We built a program in this isolated corner of the world that gained some recognition, and people began being a little excited about it. During that period, I came to realize that an awful lot of people are standing around waiting for somebody to say, "Why don't we?" And in turn, because people infrequently say that, we end up not doing much of anything. If somebody has the inclination to say, "I wonder if" or "Why don't we try"....

At one point in time, I was working with a gentleman that runs the bus garage in the West End of Montrose County. I found that he had been really excited about stock car racing when he lived in Albuquerque [New Mexico]. Over a cup of coffee one day, I asked what it would take for us to have a stock car track here in the West End.

He said, "Basically, we need a piece of flat ground. You cut a track in the dirt, put up a wheel wall to keep a tire from going into the crowd, and tell people about it. I said, "Well, what would it take for us to round those people up?" And he said, "Well, let's write a letter." We printed out a letter—50 copies—and put it in the local car parts outlet saying, "We're going to have a meeting."

Two weeks later, in January, we had the meeting. There were over a hundred people there. They put together the preliminary rules and we had our first stock car race on Easter weekend! The issue is how people respond to that dimension of urging that says, "There's something that's really possible to do, why don't we do it?"

During that period of time, we [learned] there was another federal financial source for innovative programs. I went to work on the application and we were granted $100,000 for this innovative program. My idea was built around the idea that we could create a simulation of the "broader world experience" within the West End educational community, so that our kids would not have that extremely narrow sense about what is out there and what is possible.

For the first year, the pilot program involved gathering really interesting people from all over the place and bringing them into the West End for special events, for kids and their parents to participate in. We had so many people participating that we had to set up a television in one room and the camera in another so that there would be enough places for people to sit.

For people interested in theatre, how about a Reader's theatre? We brought Western State College's drama department over to do a Reader's theatre presentation, and it became one of the biggest events in the community in years.

We brought in a professor from the University of Colorado to talk about the crisis in fossil fuel. That crisis is something that's stuck with me all these years: fossil fuel is finite. It is ultimately going to be gone—all of it. Once it's gone, it's gone.

I think we had about a dozen experiences that the kids and the parents could engage in, and out of that began to grow this sense of possibilities—this sense, again, that all you've got to do is say, "What if?"

From the groups of kids that I had as sixth, seventh, and eighth graders, we ended up with dozens of college graduates. Before, in our community, probably not more than one in 10 kids made their way into higher education. These kids became engineers, nurses, doctors, business majors—kids that have experienced some real success in their lives, professionally and academically.

I had been teaching for four years and I had also become an assistant superintendent in Grand Junction, but I [then was required] to get the degree that qualified me for the job I already had. While I was completing my master's program in school administration, I sought to learn something that would be helpful to me in the special education field, something that would be helpful to me in the administration of federal programs, and something that would be useful in dealing with parents and the politics of public schools. The fact of the matter is that I came out of that program feeling like I had [only] three good courses: one of them was a Sociology class and another was a class taught by a superintendent of schools from Gunnison. He actually knew something about what was going on in administration.

Otherwise, this experience seemed to me about as close to a waste of time as I could have gotten. All I got from this was a license to practice. I did not get that kind of training and expertise that is useful, that I desperately needed. I was learning the business through the school of hard knocks, clearly one of the best ways to learn, but it violates what we want to expect of higher education in terms of how well we perform professionally.

At my oral review, before I was to receive my master's degree, I was invited into a room where, sitting around, were all the deans and major advisers from my three summers in that program. One of the first questions was how I felt about the program at Western State College.

I said, "Truth be known, I'm terribly disappointed by it." They didn't expect to hear that. I said, "I couldn't even get a law course that provided any knowledge or had relevance to the issues of the emerging federalism in public education."

"Well, what do you think needs to be done about it if you're that disappointed?"

"I think we kind of start by flushing and starting over." Again, that didn't go over where the hoop was. I'd had straight A's in my program, and they couldn't very well throw me out for having this opinion. When I finished my conversation with them, they said, "We have some grave concern about you" and sent me out in the hall, and left me out there for over an hour and a half. When I went back in, they said that they were going to grant me my degree with serious reservations about whether I was a good choice for this field.

That's how I came out of that master's program. And [even] in additional graduate work, rarely did I find an experience that was enhancing. The key to my learning was that "trial-and-error, school of hard knocks process" that we tend to go through. We learn a lot from one another.

The third summer I was working on my master's, I ended up in a dorm at Gunnison, and the guy in the room next door happened to be the superintendent of schools in Grand Junction. We struck up a friendship and, towards the end of the summer, he [asked if I would] have any interest in Grand Junction." Within a few months, [he called and] said, "I've got something coming open."

He offered me a special education position. I felt a real connection to special education after I had gotten into the administration and the building of the program in the West End. And, frankly, we had developed a pretty good reputation for what we'd been able to do with a very small community. Now the question was, What can we do with a larger community? So, I announced to the people in the state certification office that I was going to be moving to Grand Junction as director of special education.

There was a fellow who had over 20 years' experience in special education in Grand Junction. He looked me right in the face and said, "Your moving to Grand Junction will be the worst mistake that you will ever make in your career, because what you have there is the most inflexible, unavailable politics that you can imagine. That community will never put the resources into special education services that's going to be required to have a successful program. They have the Regional Center over there and they expect kids with disabilities to go [there].

And that's that." And I looked at him and I said, "I'm afraid I'm not willing to believe what you're saying to me, and I don't want you coming to Grand Junction to influence the attitudes and perceptions of the people there." He later became a good friend, but the fact of the matter was, Grand Junction was seen as a hard nut to crack in terms of services to children with disabilities.

The Grand Junction Regional Center at that time had a population of 1,800. Today it has a population of about 100, maybe 150. That was the extent to which the institutional context was being abused. The special education staff in the entire school district was about 28 people, and that included one-and-a-half psychologists, seven nurses, two attendance counselors and a handful of resource teachers that were paid half by federal money and half by state special education reimbursements—so they weren't costing the school district anything.

There was a centralized program for a group of about 60 kids at Riverside Elementary School, with a handful of five or six teachers there that were dedicated people working with a challenging population. There was a junior-senior high school program that was called the "Occupational Training Center" that was kind of like a sheltered workshop. It had so isolated students that the kids were unwilling to even interact with non-handicap kids.

It was a pretty desperate situation. I didn't realize how desperate it was. When I went in, the primary identifier and diagnostician had a stack about 10 inches high on his desk of referrals for psychological evaluations. The one on top was the newest one. The one at the bottom was three years old.

I had to agree that this was a tough starting point. The assistant superintendent in Grand Junction sat down to talk about my expectations for the special education program. He said, "I [can] tell you how you can meet my expectations. If you can keep the parents from being on my tail, then I'm going to regard you as a success, because I'm so tired of dealing with angry parents of [special needs] kids."

And so, we launched into an evolution. First thing we had to do was give the system some credibility for people who had not been supporters. The administration, the board of education, and the community were beginning to feel kind of pushed around by state and federal officials, regarding the passage of some legislation mandating appropriate services for kids with special needs. And they were resisting the sense of that mandate.

So we started out with a message: I guaranteed to the board that I would work diligently to keep the system on track within the law, but I would also be a vehement opponent of anything that didn't make sense—things like regulations that require processes and procedures that are superfluous and wasteful. "We'll try and treat children in this system no better and no worse than you would like to have your own child treated." That would be a defensible system.

Most of us can't relate to the challenge a child with significant disabilities may represent. We can see a little bit about how tough it would be to have a deaf child, or an autistic child, or a child with low intellectual ability. But unless you've experienced it, you don't know it. What you do know is that you want the system to serve your child in a responsible way, to spend what is reasonable, and you expect your child to be allowed a degree of dignity.

[There was a new] superintendent of schools [hired], between the time I accepted the job and my arrival in Grand Junction, [that] I didn't know from Adam. So the superintendent that hired me, that was my inside track to acceptance within the administration, was gone. The new superintendent came down to my office in Riverside Elementary School, looked over the program, and said, "This is a disaster." And I said to him, "I couldn't agree with you more." His name was Don Oglesby, and he really helped with that early development of the system, including going well beyond the call of duty. He facilitated the opening of doors and the hiring of people that we needed but couldn't afford.

This was during the era of deinstitutionalization and the pressure was on to move the most challenging population from the Regional Center into the schools. And we didn't have a system to receive them. We were perceived by the Regional Center as being oppositional. Our message was: as quickly as we can have a system in place to accommodate the challenges of this population, we will be delighted to move in that direction, but to approve a wholesale relocation of a population now served by the Regional Center would be taking them from a system that is, at the very least, providing something, and putting them into a system that is capable of providing nothing.

We had some real talent among the people we had—there just weren't very many of them. And so we began competing to find and hire quality staff. A little bit here, a little bit there. It kind of grew like you might picture a mud pot: the bubbles [were] coming to the surface [but] scattered out, and it didn't seem to have much logic to it. But it did grow. And we had the blessing of being able to find and hire teachers—professionals, special educators with tremendous credentials and tremendous talent—at a salary that was below the salary they would get almost anywhere else they went.

During [about a 15-year] period of time, we accumulated a staff of truly, truly potent people attracted to us—at least in part—by one of the messages we try to use with them:

> "You are looking for a job to do something that you
> regard as very important, as part of your career, or for
> the good of mankind, or the well-being of families.
> We are building a system to work. That's the ultimate
> bottom-line test of it: Is it working? And if it isn't,
> let's fix it. We believe that you have more expertise
> than we do right now, in determining what is the best
> way to make this thing work. Our role is to create a
> structure in which you can operate, and your role is to
> do the job and never be satisfied."

Whenever I did an interview, I was a recruiter. And over a number of years, I had the privilege of being, pretty much, the final say on who we hired. Discomfort is that seed for improvement. If a person is comfortable with where they are, there is no urgency to find a better place to be. This same principle applies to almost anything you choose to learn or do. If you're a smoker and you're not uncomfortable with that, you are darned sure not going to quit. If you're overweight, and you're uncomfortable with it, you'll do something about it. If you are teaching in a classroom and you don't know how to deal with a problem, and you're uncomfortable about it, then you are motivated to find a way to fix it. If we can spread the dissatisfaction with the special education system overall—our disappointment because we know it can work better—that dissatisfaction, that discomfort, will drive the future of this organization.

It is also empowering to acknowledge to a new hiree that though we are terribly understaffed, we will configure, as best we can, the manpower that we do have to the greatest possible productivity. We can't use the excuse that there [are] simply not enough resources to do this job. It is our responsibility to use the resources available in the most productive way. We can't accept the position that, "You just can't get there from here."

During the evolution of this special education system and the collection of this marvelous group of talented people, our manpower became in excess of 160 employees with the skills and talents to take any child with a disability and provide a system that was in tune and responsive. That is almost a miraculous place for an educational system to get to.

I believe that some of the finest educators that this system has in it today came out of the recruiting of our special education staff during that time. At one point, I had become so discouraged by the sense that I was in a continuous battle with the parents' expectations, that I considered leaving the special education field. At about that time, I encountered the Boelkes—Glen and Eula—two of my favorite people on the face of the earth. The encounter with Eula started with her charging into my office to complain about a school principal who had talked down to her about their daughter. Eula came into my office unannounced, walked right past my secretary into my office, and just unloaded on me about the way she felt she had been treated. A blessing: instead of being defensive, I empathized with her and said, "I don't blame you for being exasperated." That enabled us to make a linkage which grew into one of the most important things that occurred in my entire professional life: the necessary coalition between parents and servers.

The creation of the Roundhouse Conference was Eula's brainchild. It was fueled by the collection of a pediatrician, us in the school district, her as the parent representative, and other parents. [It was] a system to bring educators and caregivers and parents together to talk about what was important. That system actually persists today. Its primary function was and is to teach parents what educators go through and [to teach] educators what parents with children with disabilities go through. It gives them a foundation for empathy with one another, and a foundation through which they can be supportive of one another. Frankly, it had a miraculous impact on the special education system in this community, and we became bonafide partners: parents who helped us lobby our own board of education; parents who helped us seek resources that we needed; parents who helped us deal with the needs and challenges of other parents in a difficult situation. It was a support system for parents and a support system for us.

This dimension [the Roundhouse Conference], over the last 10-or-so years that I was in the special education field, became a most recognized, positive dimension. It became something that others around the country sought to model. In most systems, that relationship was being driven by due process procedures and the adversarial context that due process procedures call for in resolving differences in the matter of services to children with disabilities.

It also taught us about the relationship between Kübler-Ross's [*on*] Death and Dying concepts and the plight of the parents who become aware that they have a child with a disability. When a child is growing up as a Gerber baby, and you find that the child can't hear, or that the child has autism, or has some condition, suddenly the Gerber baby is lost, as if the child had died.

After 15 years, I was offered the job as an assistant superintendent in this district, and after much thought, I took it. During the course of that time, we launched something called the "Futures Conference." The Futures Conference was a collection of people brought together for the purpose of looking critically at the structure and nature of education, special education in particular, but education in general, to see what change should be possible.

We used an approach that basically said, "What we're going to try to do with these conferences is to stimulate discomfort, and from that discomfort, give people a foundation of where to look to find another way." To this day, I think it is one of the most brilliant approaches to staff development. We sought out the foremost, revolutionary educators—thoughtful, progressive educators—in the country. We either interviewed them on the telephone or sent people personally to interview them. Ted Sizer at Brown University, Mortimer Adler in Aspen, and the list, frankly, goes on and on.

Then [we] took the tape of the interview to a conference and played it as a stimulus. Then we called the person that we had interviewed and, on an amplified telephone, we'd have a question-and-answer session. The total cost of this [was almost nothing]. We had the best people in the country talking to a collection of people, many of whom were our own administrators, teachers, special educators, and a handful from neighboring communities. We did this for eight consecutive years in the summer. This was a week-long event, and people came from all over the country to participate—and paid their [own] way.

I have some real mixed feelings about the educational system which we have today, particularly the presumption that accountability is the vehicle with which we're going to find the solutions to educating children. I'm absolutely convinced that [that's] starting in the wrong place. It's not capitalizing on the gifts and talents that our teachers bring to the classroom and it's not capitalizing on the positive aspect of finding a better way. It's building something on a coercive mechanism that has people not only fearful, but unreinforced by what's happening in their profession.

Tell me a last, final story about someone or something unique and important that happened in your career.

The Judi Parker Story

When I was administering the program in the West End, I knew this person named Judi Parker from Delta. I had watched her throughout her early childhood, travel-bound in her wheelchair, and I knew that she was set on becoming a teacher. She was something like 32 inches tall and weighed about 35 pounds. She wasn't supposed to live past two years of age, and then she wasn't supposed to live past her teenage years. But she was still going along and she got into college. Nobody could imagine she could possibly be a teacher.

Judi had applied to over 50 places for a teaching job and she didn't get a single response from any application. I found out that she was looking for a job and we began talking. I got acquainted with her from a professional standpoint and hired her into her first teaching position, at Nucla Elementary. From that point on, she just blossomed and showed us what a tremendous talent she was.

Then I had the opportunity to hire Judi into the Grand Junction school system. Later, I also had the opportunity to work with her in developing a presentation describing her life and her career, [which] was called "The Little Engine that Could" [modeled on the story of the same name]. She is a marvelous illustration of what the Little Engine That Could was. I regard Judi as one of my very close friends. We took a situation that didn't look very encouraging and saw it turn into a wonderful success story.

Merritt Vanderhoofven (Van) and Howard Littler ----

A Reprise

May 28, 2008.

Howard and Van gave us the benefit of their wisdom and their definition of success in other chapters. Because they spent a number of years designing plans and programs together and benefiting children so greatly, I believe we can enjoy their joint stories as well.

I believe very strongly that success is never satisfied. A person may be regarded by as gloriously successful, but the odds are they are never satisfied. There isn't a "getting-done-being-successful."

But I know that what really came out of that lawsuit was the door opening between the minority communities and the Anglo community that has been in this valley for years. Some wonderful relationships have been built, and the sensitivity of both the parents and the school system has dramatically improved.

You can't solve a condition, but you can make a condition into a problem, and that's what the focus of Futures was: to create discomfort and give people permission to 'blue sky,'—to think, to brainstorm, to visualize, to guess at what might make a difference.

How did the two of you come to work together?

Howard:

Well, it was in the spring of 1980. I was living and working in Colorado Springs and noticed a job advertisement for assistant directorship here in Grand Junction, in pupil services departments. And I applied for the job kind of on a whim. A colleague had moved here and was assistant superintendent. He and I had a pretty good working relationship, and so I chatted with him on the phone. It so happened that Van was in his office at the time. That was our first interaction.

Van was on his way to Colorado Springs for a conference, and so we met and visited. He was looking for his first assistant director [in the department of] Budget Approval which, in retrospect, was desperately needed. I was not necessarily looking for a job, but we visited, and then met again on a couple of occasions. It was pretty amazing to me that it seemed to fit for me, what I heard Van talking about.

Van:

I had actually been looking to fill that position for several months. Bob McCormick was superintendent here in the district at the time and he had persisted in throwing names on the table and encouraging me to consider them, and I was finding no one that I regarded as really fitting what I thought I needed. And frankly it was a pretty personal kind of thing that I was looking for—some administrative orientation that was strong, someone who had special accountant skills in attending to detail, and problem solving with groups of people.

And when the assistant superintendent indicated that maybe I ought to give a shot at talking to Howard, we hit it off from the get-go. And from that conversation, that rather amazing conversation in The Three Seasons [hotel] in Colorado Springs, I went away saying, "I've found my person. Now the next step is to recruit him, to get him to make the decision to move from Colorado Springs to Grand Junction," when he hadn't had any intention— he wasn't looking for a job. He had a darn good one in Colorado Springs.

And somehow or another, we found that we had opposites about us that complemented one another in a tremendous way. And at the same time, we had interests abundant that we shared in common. As a matter of fact, that's evolved over the years to where we have all kinds of activities that we, on a social level, have very much enjoyed participating in.

Howard:

It was a rather unique interview, as I am recalling now. Unique to the extent that, when we met and visited in Colorado Springs, it was for about an hour, an hour and a half perhaps, and he did all the talking, it seemed to me. And then I came to Grand Junction and met with a committee of administrators and left, then a few weeks later, was contacted. And so I uprooted the family and came to Grand Junction. It was one of the best decisions that I ever made.

Van talks about how we complemented one another, and I would put it in a bit of a different perspective. Van is a dreamer, and we need lots and lots of dreamers—not to suggest that he isn't a doer, as well—and an implementer—but my skills, I think, complemented that to the extent that I enjoy management kinds of activities. I enjoy implementing programs and developing programs, working with people from that perspective. And so he was quite patient with me and gave me time to get up to speed. I was shell-shocked for a good portion of the first year or two.

Van

That shell-shockedness was not particularly apparent. He just picked up every ball I threw to him and ran with it. He was a natural talent in that regard. And from a philosophical standpoint, that stuff that I had talked to him so intensely about during the interview were pieces of a theme that he handled very, very well—stuff that I don't think you could begin to do unless you started with the predisposition to work in that direction.

With the less-compulsive administrative structure that I operated, he was able to pick up and run with; he could take any part of the organization and go with it. And so we really didn't lay out a structure [that said, for example], "This is exclusively my bag and this is your bag, and never the twain shall meet," but, rather, "We, together, carry the administration of [the] Pupil Services Department as a team." And it seemed to work out wonderfully.

Howard:

One of the things that occurred here in Grand Junction prior to my arrival was the approval of a fairly massive bond issue. That was kind of a first for Grand Junction for a long period of time. And at the time, Grand Junction was growing very rapidly, the oil shale industry was booming, and so forth. Another factor is that the state had at that time three regional centers where they placed students with severe disabilities: one in Pueblo, one in Ridge Center in Denver, and the Grand Junction Regional Center. The state tended to put school-age kiddos here in the Grand Junction Regional Center. We had about 150, perhaps 175, school-age youngsters who were institutionalized at that time.

And so the bond issue that was passed provided for what we called "deinstitutionalization"—,bringing some of those kiddos out of the institution and serving them in the public schools, as well as closing the old Riverside School which at that point housed students with disabilities that probably couldn't be served in what we at that time called "the mainstream."

Van:

This was the first time this school system had provided physical plant accommodation for the expectation that there would be a special education program operated through the public schools. Prior to that, the spaces occupied by special educators in school buildings, be they speech therapists or resource room teachers, or self-contained programs, or whatever, literally went into spaces that were left open, or the spaces that could be converted from storage into spaces for which we could create programs. And with this, it opened the door—a wonderful opportunity—to plan some very fine facilities for this special population.

Is this the point in time when the state said, "Not only must you deinstitutionalize, but you've got to do it now. And we're not going to tell you how. Figure it out yourselves."?

Howard:

That's exactly right. And it almost happened overnight, literally. There was hardly any additional funding. Grand Junction Regional Center had about 125 youngsters which we integrated into the public schools—in a single school district. Ridge Center had the whole metropolitan Denver area with [only] about 125 kids. So you see the difference and the impact that it had for us.

And so one of my first projects when I arrived was to get involved in what we called "squatter sessions." We met with architects, and there were committees of us that worked on the planning of the new facilities for the kiddos right down to "Where are we going to put the light switch so that it's accessible for a kiddo in a wheelchair?" to ramps, to accessibility to changing tables, specialized bathrooms, kitchens—so that we could teach kiddos home skills—to laundry facilities. So we were able to build those kinds of facilities into several schools that were being newly constructed, as well as major remodels at Grand Junction High School, for example, where we would be integrating the older kids.

And we spent a couple of years, literally, before construction actually began, as I recall, and it was an incredibly exciting time. We put in incredible hours meeting with parents and committee people. It was a massive project. And I can remember closing the old Riverside School that was still functioning at that time, the first year that I was here. What an exciting time!

Another major issue that we were faced with at that time [in addition to the physical plant construction] was the business of convincing building principals, regular educators, superintendents, board members, parents—even parents of kids with disabilities,—[because] they were frightened too. They didn't know if they wanted their kiddos to be in the real world. And so we did a lot of work in terms of planning, meeting, and convincing.

Van:

Involving them in the process. Yes…

Howard:

Go right ahead. It's exciting to talk about it.

Van:

Yes. It *is* exciting to talk about it. Among the greatest challenges for us was the issue of the biases. There were tremendous biases that had to do with "why." The history of special education was segregation. And frankly, there was little going on in this community and in public schools [to] change that.

People literally would look at a plan and say,

"You mean this room, this room, and this room are going to accommodate a special set of special needs kids?" and

"There's going to be the expectation that these kids will be involved in these regular classrooms"; and

"These kinds of things are going to happen"; and

"What on earth are you going to do with a kid who has a seizure?" and

"How are you going to handle the feeding dilemma that you're going to face with this population, [when] some of them are virtually wheelchair [bound] and almost bedridden and…?"

Howard:

"You mean to tell me, you want us to put these kiddos in the lunchroom with the real kids? Come on now."

Those were the kinds of bumps and hurdles that were incredibly challenging, and [this is] not to suggest that we didn't have a lot of partners in that effort, both colleagues in the special education world and lots of committed folks, building administrators, and others that were right on the bandwagon and did marvelous things.

Van:

Our board of education had come so far. I remember Peggy Lippoth [a school board member] as a particular character who had been a friend to the evolving special education program long before this dramatic move occurred. The fact of the matter is, she had been the influence who had said "yes" to this expansion of the program, the system of service—a horribly expensive program. Having people with no personal experience—Peggy Lippoth, Lou Grasso, and numbers of other people—but who had that openness, that foresight, [and] the energy to move the system forward was a gift. It was absolutely a gift, because this was an insurmountable obstacle in the organization.

Howard:

I remember two or three building principals, particularly at the elementary level, who, at least in my opinion, were some of the most anal-retentive, hard-nosed folks about, and I considered them some of our biggest challenges to accepting these youngsters and treating them with respect and dignity. And it wasn't long till some of these folks became our biggest advocates. People like Bud Roberts, people like Russ Connor, John Fulham, a list of other folks that simply stepped up to the plate and said, "This is the right thing to do. And here we go."

Van:

"And we *can* do it. And whatever is it, we're going to have to learn to do it. We're going to do it."

And they were stars also in bringing parents along, both with the special education and the non-disabled population at the same time.

Howard:

Another event is what became known as the Roundhouse Conference. We held 20 of them formally over a 20-year period, and I was involved in 18 of the 20 annual Roundhouse Conferences, as was Van. Talk about the Roundhouse Conference.

Van:

Roundhouse Conference grew out of a realization that parents of children with disabilities felt like they were the outsider and even the adversary to the educational system. They felt like they were discounted, that their knowledge was insufficient to be a full player and to participate in decision-making regarding their children. They didn't have a great deal of trust in educators. They saw us as rather self-serving.

We were lucky enough to hook on to a number of people in the community who thought we could do something about that problem. We thought we could begin to create some kind of a mutual dependency and positive working relationship among the medical community, the parent population, and other agencies that were dealing with children with special needs. And so the question was, "Well, how do you go about attacking these problems?" So, ingenious folks like the Boelkes, Glenn and Eula, and Sherry Sjerven had some real—frankly, they simply came clean with us in terms of describing the dilemma that we were faced with.

And we concluded that what we needed to do was to create a conference that enabled parents to be just as high status, just as important and their contribution just as important as any of the "professionals." And we called those parents "professional parents," because that indeed was what they were.

And the content was selected based on what parents said they needed, what teachers said they needed, and what the medical community people said they needed to improve their understanding. Back during that year, we'd, for the first time, made that relationship between the Kubler-Ross Death and Dying Model and the plight of the parent [of] a child with a disability going through the loss of the Gerber baby. [Editor's note. Elisabeth Kübler-Ross, "On Death and Dying", (1969), describes the five discrete stages, the process, by which people deal with grief and tragedy, known as the Five Stages of Grief.]

That became a crucial theme, but beyond that came themes such as,

- how can parents find support systems for themselves?
- how can we expand and improve the process of communicating with parents in the staffing procedure?
- how do we get educators to speak the parents' language when they are trying to come to grips with what might otherwise be a conflicting kind relationship?
- and over time, to talk about partners.

Parents and educators in this system became amazingly good partners. Frankly, an awfully lot of regular educators became a part of that partnership as well.

Howard:

And we became partners with the medical community. A pediatrician, his colleague, and several others in their practice were major participants in the Roundhouse Conference and would present workshops on issues. And lots of these workshops were fairly unique in that they would have a physician and a parent doing the workshop together.

I recall also an incredible event that I attended at a workshop session at Roundhouse. I had gotten the permission from Glenn Boelke to attend a session that he did called, "Just For Dads." Nobody else was allowed. Dads kind of got the short end of the stick, I think, in a lot of ways. They tended to be less of a participant in the kiddos' education, for whatever reason. Moms generally got stuck with all the "stuff." And so dads had special kinds of issues that were hard for them to talk about. And so it was a neat session.

Glenn got a couple of six packs of beer and we sat up in one of the conference rooms and drank beer and laughed and cried, and told stories, and got to know one another; and in the process, got to talk about what dads needed relative to trying to manage a child that had a disability.

Van:

Another benefit of this entire process involved the Adversarial Conflict Resolution mechanism that's built into special education law, called the "Due Process Procedures," that parents had available to them as a [way] to call the system to account for how well it was doing its job.

Around the country, school systems were spending hundreds of thousands of dollars on the costs of Due Process Hearings. And these were, in some systems, occurring hundreds of times a year. In our system, the tempering of that barrier between educators and parents was just unbelievable. We went for several years without ever having a single solitary Due Process Hearing. It didn't mean we didn't have conflicts; it was just that we found other ways of attacking those conflicts.

One of the things we used when a parent was concerned, the system—in conjunction with our parent organization—would supply a resource person—another parent with a child with a disability—who would accompany the parent to the conference, help ask the right questions, and help understanding. We prided ourselves as being one of the few systems in Colorado that, for a number of years, had never had the process go all the way to a Due Process Procedure.

Our neighbor school district, just down the road in Montrose, was in a battle with the family of a child that was being excluded from some school. It was costing the district a couple of hundred thousand dollars. The district bowed its neck and the parents bowed their necks, and [they] proceeded to spend that fortune on it. Well, [we were able to] use [our] money for something other than the adversarial problem-solving.

Howard:

Up until my retirement in 2000, and I don't know the history from 2000 to date, but to that point, we had only one Due Process Hearing. It cost the school district $50,000 for attorney fees, hearing officer fees, transcript fees, and other fees. And when it was finished, everybody went away angry—there was no problem solved.

And so we felt like we had done the right thing previously in not pushing to go to Due Process Hearings. We were convinced. And so, as Van said, we really prided ourselves on figuring out other creative ways to get the job done.

Part of the dilemma we get into is the "fix it" mentality. That's a trap that parents get into often. Because of their shattered world, they need to blame somebody and, oftentimes, the school district or the medical profession or other service providers—caregivers—get that blame because they can't fix the child. And I think that's how school districts get into Due Process kinds of events that generally don't solve very many problems.

Van:

At one point, the school district was sued in the Federal Court for failure to respond to the needs and challenges of children who were bilingual or had English as a second language or, in some cases, had not acquired English.

The contention was that children of Spanish surnames and perhaps others were being inappropriately placed and labeled as disabled and placed into special educational programs as the sole method of responding to the fact that it is difficult for regular classroom teachers to meet the needs of these children. This interesting lawsuit went all the way to Federal Court and the school district invested [substantial money] over the course of a year and a half. The plaintiffs had a lot of federal money supporting their lawsuit effort to force a school system into some kinds of changes that school systems appeared reluctant to participate in.

During that two-week trial—it was an amazing experience—we saw the plaintiff with seven attorneys sitting at the table and our school district defense sitting with [two]. The school district had practically no bilingual or Spanish-speaking employees in the whole district, much less in the special educational program. We had no psychologist that could test a child in their native language. The allegation was that this obviously meant the system was not well-intentioned and was deliberately doing harm to this population of kids.

The relationship between the Hispanic community in Mesa County and the school system became intolerable. It became such a continuous cacophony of confrontation that there could hardly be a civil conversation between the school system and that parent population.

Along came some folks who stirred it up but made it better in several ways. A family from Fruita was incensed that children's needs were not being met and were passionate in their effort to move us toward being more sensitive. Another woman, a member of the plaintiff's team, was very angry. I remember, vividly, going in and out of the courtroom and she would have this angry look on her face—all she had in mind was confrontation and seeing us as the bad guys.

But we ended up hiring her into the system. She became a leader in our school district and a strong advocate in our deliberate, purposeful effort to do the best possible job.

The Fruita family, even though continuing to be critics, became advocates and problem solvers in really converting the kind of conflict that once existed.

Now, I'm not suggesting that the conflict is completely gone, but it certainly had turned a corner, and we are no longer in the process of arbitrarily spending money. We've both been out of [the system] for a while, and we really don't have a good sense about what they're doing today.

But I know that what really came out of that lawsuit years ago was the door opening to having relationship and community between the minority communities and the Anglo community that has been in this valley for years. Some wonderful relationships have been built, and the sensitivity of both the parents and the school system has dramatically improved.

Howard:

It was a process—a process that organizations go through. As we get back to the issue of success in creating a functional system, those processes are necessary, and when you gain the most success is when you can look at those processes and not be mad but gain from it. I recall that we began to put quite a bit more effort into being sensitive about the needs of our minority kids. We went about the business of searching for staff members, although tough to find, who were able to deal with the bilingual issues. We wrote some grants and put some funds into training and testing materials to try to be sensitive to some of those needs.

Van:

I don't remember if we talked about Futures. That was another conference. We've been talking about the importance of relationship-building, determining what works, finding ways to solve problems. One of the things that we inherited with this school system was many

Steve Gammill

solutions that really weren't solutions at all. They were simply the ways schools had done business for a long, long time and no one had questioned them.

[Some] of what schools were trying to do was simply off base and had never been good. In an effort to open some avenues and to explore this dilemma, we put together a conference that we called The Futures Conference. It had an eight-year life. There were eight consecutive years that we brought people from around Colorado, from back East, New York, and all over into proximity with our staff and other staff members. We exposed people to questions.

Howard:

Not only did the outcome of a number of Futures conferences impact special education, [but] quite frankly the vision probably had a greater impact on regular education than special education. We thought we had some pretty good things going in terms of working and problem solving with kids with disabilities, but we sensed—and Van particularly sensed—the need to throw problems on the table and irritate people. Quite frankly, that was the goal: it's to irritate some folks.

Van:

To "foster discomfort".

Howard:

Yes. You can't solve a condition but you can make a condition a problem, and so that's what the focus of Futures was: to create discomfort and give people permission to "blue sky"—to think, to brainstorm, to visualize, to guess at what might make a difference when they took some of these thoughts back to their home school or to their district. There were a number of fairly significant changes in how we did business that came directly out of the Futures conferences and we would work on those and come back together a year later to talk about them and create other kinds of problems for people to solve.

Van:

Kind of puts people in touch with the possible as opposed to always seeing resources as the deterrent, to allowing things to be different, to see the potential reconfiguration of resources as the mechanism with which we could find better solutions, better approaches; things that work as opposed to things that either don't work or don't work very well. Even things that work can usually be improved if you look at them critically and reconfigure your resources in a way, to enable us to find solutions.

We see a process going on today. The New Emerson program out on Orchard Mesa, for example, was established as an exploratory effort to find some better ways to serve young children. It started as a collection of hypotheses: maybe if we do it "this way," children's growth will improve. One consideration was, how great will the impact of full-time kindergarten be on a child? We can follow the child through his first six or seven years of school and see how he performs when he hits middle school.

Another was, What's going to happen if we enable a classroom teacher to have uninterrupted time in working with a classroom full of kids? We're operating in a day and age when there are so many interveners coming from different directions, be they the special education resource teacher, the speech-language therapist, the behavior management specialist, the occupational therapist, the remedial reading teacher, the bilingual specialist—all of these players trying to do their best to help a child grow and perform at grade level or to his potential. Then we look at the plight of the regular classroom teacher as this multi-faceted mechanism is trying to do its well-intentioned best effort, and realize that the regular classroom teacher has continuous interruption and almost no continuity of time to deal with the children. When do kids go to P.E. and Music and Art? Here's the classroom teacher, primarily responsible for the academic instruction of a child, having, if lucky, two or three hours of sustained engagement with those kids in the course of a day.

Howard:

The teacher is there as a conductor with a baton in his or her hand, and no one is paying attention, because everybody's going a thousand different directions.

Van:

And so I believe that one of the primary things that New Emerson has taught us is, "You betcha, a full-day kindergarten is going to have a significant impact on kids." You're going to have to start with a good teacher working with that population of kids, but kids are going to grow. And another thing that's going to make a difference is when you realize [that] those kids are going to school and having easily five to six hours a day of sustained engagement because those teachers don't have art teachers and music teachers and that support mechanism. They're basically with a teacher's aide at their right hand working with the entire population in continuity. They can start something and finish it and use processes.

People have suggested that New Emerson has an unfair advantage over other schools because it has a very carefully selected gifted population. The truth be known, that is not the way they put together the population. It's much more of a random [selection]. The process results in a pretty random, general population of kids, and we're seeing what happens when you have that kind of focused effort, that absence of interruption.

Referring again to the Futures Conference, if someone said, "That's a great idea, tell me how to do it," how would you physically structure or populate the Futures Conference?

Van:

Concrete sequential.

Howard:

The first thing that we wanted was folks that were fairly black and white in terms of their approach to how they do business —"concrete sequential" kinds of personalities. We absolutely drove them crazy because the "structure" was probably best described as "lacking structure."

We would have a stimulus, or a topic, from a general perspective. We would bring in an "authority," in some cases nationally recognized and well-known folks in their field, and have them do a presentation. Then we'd break up into smaller groups and brainstorm ideas on a flip chart. And then, after a series of these kinds of events over the course of the day, we'd bring the folks back together. And we tried to keep it small—under a hundred participants or so. We begin to lose when things get too big.

Van:

And we were pretty good at that. As an illustration, Ted Sizer is a world-renowned educator at Brown University who was the ramrod of an educational research project [called] "Effective Schools."

They did an analysis of schools and determined what common variables were identified in those schools. So we asked Ted Sizer to give us what he thought was really most important about improving the quality of education. He did that for us, and then we broke our group into discussion groups and debated and discussed what we thought were the most crucial considerations, and basically gave one another permission to think in terms of how we could make it better.

Do we have enough physical engagement in the process of teaching and learning? Do we have other strategies by which children who have limited language skills can accelerate their acquisition of language? Do we have special ways of giving mathematics instruction a relevance, a meaningfulness that allows kids not just to think in terms of the abstract numbers, but in terms of the utility and functionality of the math?

[We didn't want] anybody coming back and saying, "No, there is an answer. See, here's the answer. It's one answer, and as soon as you guys figure out what this answer is, then you'll be right."

187

But, rather, [we wanted to explore], to say, "We don't have the answer. We have a lot of research that points us towards various answers. Some of that research even conflicts with other research. Let's talk about them simultaneously and see what we find in that regard. Let's empower people to think outside the box."

Howard:

One of the things I remember so specifically, and I think it was a bit of a revelation to a number of people, had to do with learning style. "Learning style," several years ago, was a new concept, and for lots of folks I think, probably, a new concept today. But it's a simple little concept: teachers teach the way they learn. We all have our own learning style; we're auditory or we're visual or we're experiential, whatever the case may be. My God, what a revelation to suggest that 30 little kids in this classroom all have different learning styles. But the teacher goes about the business of teaching all of these kiddos the way [the teacher] learned their own learning style—because that's what they're most comfortable with.

Well, that was one of the revelations of the Futures Conference. A number of participants went away saying, "My gosh, I have to do some major adjustment on how I'm doing business. Not everybody learns the same way, for crying out loud" and "Let me go back and take a look at this and decide how these little cherubs are functioning, and respond." Those are some of the kinds of events that I think made a difference.

Howard, can you tell us about your management teams and your philosophies?

One of the lowest points in my career here in Grand Junction was the day that Mr. Vanderhoofven [Van] walked into my office and announced to me that he was leaving. He was going to become the assistant superintendent.

That was good from the perspective that we needed all the support we could get from the big boys. The bad part was I really didn't want the job as director. I was delighted with the role and function that I had at that point and I enjoyed our partnership.

Van and I sat down and chatted about what might make sense in terms of a different management style or different management team, with his leaving, given his skills and my skills. What would be the best way to organize the department.

We decided that an assistant director probably wasn't the direction that we wanted to go, and so I went about the business of hiring four or five staff members to work with me, and we reorganized the budget in a way to accommodate that. I was able to surround myself with some of the most talented people you'll find on the face of the earth quite frankly. To name a few: Judy and Craig Thornburg, Dave Rakiecki, Sally Manahan, Jan Blair, and later on, Richard Hoctor, Richard Hartman, and Lee Searcy.

This team for me clicked kind of like the way Van and I clicked. I hired these folks given their backgrounds and talents in the areas [where] I felt I didn't have sufficient knowledge and background, such as focusing on kiddos with emotional behavioral disorders or kiddos with severe and profound mental retardation.

Then we went about the business of organizing groups to go out and be in the schools—not sitting in the office—be frontline teachers of teachers, and along with that, working with parents, problem solving, program development, curriculum, all of the things that go along with that. We would have management team meetings once a week which was, quite frankly, my highlight of the week. We would meet for a couple of hours, brainstorm, plan for the coming week, and problem solve the issues of the day. The best way to manage a team like that is to get the hell out of the way.

Van:

Empower them and turn them loose.

Howard:

Once again, the teacher of teachers concept. One of the things that Van taught me so well is [while] we're going to work hard, we're also going to laugh and have some fun. And we needed to do that at least

Steve Gammill

once a day, and we did. That was a process that I did for the remainder of my tenure with the district—almost seven or eight years.

What is the essence of success in terms of what we've been talking about?

Van:

My contention for a long time has been that there are some foundational perspectives that foster success, that fostered a feeling of success in me, whether while I was a student in school or just because somebody said, "Good job."

What [becomes] the essence of success, and to what extent is that essence pertinent to the operation of an organization like what we've been talking about all this time? I believe very strongly that success is never satisfied. A person may be regarded by as gloriously successful, but the odds are they are never satisfied with the quality or quantity of what they're engaged in, of what they're doing. There isn't a "getting-done-being-successful." It's a journey, not an outcome.

It kind of fits into a category with "diligent effort," with "doing your best." You can work your tail off for all the right reasons and with all the right stuff, on something that doesn't work. The fact that something didn't work doesn't mean it wasn't a successful venture: the success is in the diligent effort and doing your best.

Another element is that it's a sharing of achievement. Success, by whatever definition we give it, is meaningless individually. It becomes meaningful as a shared process and venture. People become inspired by, engaged deeply and profoundly with, a purpose. And that engagement is an essential element of success, regardless of the ultimate achievement.

Another [element] is persistence, rolling with failure. The best baseball player, the best batter in history, failed more than 50% of the time—about six out of 10 times when he went to bat. Yet, was he a success? The fact is, it's not the keeping score: it's something more.

The most exciting moments in my life experience, in my professional career, have been the partnerships—the marvelous partnerships, the marvelous role that others have played in everything that I've ever

190

done that anyone would choose to describe as successful. I have not done anything by myself. I'm a guy that couldn't work by myself for an extended period of time without having to get up and look for somebody else in the building, because the sharing and the partnership [were] almost more important than the task.

Howard made a comment earlier about the distinction between problems and conditions.

Bureaucracies, be they school systems or governments, spend tremendous amounts of time and energy trying to fix conditions. One can realize that conditions are a certain way—things like the weather, or you have only enough money to buy 100 books but you need 1,000 books. So is the problem solvable? Or are we dealing with an unsolvable problem?

As an illustration, I'll relate [that a great many] years ago we initiated the Resource Teacher Program. We had six resource teachers in a school district of 12,000 students. And we had somewhere on the order of 5% to 7% of that population with a disability that should be supported by a resource teacher—six for 12,000 students.

And so we could say that this is a condition that we can't deal with, or we could search for a solution to the problem. The problem was insufficiency; the issue was that we needed an alternative delivery system in order to make it work. So, we structurally created a system we called "the traveling resource teacher," who worked through regular classroom teachers in order to solve the problem. It didn't work as well as we wished, but at least it enabled us to attack the problem and to move forward. You can grind yourself to a nubbin trying to change and fix a condition; but you can darn sure get something done when you attack the problem.

What areas of accomplishment that you did together give you the greatest satisfaction?

Van:

The greatest achievement of my lifetime was [one] that occurred hand in hand with Howard. We, in fact, were able to see a delivery system come together in this school district—a special education delivery system that could all but accommodate any child who walked in the door. It became one that was sufficiently comprehensive, that [had] sufficient quality, with sufficient intensity that you could not go elsewhere and find a better effort to serve the needs of special needs children. And that was from a system that could not serve the needs of almost any child when it started.

As I saw the program and as Howard carried on with it after I left the department, it absolutely became a showcase of quality programs. If you were going to have a child with special needs, you would want to have that child enrolled in this school district. And, frankly, I don't know what I could have asked for in my lifetime that would have been any more important than that.

That is, of course, a sandcastle, in that we build them with all due diligence and then we step away. And then the tide comes in. And then somebody else builds the next sandcastle. If they want it to work they have to build it, and I believe that people who build a plan will make it work. People who are not a part of the building of the plan frequently will help it fail.

Howard:

I have had a wonderful opportunity to participate and to learn from Van—he's still my teacher—and the opportunity to be able to walk away after 20 years here and feel good that I was able to help kids and [families] along the way.

I can't quite imagine some of the problems facing our schools, and in particular our special education programs, today. I know that the whole issue of autism has just flourished, almost like a measles epidemic. That is one example, and I'm sure there are a number of others facing educators today in terms of "How do we get there from here? What's it going to take?" What I would hope for is that they are able to surround themselves with quality people who are dedicated and willing to risk the sandcastle. That analogy is so real—we build those castles.

What, if anything, remains unfinished in this area for you?

Van:

You know, as retirees, there is a joy in putting down the burden of the responsibility for making it what it can be. It's literally a relief to be able to say, "That's somebody else's issue and there's not a lot I can do about it." There is from time to time an opportunity to sit and confer with some of the folks in the trenches and to express an opinion, and maybe to talk with someone who is exploring a career in our field.

I can tell you one of my biggest frustrations right now is that Howard decided he didn't want to play golf with me, because he tried it for about three years, and he just became sufficiently exasperated by it that he went to some of the other super skills that he has in restoring furniture and rafting.

The truth be known, I'm not driven by the responsibility of it [what's going on in our school system]. I'm driven by sadness that I feel from time to time because of the sense that the challenge, maybe, goes unanswered. As hard as people try to fix it, it doesn't stay fixed.

I played with that thought of being on the board of education and bringing ideas to the table. But I've had a front seat on changing the organization when I was assistant superintendent. And I found that none of the problems were easy. People that are trying to fix something [of this magnitude] better well bring their lunch, because school systems don't change easily.

But I'm glad that somebody else has the burden now. I'm soon to be 67 years old. I just did a 75-foot-deep scuba dive in the Caribbean and had an absolutely lovely time doing that. We're on our way to the Yampa River to do a raft trip; then, in the middle of June, I'll be in Kentucky with my Tennessee grandkids and family for the Fourth of July, and then back to Kentucky for the Ryder Cup Golf Tournament in September.

I wish I—I sometimes regret that I'm not driven by writing a book. Writing a book about a lot of the things I have really strong feelings about had seemed to me for some time to be a possible option.

Howard:

Van is an incredibly talented writer. If you haven't had the opportunity to read some of the things he wrote—he got kidded about it sometimes, because of his long-winded memos.

I think there is potential. I think it would be therapeutic for [Van] and it could be instructional for some of the rest of us.

What remains unfinished for you Howard?

Howard:

I would not be a good school board member in this district or any other because there are so many issues that irritate me. I have recited little speeches in my mind that I would give to the school board on occasion, and I've written a number of letters to the editor that I never sent, all in my frustration about some of the directions I see education heading today.

We hope that some of this ridiculousness will run its course, and most times it does. This whole issue of "By God, we're going to test everybody until they drop dead" seems to be lasting a lot longer than I anticipated. We have to put some sanity back into our schools relative to that whole issue. We need to be accountable, and we should be, but there are other ways to get that done.

Van:

That are less wasteful.

Howard:

And a lot more functional.

The one thing that I am involved in to some extent, and can perhaps have a bit of influence, is doing some monitoring and reviewing of some of the state's special education programs in different school districts. And I participate a little bit in that. So I keep a little bit more involved than I had anticipated. Beyond that, no burning desire. I'm anxious for the raft trip and some sailing that I have in mind for the summer, and that's kind of where we are.

Terry Fine

November 8, 2007

The three basic goals of my professional career have been quality of care; developing a quality-of- life experience for my staff, to make sure that they wake up in the morning and say, "Hey, we get to come to work"; and to make sure that we're viable so that we can continue on with the successes that we've had....

I'm giving you my heart and soul here, man. I think it centers around continuing to have a vision—looking forward, not living a shoulda-woulda-coulda-kind of life,—but to look forward— having dreams and sharing that with your wife or your family.

Terry, when you were growing up, what did you think it meant to be professionally successfully?

I guess the first thoughts were from my father. He was an engineer and he was really kind of my only role model. Professionally, he was a hard worker. People looked [to] him for advice. He had a hard-work ethic, and I guess I looked up to him [as] a basic role model when I was younger.

Then when I went through school, teachers were role models for me. I looked at them and looked at them as being professional [people that I] wanted advice from.

I had a chemistry teacher that I used to spend hours [with] even after school, just talking to him, dreaming with him. He helped me explore, you know, different professions and [offered] different thoughts about what I wanted to do when I grew up. So he was pretty influential in my life and kind of helped direct or give me some basic ideas about what professionalism was.

[When I went] to Vietnam and spent some time in the military, [there] was a dentist that was there [who] took me under his wing. I saw how he would help people and how people looked up to him.

So professionalism, I guess, when I was a kid was all about having people look toward you for advice and for leadership, guidance, and counseling.

Do you remember any particular conversations with your chemistry teacher that stand out as meaningful?

We used to sit after class when school was over and I'd ask him questions about chemistry principles. And he saw that I had some interest in that and he would ask me questions like, "What do you think about being a chemistry teacher?"

He would keep asking questions and probing me to make me think about what my dreams would be about the future. And we kind of looked toward pharmacy and staying in the health care field, because I guess I had a passion for, or an interest in, that and he would help me— make me think outside of me about what the future might bring.

So learning how to be goal oriented, focusing on dreams and passions, helped me to develop by simply asking questions and having those kinds of conversations. I don't think he really shared a lot of philosophy; mostly he was a guy that would ask the right critical questions, and [he] made me work on what it was that I needed to do for myself. I think it worked.

Thinking back to your dad, what do you remember about his office or his place of work?

I never really saw it. He would get up at six in the morning and be off to work, driving 50, 60 miles. And he would work there all day long. As a civil engineer working for [the]Bureau of Reclamation, he was [always] on some government project. We moved around an awful lot, from place to place, but his focus was always to work hard, to provide, to be the breadwinner of the family. And I really didn't—I just looked at what he did—I really didn't know my father that well. I just know that he was there, that he provided and he worked hard. He had certain standards of excellence, certain standards of performance, that were expected and he was pretty strict [about them]. But I really think—I really didn't know my father or what he did professionally or what his office looked like.

What is your definition of professional success today, and how does that compare to other people's definitions of professional success?

Well, if we define professional success as [being] in a position of influence and you were able to give advice, give direction, have certain leadership qualities—I don't think that's any different [from] what other people would think professionalism is. I think that it's important to have a vision of what [is going] on and to be able to share that with [my] staff. The only reason that I've been successful is not because of what I do alone, but [what I do] by developing a team and having a circle [of] staff members that share the same vision. We work toward goals.

The three basic goals of my professional career have been quality of care, making sure that [I] provide the very best care that I can here in Grand Junction; developing a quality of work or life experience for my staff, to make sure that they wake up in the morning and say, "Hey, we get to come to work" and "We're excited about what we do and we have a passion for being a caregiver. " And [the] third thing would be to make sure that we're finally viable so that we can continue on with the successes that we've had the privilege of having.

Professionalism is being able to give good advice to your patients and to your staff, to lead by example; to make sure that you don't manipulate the situation because you are in the position of power, and to make sure that you give accurate information. Give people choices. Give people options. Empower and share with them and try to make their decisions work. Make sure that they become successful. I think that's empowerment. As a professional, I think that you have an obligation to do that for people and to be able to give of yourself to help other people be successful. If I can do that in my practice, then I feel like I've been successful as a professional.

Do you remember how you came to the conclusion that you needed to communicate that philosophy to your staff?

I think [it was] with all the experiences that I had in Vietnam, and watching my commanding officer handling people—those that worked underneath him, [his] patients, small villages of folks, [people at] sick call—and how he would sit around and not really talk about the tasks that needed to be done. But it was how he became passionate about what he did. We talked a lot about his feelings, and his thoughts, and his dreams—and, yeah, I think it's really cool that he was able to share those kinds of thoughts and feelings.

And then when I first started a practice, I spent an awful lot of time in the behavioral science approach toward management and a lot of work in organizational development. I had a consultant that came in, Wayne Boss, who was probably one of the most significant people in my life. He was able to share some of the philosophies and principles of organizational development, and I incorporated [them] into the practice. I think that that's really been one of the most significant things in my life—that consultation and that time that I spent with Wayne Boss.

We talked about empowerments, we talked about visions and setting goals and how [to] hold people accountable. How do you deal [with] conflict management? Those principles that really make a practice [a] success. It's not the dentistry that really makes a person successful: it's the people that you [surround] yourself with and [that you] help. It's really the staff and the people around me that [have] made me what I am today.

Never stop learning. Always work toward standards of care that make you excellent. I don't think that's an end thing, but it's a process of working and getting there. It's not something that just happens. All I can tell you is that I'm in the process of trying to be a better professional, a better person, a better leader, a better boss, a better caregiver—and you do that through continuing to redefine your vision, sharing that vision and setting goals that are measurable so that you can have some [way] of knowing that you're moving forward, or backwards, or sideways.

How long have you been a practicing dentist? And, financially, could you quit if you wanted to?

Thirty-one years. I know I'm old. I'm an old dog. I don't think that success is measured in money. I don't think finances are the key ingredient [in] wanting to quit or to continue on. I think I'll always be a professional, that I would always want to learn and try to have some influence in whatever I decide to [do].

It doesn't necessarily have to be dentistry. I think there are lots of different chapters that you can have and lots of other endeavors that you can do in your life. You can be…whatever you want to be. I like welding. I mean, I think that I could fit the [mold]—have some great success in doing that also.

So I think that I'll always want to be able to do something to be productive, and one of the ways to measure production is to be able to generate or supplement one's income throughout your life: to teach, to be a consultant—I mean, there are lots of dreams and lots of chapters that we can go [to or do] as we get older, besides being a clinical dentist. [To be able to] stop and say, "I am financially set for the rest of my life," is not how I would define success.

I think success is a process of keep[ing] going. Keep dreaming. Keep looking forward and setting goals. That way you're more successful. If you do the right things, the money will come. I don't think that you ought to focus in on the money. I think you ought to focus in on doing the right thing.

What remains unfinished for you to do or accomplish in the sense of professional success?

Oh, everything. I don't think that there's ever an end. I've got a lot of things I still can do and [am] excited about doing, and, like I said, I'm not trying to finish. I maybe have finished a chapter but the book's not complete, and there's lots of things that we can continue to do in our lives, professionally. The teaching ideas are great—to be able to do some humanitarian things which I've not done in the past, but have visions of doing in the future. I mean, those are dreams and goals that will happen as I get a little older and work toward those ideas. There's lots of stuff to do. It's not an end—it's an ongoing thing. I don't think that anybody should stop being all that they can be.

199

What do you believe constitutes success in learning and in education?

Well, I think that getting good grades and going to college were things that were instilled by my mom. And we used to sit at the table and do homework together and make sure that the homework was done. She would keep picking at us until we got it done. And she would always philosophize about going to college. She never went to college and she thought that getting a college education was the thing that needed to be done. We used to sit around [at] the corner of the table and talk a little bit about how to be successful—and that was basically getting good grades.

I think that [it] was instilled that education equals success. I don't necessarily agree with that, but I think that that's what was instilled in me when I was young, because as I grew older and education be[came] important, [I realized that] it was within me to learn.

I always felt that I never knew enough, that everybody else was smarter than me, that they had the answers to the world and I was just a nerdy little old kid. So I always wanted to learn more [about the world]—not only book-wise, but socially, you know—and to know what was going on. To be successful in education—to me, *passion* equals success. Having a passion to do something, to grab ahold of a concept or an idea and learn about it or to experience it gives success more than book learning.

I don't think that education in an educational setting is what makes one successful. I think it has something to do with what's within you and what your passions are. I love what I do and I've been lucky: I will always be a student. I'm probably more of a student than I am a teacher. I always want to learn more things from more people so that I can be a better person.

Can you remember any particular conversations with your mother at the table that instilled some of these ideas?

She used to talk about our grandfather, about how he was a farmer in Missouri and how he would work hard but never could get ahead because it was just a struggle. I think it was during the Depression.

Most times, she would tell stories about the [grocer], the lawyer, the doctor. She even talked about a dentist that she knew that flew an airplane—that was able to have an airplane and fly from place to place. She thought that was just marvelous. But all her examples and all her stories [were] related to professional people or educated people [who] went to college, and the only way that I was gonna be successful was to go to college. And she was basically sitting and talking about people that she [actually] knew.

She [had] started college but then the war came, she got married, became a mom, and was a mom all the time. And I think she's always, inside of her, wished that she had finished her education, had gone to college.

What do other people that you know think it means to be successful in learning and education, and how does that compare to your own ideas?

I don't know if I can answer that. ...I don't know if I can compare what other people think, because I really don't know what other people think about education. The people that I see that are successful are not necessarily scholarly. Again, I think it comes back to passion. The people that I see that are successful in education or in learning have something to do with what they love to do, what they've found to do. Some of the most successful—you know, people that [own] restaurant chains or own a series of Taco Bells or that started off owning [an] irrigation system and end up owning Grand Junction Steel—*those* people. You learn that stuff not from school, but from life experiences, and those aren't really people that I would say are particularly more educated than I am or more successful than I am, but they have had life experiences and learn from those things.

Education is an ongoing thing, and when you stop learning—when you start looking backwards and stop looking forward—then the chapters are done.

When you were growing up as a child, what did financial success mean to you?

Oh, man. I remember walking down this gravel driveway, walking toward a house that my dad was building in the country in Utah. It was the first house for the family and he was building it, and we were walking down this driveway. I guess I asked him how much money he made. And he said, "Well, I think I make about a thousand dollars a month. " And boy, I thought that was a lot of money. And I thought, "Well, man, if could make a thousand dollars a month, make as much money as my dad, then I would be successful. " And that, to me, was a measure of success. And so, I kept wanting to make a thousand dollars a month.

I had a part-time job when I was in high school and then in college. I mean, I've always worked, and when I finally made a thousand dollars, the first thing I thought about was my dad and walking down that gravel driveway, and [I said], "I made it. " You know, I felt good about that. But I knew that that wasn't the end. I mean, things change, as you know. Things cost more and we have inflation and different standards of living.

So today, what do you think it means to be financially successful?

Probably the most important thing is to make sure that I'm not a burden to somebody else. I don't want to be a burden to society and I don't want to be a burden to my kids. Those are really important things and would be a measure of success.

I'd like to maintain [my] lifestyle. We've worked hard to [get to] where we are now, and I'd like to continue that on through time and also to continue supplementing income. [Hopefully] we'll be able to do that. To be out of debt is a biggie, [at least in part] to not be a burden and also so we don't have the pressures of owing people a lot of money. And, as time goes by, to maybe create a small legacy for my kids. I don't necessarily, philosophically, believe in inheritance [in and of itself]. I don't think it's a healthy thing for kids. It creates conflicts; I think it makes kids lazy, or they don't have their own personal initiatives to be driven to do things. So I keep telling my kids that I'm gonna die broke, and that the last paycheck I'm gonna give to them—or the last check [I give to anyone]—is going to be to the undertaker, and it's gonna bounce. They know that I'm working on trying to be able to enjoy our lifestyle, to continue to go on the way we do, [to] learn, [to] be able to give back to the community, to be able to make some donations or volunteer a little bit—and not to accumulate a lot of money.

Do you think that other people around you share that definition of financial success?

My wife and I talk about that a lot. We have dreams and goals and have talked to the kids about our thoughts. I think we have some friends that measure their financial success on, basically, how much money they have and how much money they are going to be able to leave to their kids as a legacy. I don't know if I necessarily agree with all that, but I think people have different ways to measure their financial success. The way we measure it is to be out of debt, to be financially stable, to be able to continue our lifestyle, not be a burden on society, and to be able to give back to the community.

What advice can you share about how to achieve financial success?

I think that if you follow your passions and you do the things that you want to do in your life and you work hard toward being successful professionally—being successful in what you learn, be successful in family, be successful spiritually—whatever ways that you measure success, the money will come. I don't think it's the other way around. If you focus in on the money, I think you will be a slave to that and I don't think that's a good, healthy thing to do.

Terry, what are some examples of successful relationships that you have known?

Well, this is the hardest part of this interview, because I don't think [I've been] successful in relationships at all. I am no expert on relationships. I've made some major mistakes as it relates to that, and those are probably some of the biggest regrets that I have— not really spending the time and energy in developing good, healthy relationships.

I wouldn't say that my mother and father, in my definition of relationship, would be healthy—and that would be [the] first thing, I think, that I'd look at.

And I don't think that the percentage of divorces that we see has really constituted a healthy situation. I'm not inclined to think that there [is] a perfect relationship: that's something you have to continue to work at and that's between two individuals. The things that make a healthy relationship are [things like] talking about feelings, talking about situations, having common goals and interests.

One time in Mexico, we were sitting on the beach, just watching people walk by. And there was a couple—80 maybe 90 years old. He had a little Speedo on and his wife had on a little swimsuit. And they were walking down the beach holding hands. That was very moving to me: that, after all the years and being the age that they were, they could be who they were and love walking down to the beach, holding hands—it was real. It was such a real, real thing, and I looked at Linda and said, "You know, I hope that we can do that when we're 80 years old. " And I think I said that it was a cool thing. I liked that.

We [often] sit and watch people, you know, at a restaurant or a bar, and there'll be a couple, just the two of them, sitting like you and I are in the corner, looking at each other and having a quiet conversation over a glass of wine, intently and genuinely enjoying each other's company, and being partners in whatever endeavor they're doing. Those things are measures to me of what a really good relationship is.

To be able to laugh, to have your kids come over and play dominoes at the table and laugh and tell stories, and share those kinds of times with kids are important in relationships. Family—and I think that the biggest regret, like I said, is probably [that] I didn't spend as much time as I needed to develop those things with my kids and my wife.

I sacrificed a lot of that time with [my] kids to be successful as a dentist. Work got in the way; [I was] driven to do those kinds of things. So I think that's one of the things that I'm probably more driven to do now, as I get older— to not sacrifice [them].

Spending time with the kids, watching them grow, sharing their experiences, and living through them vicariously—those are successes in relationships that I have now that I didn't have when I was younger. They are probably some of the most important thing[s] in my life right now. It's not the professionalism. It's not the money. It's not the education. It's really family and spending time developing in those relationships and with friends, as well—you know, spending time doing those things and learning those skills. Learning: learning how to be a friend, learning how to be a father, learning how to laugh spontaneously and share quality time. Those things are the most important to me.

Am I hearing you say that there is a difference in how you view your relationships now and how you viewed them when you were younger?

I think that there is a major difference. I'm not as angry as I was, or frustrated, or forceful or controlling. I think I just let things happen and try to be part of that. I think I've changed as it relates to those kinds of things. I have more fun with my kids now than I've ever had. I have [been married and divorced and remarried], and now, having a new life, having fun and learning how to have good, healthy relationships is really an exciting thing for me. So yeah, I think I'm doing a lot better than I did in the past.

Looking back over your whole life , what areas or accomplishments give you the most satisfaction?

Well, I think it's what I call "The Cross of Life." It's trying to balance your life with your family [and all the other components] successfully. I raised two great kids, I have a granddaughter and a great wife—and they [all] still hang out. We still do things together. Family is one of the [four] points on the cross.

The next point would be personal learning—being able to continue to learn and to be excited about learning new things. [For example], look at [my interest in] the welding; my learning a little bit about [the] stock market; my going to continuing education classes [such as] Plantology and some new things in surgery, and still having a passion to do that. I think that's a great accomplishment.

And then another point on that cross would be professional—continuing to be a professional person. People will look to you for advice and you will have an influence on them. So make sure that you give accurate information and give [them] choices and options in their care or their decisions. Being able to act professionally, whether working with my young son, or a patient is a great accomplishment.

Last, but not least, is [to] continue to work on spirituality. There is more to life and more meaning than just the physical accomplishments that we do. To have a relationship with your God is an important [thing] that you need to continue to [think about] and work on. It's probably one of the weaker areas of my four points of life. It's something I am definitely interested in pursuing and continuing to work on.

Can you tell me when you first became aware that a spiritual relationship with your God was an important piece of life?

Well, it certainly wasn't when I was younger. I mean, we went to Sunday school and had a Christian Protestant upbringing, but I don't think —I think it was a task, something that we had to do. I don't know if it brought spirituality into my life. When I went to college, I was on my own. And spending time in the '60s, identifying who I was and what I was—exploring and questioning the meanings of life, trying to figure all that out—probably brought spirituality into my life. I was practicing from Buddhism to Hinduism to Christianity and was able to sit around and talk about [them]. And, you know, [I read] old books like Prophet Imran's philosophies on *Atlas Shrugged* and on capitalism—all of those things were things that put together how I fit in the universe.

I figured that this couldn't have all happened without some grand plan and somebody overseeing all of [it]. I guess I really believed deep inside of me that there was a God and that I wanted to explore more meanings of life—how people in the world live, how they exist, and the universality of man.

Have you found any downsides to achieving successes?

Time. I think sacrificing one of those points for another, focusing so much on trying to be financially successful or professionally successful and sacrificing your family for that is definitely a downside. You have to continue to learn and work on trying to balance your life out.

With whom do you want most to share the successes of your life and how are you planning to do that?

Well, I think that's a process. I'm sharing all these things. My relationship with my wife is fantastic and we're having a lot of fun. We sit here [around] the corner of the table and we dream, and we philosophize, and we analyze what's going on around us. We make plans; we share time with the kids and help them to be successful; and share our enthusiasm with our grandchild, with our kids. I think that family is the most important thing in one's life. I mean, that's who I'm probably sharing all of this with—more with my wife than most anybody. Our dreams are to travel, to go do some humanitarian stuff in the future, to be able to work together in our financial, professional efforts, to be partners, and to work together to help each other be successful in the future. My best friend, my partner, my life, my soul is my wife.

So what it's all about to me is being able to share those successes with somebody, and if there was one person, it would definitely be Linda. But we also try to incorporate into the bigger picture the kids and our friends. Those things are important to us—relationships. Just because it wasn't important in [my] earlier years, probably makes it more important now than anything.

What more would you like to say about any of these ideas?

I'm giving you my heart and soul here, man. I think it centers around continuing to have, you know, a vision—looking forward, not living in a shoulda-woulda-coulda-kind of life, but to look forward— having dreams and sharing that with your wife or your family, and working together toward accomplishing other things in your life: travel, more experiential living, learning, worshipping. I mean, all of those are things that we need to continue to look forward to.

I think it is most important to have that passion or that drive within you to continue to look forward and not to look back. I think that the shoulda-woulda-couldas in your life are not the right direction to take. [We] ought to look forward and have the dreams and visions to move forward to the next chapter of our lives. That's the important thing. That's what success is all about: the process. It's not the end result, it's just the process to get to the end.

Sally Henry

August 4, 2008

I think that ShareFest is one of many things that came out of that reflectiveness—that time of reflection where we, as a church, looked at ourselves and said, "Hey, we don't want to be about just ministering to ourselves and ministering to church people and waiting for people to walk through our doors. We want to be about what Jesus told us to be about, which is loving God and loving other people and not just people that are like us." And so ShareFest is like the culmination. We'd been moving in that direction.

I saw financial success as [making] enough money that you could do stuff, you could keep doing it, and you could keep it—you wouldn't have to sell it or give it away [in order to] keep going.

...the whole HIV/AIDS thing and how the church is finally, just now, acknowledging that it's out there. That's the leprosy of the twentieth and the twenty-first centuries. And if Jesus were here, he'd be right in the midst of it all. What is the church doing? Nothing. I'm already feeling the fire underneath me going, "We've got to do something."

When you were younger, what constituted success in learning and education and who taught you that?

I think of my mother constantly reading, and it just seemed like she always knew so much. And I admire her for that. I don't know if I had put the word *success* to it, but I was just always amazed by how much she knew.

In school, I was an average student, and so I always thought the successful kids were those that got A's and all the E's in elementary school. I don't think I was as aware in elementary school as I was later, when you get A's, B's, and C's.

We got paid for our grades. It was very minimal—$2 for A's and on down the line—and so in some sense, there was that definition that success [meant] getting A's. But later in life, when I was homeschooling my own kids, success for me, then, was that they would know *how* to learn, that they would know how to educate themselves.

Part of what we did when we homeschooled was called "unschooling." That meant following your areas of interest. And so if Sean [her son] had a thing about weapons, we could totally dive into every weapon there was and go to books and find clubs and find friends that would provide information and who usually had really cool things that he could touch and feel, because that's the kind of learner he was. And so, later in life, success in education [became] that you knew how to learn and that you knew where to go if you needed to learn about something.

You said that your mother was an avid reader—can you think of an experience that caused you to equate that with her thoughts on education?

My mom reads a lot of New Age-kind of books. And she would tell us all about them, and that equated to reality for us. It wasn't just information to be learned. It was like, "This is how the world is," and so it entered our spiritual lives and other aspects of who we were. It didn't enter the educational end of things, as such, for her. I saw reading and learning as equating to application in life. When I think of education, I always think of formal education. But when I really stop and think about education, it's more learning and applying.

In what ways do you think that "learning" may differ from "education"?

I think of public education and I wonder how much *real* learning happens [there], because of all the other junk that's going on in kids' lives before they ever get into a classroom. And then working at the church [First Presbyterian Church in Grand Junction, Colorado], I see so many different ways that kids and people learn that have nothing to do with a classroom, that's more life-learning—the kinds of things that are so much more valuable than information that can be learned in the classroom.

I think of teenagers that hang out with adults doing a project, like during the ShareFest Weekend where they did stuff together. Just by spending time together kids learned skills at whatever project they were working on, whether it was painting a house or repairing a deck. They would learn something that way, but they also learn that not all adults are out to yell at them for one thing or another—that adults are actually kind of fun to hang out with—they get something out of that, and they're valued.

In what ways are you already a success in learning and education?

I know how to learn. I'm passionate in certain areas and can just devour books, DVDs, and CDs on a subject and then apply it. Usually, there's some kind of application, because it's what I'm interested in. A lot of what I'm reading now has to do with my job, which I love and I'm passionate about.

What are some keys to achieving success in learning and education, and what is an example of when one happened in your life?

One key is hanging out with people that you see are good learners themselves, people that seem like they're going in the right direction, in the direction that you want to go; and also people that build you up, add value to you, and who value you as an individual.

That happened to me when I first started going to a women's Bible study. My motive for going was for adult conversation, and Kim [her husband] was in Gunnison, Colorado, at the time. So my motivation wasn't necessarily to learn, but I thought it would be a great time to connect with other women. And then, when I started going, my appetite grew, and grew, and grew. And I just wanted to hang out with Karen Stewart [the group leader] all the time. She was so full of wisdom. She knew the Bible. She had her own story that she shared with us and I saw that she was living it, that she was walking her faith; I wanted more of that.

And so, what better way to learn than sitting at the feet of somebody who you feel like has it down?

What remains unfinished for you in this area?

Formal education. My plan is to go to seminary in a year. In a way, that's really exciting; and in a way, that's very daunting and overwhelming. I've heard horror stories of how hard graduate school is. But then, there's a part of me that says, "Yeah, but this is ... the subject matter that I love." I'm sure there are going to be areas—you know, Hebrew and Greek—that aren't going to be as exciting, but the motivation there is that I've got this goal.

And just the ongoing learning. When I'm done with graduate school, it's not like I'm going to stop reading books and stop learning about the up-and-coming generations that I'm going to have to minister to and with. I love learning and I love learning about people.

If you were, for some reason, unable to complete your formal seminary degree, would you feel that you had failed in learning?

No, I see seminary as a means to an end. I'd like to pastor within the Presbyterian church, but I know that there are a lot more options out there that don't require a formal education. For the past seven years now, I've been extremely satisfied at the job that I've been doing, which has been ministering to and with people, without that formal title. And in a way, that was kind of the best of both worlds. I got to do a lot of the things that a pastor would do without all the responsibility, and so that was kind of cool.

Can you give us an experience or an example that causes you to say, "I am extremely happy with what I do"?

I look over the last six or so years and it's been such a journey of growing and being stretched in learning through difficult times. When we [at our church] were in-between pastors and people were leaving the church—going to other churches, just leaving church altogether—it was so painful, and we worked so hard at building up the leadership that was staying. And there was one man, an elder, and as people were dropping like flies, he said, "Well, you don't have to worry. I'm not leaving here, and if I have to be the last one to turn the light off, so be it."

And to me, that was just music to my ears. It was so heartwarming that here's somebody that's going to stick it out with me and go through the gauntlet, so to speak, because it was just a rough time. But in hindsight, now that times are so much better and we've gotten to a healthy place in the church, I can look at that time and know that even in the midst of it, I knew that it was valuable—it was hard and it stunk, but it was valuable—and I was going to learn so much from it.

When you were a youngster growing up, what did financial success mean to you, and what personal experiences contributed to what you understood financial success to be?

When I was a kid, financial success meant that you got lots of extras and you got to do lots of cool things. My entire childhood is characterized by finances always being tight in our household.

We still did lots of great things. We owned horses and we built a house in the mountains. But some of those were short-lived, because finances got in the way. So I saw financial success as [making] enough money that you could do stuff, you could keep doing it, and you could *keep* it—you wouldn't have to sell it or give it away [in order to] keep going.

Our house that we built in Evergreen [Colorado] is an example. My folks owned some property with some friends. We owned one lot and our friends owned the other. Eventually, we all decided to build houses. We had the shell of our house built and it was supposed to be done, or done enough to move in, by the summer of, I think it was, 1974. But then it wasn't quite done. So we moved into our tent in the front yard. That summer was the rainiest season in history in Evergreen—I think

213

on the whole Eastern Slope. So we ended up moving into the house. There was a roof over our heads and there were walls—just studs. Ellen, my older sister, and I learned how to put up insulation and to mud and tape drywall.

We lived there for two years and, in the midst of that, my dad was also trying to start in his own insurance business. All of his customers were in Denver and the commute got to be too expensive—it was just too much—and so, we ended up selling the house and moving.

Today, what do you think it means to be financially successful and do you think other people share that view?

If you can cover your bills and have a little extra for a vacation every now and then, that's just great.

If you've got even more so that you can be gifting people and helping others out, [that's] even better. I think that's when I would probably consider myself [to be] financially successful: when we'd have enough money that we could give it away and it wouldn't hurt. But then part of me goes, "Yeah, but there's something about when it hurts to give it away. It means more."

Can you describe the difference between sacrificial giving and just generosity?

It seems like most of our giving is sacrificial giving, because we never seem to be overflowing with cash, or, the cash that we give is really not extra. It's giving up something that you, yourself, would have gotten otherwise. It's giving up that dinner out or maybe it's giving up that weekend away. It's giving up something that you would've enjoyed so that somebody else can maybe have a necessity. I keep thinking of these renters that we have. They're scraping. He had a good-paying job when they first got in the house, and then he lost that job. He worked at a printer's and made a couple of mistakes—they were big mistakes—and so he lost his job. And now, he's working a job that pays $10 an hour and he's supporting a family of five. It's not cutting it.

So for a couple of months, we covered part of their rent. And for us, it was getting close. We were getting down to our last little bit. But you know, you want to help them. You want to see them succeed, and so we helped them, despite the fact that maybe we could've done something a lot more fun with that money, or maybe we could've paid off a bill.

What more do you want to achieve in the area of financial success?

Kim and I have sat down and written out goals before, things like, "We need a new roof" or "We need to replace this" or "We want to go on a vacation." And without even consciously trying to take steps to meet our goals, usually within a year, they'd be met. When we moved to our most recent house, we came across one of those lists. And it's like, "Remember this?" They seemed so out of reach when we wrote them down, but then they just happen.

In talking with your children or grandchildren, what advice can you share about how to achieve financial success?

Don't get stuck with credit debt: pay cash whenever you can, because what [credit debt] does is it takes away your freedom and your choices. But then, the other end of that is to do what you love because otherwise, all the money in the world won't make a bit of difference. Both of [our children] have credit debt right now, but it's for school.

Tell us of a time when you told one of your kids, "Do what you love."

Well, I was constantly telling them that. They grew up watching their dad go to a job every day that he hated, but he did it to support the family and so that I could stay home with the kids and homeschool and do all the things that we did. It was tight, but they saw that and took it all in.

And also during that time, I was learning about how each of us have gifts, talents, and passions that God has put into us, and we need to follow those. He gave them to us for a reason, and so I always encouraged them to do what you love. And after watching Kim all those years, they were highly motivated to do that, because they didn't want to end up going to a job every day that they hated.

What are some examples of successful relationships that you've known?

I'd say that my relationship with you and Jan [Gammill] is a good example of a successful relationship. And I would say that it's successful because we know how to be real with each other, transparent, and we can really say what we feel. There are no issues or head games.

Another relationship of mine that's successful is with my older sister, Ellen. In some ways we're very much alike, and in some ways we're very different. And our biggest difference is that I'm a Christian and she's not. When I share that with people and share some of the conversations that Ellen and I have together, people are just really surprised and even shocked that we can have these conversations and still be friends and still have the close relationship that we have. It's easier to have relationships with people that you have much in common with; I think it's harder when you have less in common.

What lessons has life taught you about how to achieve success in relationships?

I think that there has to be a lot of grace to have successful relationships, and I say that because I have some relationships in my life that are not the best that they could be. And I think it's because I haven't extended grace. I'm requiring way too much.

The relationships that I struggle with the most are with my parents. We think very differently. They're very set in their ways and I'm getting more set in my ways. And there's probably baggage that goes along with that, too. I'm just requiring way too much of them. And because it makes me too uncomfortable, I just avoid, avoid.. You know, like most middle children, I don't like conflict.

There are lots of things that we should've talked out—stuff from my childhood, my dad's reactions. He will flash and get angry and the kid in me [doesn't want conflict, doesn't] want a raised voice, so I just avoid that. It's frustrating and disappointing and I'm disappointed in myself.

What advice would you give to someone who found themselves in that situation with someone they were close to?

Speak the truth in love. I think in so many situations, our fear of what's going to happen gets blown up to be bigger than it ever would be, and it keeps us from doing what we know we need to do. What if we had just dealt with things along the way? Then there just wouldn't be all these underlying [issues]. But we didn't, so it's just there—hovering—and everybody is too afraid to say something. Nobody is acknowledging the elephant in the room. So I would say, "Speak the truth in love," even if it's going to be hard—even if you think it might be hurtful.

A lot of times—I know that I've done this with my husband—I don't give the person credit [for being able to] handle what I'm going to say, [able to] handle the truth, handle whatever needs to be spoken. So we won't even go there. [I's better if you] don't worry about what *could* be. Just do the right thing. Speak the truth in love and go from there. I suppose that means I have to go home now and practice what I preach.

When you were growing up, what did you think it meant to be professionally successful, and what experiences led you to that definition?

I thought my dad was a success, because he had his own insurance business in our basement. I saw him working all the time, saw him going out on calls, and saw him paying the bills. In the insurance business, they sometimes have contests: if you sell so many life insurance policies, you get a free weekend at a resort. We qualified a few times and got to go on these long weekends to a resort, like in Wisconsin. It was really fancy and ritzy. So it's like, "Yeah, my dad's successful."

Of course, we'd have that overhanging umbrella: "No, we can't do this. We can't afford it." But as a child, I thought that he was successful.

My parents are risk-takers, too, in so many different ways. Not everybody can start their own business. There's something to that, too.

What's your definition today of professional success?

Going to work, using the gifts that you have, and loving what you do. I think loving what you do and being good at it is just—that's *it*. That's the pinnacle. When I was a kid, the big thing for professional success—you know, the doctor, the lawyer—was bringing home a lot of money. For the husband, it was being able to provide for your family; for the woman, it was being in what historically had been a man's job.

But now, it's doing what you love. It's enjoying going to work in the morning. That was my biggest fear when I finished college. But, lo and behold, I had nothing to fear. Before I even graduated, I had a job at the church. On the first day I showed up, we—me and all the people that I work with—were all a-grinnin' ear to ear.

What remains unfinished for you in the area of professional success?

I think there're always new adventures. I did a spiritual gifts inventory [once], and one of the gifts that I had that was near the top was apostleship. Apostleship is starting new churches or ministries, and I love to do that. I start things, I get them going, I get the leadership equipped and strong so that they know what they're doing, and then I slowly back away. And then I get excited about something else, get that going, and then back away, and then start something else.

So for me, there's a never-ending amount of possibilities. New church development sounds really exciting, because there's so many things that you have to start up in a church, not just the church itself. Holy cow, all the different things you could be doing!

Once you get a church going, maybe you stay around for five, ten years, and then maybe you go start another one. And who knows? I could be a missionary in Haiti.

So what else? I want to be a good grandma. I want to be a good parent and a good wife for a long time. I want to help a lot of people come to know that there's this great way of living by following Christ and having Him as a part of your life. The possibilities are endless. There's so much to do in this world, and I get excited about a lot of it.

I just watched an interview with Bill Hybels and Bono from U2. [They were] bringing up the whole HIV/AIDS thing and how the church is finally, just now, acknowledging that it's out there. That's the leprosy of the twentieth and the twenty-first centuries. And if Jesus were here, he'd be right in the midst of it all. What is the church doing? Nothing. I'm already feeling the fire underneath me going, "We've got to do something."

All you have to do is look around the world and see all the hurt and despair. Expose yourself to it until it breaks your heart enough to do something.

Let me ask you a question that's not on our list. What do you think it means to retire?

To not get paid for what you're doing. [smiles and laughs.]

It might mean a slowing down. It might mean that you don't have to go [to your old job]. But I don't think that your love of doing whatever it is that you are doing ends all of a sudden at retirement age. I fully expect, when I'm around 50, to be starting my first *official* career, but [it will be] my *second* career. And I'll do that for probably at least 20 years. And then, if I'm still loving what I'm doing and my health is good, I'll keep going. If I'm getting tired, maybe I'll slow it down a little bit.

What if at the end of that 20 years that you've just described, you thought God was leading you in a different direction?

By golly, then you go. My parents are in their early seventies and they've just moved back to—Florida, packed their stuff, and drove across the country themselves. They only moved to Colorado six or seven years ago, and they're off on a new adventure. They're ready to redo this house they bought.

All three of us daughters are the same way. If it looks like fun, or another adventure and it's doable, let's go for it.

Looking at your life as a whole, what areas of accomplishment give you the greatest satisfaction?

Homeschooling my children, because they turned out to be good kids, good people, good adults. They care for other people. They have a strong faith. They chose spouses that are caring and have the same values that they do. They didn't just *survive* their childhood into adulthood. I like them. I like hanging out with them, and they like hanging out with me

I think one of my other biggest accomplishments would involve what our church went through from 2002 to 2006,[and] that I stuck it out: with the turmoil, with the transition, with going from being an organization that didn't do things in a healthy way to a place where now we do. By "doing things in a healthy way," I mean like dealing with conflict, having goals, taking long, hard looks at ourselves as a church. I'm proud of the fact that I helped bring about that transition to a healthy place.

Have you found any downsides to achieving success?

I think the downside can always be pride. That's the thing for any kind of leader, or anyone who feels like they've achieved any kind of success—an unhealthy pride. I don't think pride is wrong. Like I just said, I was proud of the fact that I helped this to happen, but I fully acknowledge, too, that it wasn't all about me. It was mostly about God, and it was also about a lot of other people, but I was a part of that. When you think everything is about you, a real downfall can happen—one that can take you to that place.

With whom do you most want to share the successes of your life and how are you planning on doing that?

The obvious answer would be my husband, Kim, and my family. But I think you share the successes with the people that you're with along the way. Hopefully you're not just working together, but you're celebrating together along the way. That's part of the deal.

It's like at the end of this growing season—when the peaches are done and the markets are all over—and Kim and I, and probably Sean and Sarah [her children] and for sure Ellen, and whoever else we can gather up that's been a part of that whole insanity of summer, will get together and we'll celebrate that it's over, that we don't have to do it for another year. You celebrate with the people along the way.

In what ways do you think God approves of what you just said?

He said to love others. Part of loving others is inviting them to be a part of what's going on, and not just in difficulties, but in the fun stuff, too. God talks a lot about celebrations. Sometimes, we make Christianity be way too serious. There's a lot of celebrating to be done—and yeah, I think God likes celebrations.

Please describe what ShareFest is and what it means to you.

ShareFest was a weekend this last spring where 20 or so churches came together and served in the community for a weekend. We planned. We created a website where people could enter the skills that they had to offer and where people could also enter help that they saw needed: a senior who needed leaves raked, or swamp coolers hooked up, or the homeless shelter needing a paint job or a deep cleaning of their kitchen.

We had around 3,000 people that went out on that weekend and did approximately 600 projects throughout the Grand Valley area from Fruita to Palisade. There was a lot of yard work and repairing of decks and other things. We had a group that worked in an elementary school cleaning desks, floors, [and] walls, did landscaping, and built sandboxes. There was another group that totally scraped and repainted a two-storey house and put a wheelchair ramp on it for a woman. It was all of these churches coming together. I read about ShareFest in a magazine that I get and told our mission elder about it—a couple of times—and told our pastor about it—a couple of times. Finally, they agreed.

So we called some people at other churches and said, "Hey, we've got this idea. Let's come together and talk about it." There were probably eight or 10 people at this meeting. From that, more were contacted—and so we kind of spidered out.

Eventually, we sent a letter to all the churches, inviting them to a lunch. And out of that, we ended up with 20 churches. We had an opening registration time—I call it a "launch"—on a Saturday where people would come to pick up information. We had a team that worked on the launch, a team that worked on getting people hooked up with projects, and one getting those projects into the database. Afterwards, we had a big barbeque potluck with 3,000 people and a band. It was wonderful.

It would have been easy to just get really prideful about the whole thing. I got a lot of pats on the back and they gave [me] a hard hat with my name on it that said "ShareFest." But there's no way I could've done this [by] myself. Yeah, I read the article and pushed that we go in that direction, but if everybody would've said no, it wouldn't have happened. It takes everybody and it takes everybodys' gifts. The more people that are involved, the more people there are to help.

I think that ShareFest is one of many things that came out of that reflectiveness—that time of reflection where we, as a church, looked at ourselves and said, "Hey, we don't want to be about just ministering to ourselves and ministering to church people and waiting for people to walk through our doors. We want to be about what Jesus told us to be about, which is loving God and loving other people and not just people that are like us." And so ShareFest is like the culmination. We'd been moving in that direction.

Chris Muhr

November 14, 2007

It's just a great privilege to have friendships that have lasted so many years. I would rather somebody take away the companies and the houses—I live here in a straw bale house on the Redlands with this kind of view. If you ask me to trade [my] friends for these really great things that I have—no way.

[Caddying] was paying a buck an hour and I remember Dad saying, "Boy, you ought to come to work down in the aluminum shop." And I did. You always wonder, "Gee, did I give up a dream just to make more money when I was 16?" But I know that I made the right decision.

Chris, when you were growing up, what did you think it meant to be professionally successful?

Oh, I think I was probably looking at people who owned large companies, who were bank managers and doctors and lawyers. Looking at those types of people who, in the community, were probably viewed as important community members and had jobs with heavy responsibilities, a lot of employees. I think that was the professional model of success that I looked at. I didn't really look at other disciplines like an English teacher, a college professor, [or] a social worker as a professionally successful person, because they didn't make the money, I guess. I was probably pretty naïve growing up.

Can you remember some experiences you had that led you to that conclusion?

I started playing golf at a fairly young age, 12 years old, and was good enough that I would go to different tournaments around the state. When you'd go to the country clubs, you'd see the big cars in the parking lot. You'd see the people that [were] well-dressed inside and you'd see the membership roles; and you'd think, "Wow, that's really where success lies—to be able to afford this kind of a lifestyle." And, of course, the membership list would have all of the business people, doctors, and lawyers, so I think that's where that notion, "Boy, I've gotta be a professional of some type with a degree such as a doctor and make a lot of money and have a lot of people respect [me] [came from]."

Does your definition of professional success today differ from other people's definitions?

I think today my definition of professional success is about 180 degrees from what it was when I was a child. I worked in the sciences for 14 or 15 years as a geologist, and I got to see the more purely academic side of professional success.

People who produce papers on various subjects, whether it be geology or, at the time, health physics with radiation, were not highly paid or highly educated people in most regards. I was interested in the fields of environmental contamination and cleanup, and I would view successful people as those who were studying different subjects that had a wide range of effect for a number of people—in other words, improving others' quality of life or protecting them in their environments as far as contaminations go. I viewed people with a profession of protecting others and trying to benefit others as highly successful, regardless of how much money they made or how much notoriety they gained from that.

Can you compare that to other people's definitions?

Yeah. I'm stereotyping, but I think if you were to look at the model of success that is put out there by the media, you would see, I think, that housing becomes the standard—"big mansions." If you don't have [one with] 4,000 to 7,000 square feet [and] a three-car garage, and if you aren't driving a BMW and a Hummer, then you're not successful.

That's where we're seeing a lot of people getting into trouble financially. It's their buying into the idea that success means possessions, and not necessarily the ability to be with your family, to improve the quality of life for your family, to improve the quality of life for your community, to have a lower impact on the earth, on the amount of resources that you consume. It's changing, but I don't think a lot of people view their immediate family, and their community doing good for others, as necessarily being successful. So long as the rest of the world sees you living in a large house with lots of nice furniture, and big cars—and that's because of the way Wall Street and the media have portrayed success: you need a bigger, faster car, and you need to have your house filled with stainless steel appliances, nice furniture.

Within your own definition, in what ways are you already a professional success?

You know, it's kinda hard to see myself as a success. I have this idea of so many more things that I want to do in life, that to take a snapshot at this point in time,—[but] I would say that I've been somewhat professionally successful in the sciences field and in my involvement in community organizations and advisory boards, like the Air Quality Planning Committee.

I've been involved with the Environmental Quality Committee and the Air Quality Planning Committee for about 20 years now for Mesa County. That's resulted in some regulations and some changes to the way things are done here in the valley, so that our air quality is protected. There's less open burning. There are woodstove regulations, and no-burn days, and woodstove change-out programs, and composting at the landfill—a number of things that benefit the community and the region as a whole. I feel that's a place where I have been successful.

I was involved with mining pollution, assessment, and litigation planning when I was with Oak Ridge National Laboratory. Now, seeing some of the national regulations changed and some of the possibilities for cleaning up a lot of the streams here in Colorado, I feel somewhat successful in some of those ways, because of small contributions that I had to the National Mining Pollution Task Force that I was on. And some of the geologic research that I've done has led to a better understanding of the natural gas reserves that we're currently exploiting.

In the business ownership arena, I think I'm somewhat successful in the fact that I've been able to retain the employees that worked for my father when he owned the company. [Some have] been there 25 years. I pay them well, I give them good benefits, and I treat everybody with respect, whether they're the shop cleanup kid or the top metal worker and welder in the shop. Thus, we have a really good work place, not just for myself, but for all the employees. I think that probably gives me more pride than to say that [for example] at the end of the year, our net income was 10% higher than last year. The numbers really don't impress me nearly as much as how customers view All Metals Welding and how my employees view working there.

Can you relate an experience when you were aware that these employees felt the way you have just described?

One of my employees just recently got into some trouble. He cashed a check for his brother, who has been a troublemaker in the past. The brother didn't have a bank account. [My employee] cashed the check for him and it turned out it was fraudulent. Well, because my employee cashed the check, he got into trouble. A number of my friends that mountain bike are attorneys. They recommended an attorney in Glenwood Springs where this occurred and I was able to make a contact for this employee. [His] family is having tough times economically, and I was able to offer him a loan to obtain the legal services. I also was able to put him in touch with another friend of mine who runs an affordable housing program, a self-help housing program. And this young man, who's only 23, now has a three-bedroom, two-bath house and his legal problems are behind him.

One of my employees whose son has been deployed to Iraq a couple of times, wanted to build [him] a toolbox, a real fancy toolbox for his truck, and to have it all loaded and ready to go for him when he got back from Iraq. He asked to use the shop to put it all together [and was willing to pay]. "You know, I'll make a list of all the materials that I use building these boxes." And I told him that I'd donate it.

I enjoy giving them things like that, just because they work really hard to provide [me with] a living. I don't know how to weld and I can't do the metal work. I merely do the quotes and the management of the place. So it shows my loyalty to them, and in return, I get a lot of loyalty. I try and help out people wherever I can.

Another employee's son was mentored by John McConnell, who established the Math & Science Center. And this son subsequently won kind of a junior Noble Prize and was awarded many dollars in college scholarships. So they have the feeling of an obligation to the Math & Science Center. I allow them to make a lot of things in the shop for the Center. I donate the materials [and] any labor that's needed, because this guy [McConnell] transformed this gentleman's son's life. He feels an obligation to give back, and I feel an obligation to help him do that.

I have incredible employees and I'm very lucky to have them.

Describe some of the environmental changes you saw happen in Mesa County.

The woodstove change-out program happened while I chaired the Air Quality Planning Committee for about seven years. I had been on the Environmental Quality Committee for a number of years, and then we changed it to an Air Quality Planning Committee because of the growth that we could foresee happening here in the valley—putting this many people in a confined space like you have in the Grand Valley.

We could see problems happening and one of the big ones was the winter. We would get inversions that would last an extended period of time. The air quality on the valley floor would be horrible, and yet 500 to 800 feet above, there would be clean, clear, beautiful air. All of the wood smoke and exhaust fumes would accumulate on the valley floor for days on end. It became a real problem. After looking at the data, what actually was causing the problems with air quality during those inversion days, we saw that 40% was wood smoke derived. So we figured the biggest bang for the buck would be to try and minimize the amount of wood smoke on those inversion days.

The Air Quality Committee came up with a way of determining how best to go about it, and that involved voluntary no-burn policies and to change out the old woodstoves that had no EPA rating, very dirty burning woodstoves. We were able to start a revolving loan fund to change these woodstoves out as a result of the Louisiana Pacific fines that were paid. We got cooperation from all the media outlets to do a no-burn day, and the health department now has a method [of] contacting all the media outlets on days that are no-burns. That system was established and, consequently, we've seen some real improvement on inversion days.

> ### When you were younger, what constituted success in learning and education? And who taught you that?

My parents instilled in us that an education is the way that you obtain a better job, a better paycheck, and a better chance for living a good life. My parents both graduated from a high school—Central High. And then my dad took classes for surveying and other skill sets that he needed for various jobs; my mom took some business classes that she needed for different jobs, and although neither one of them [had] a bachelors or advanced degree, it gave me a good example to realize the value of an education. They certainly didn't have to go back and attend classes at nights, but they did.

In college, I didn't get good grades for a couple of years, just because I was kinda wandering aimlessly, not knowing what I wanted to do with life. And then I ran into a professor when I was signing up for my last year of my business major. I ran into a professor of geology. This guy was so excited about teaching geology and what we were going to do.

All I needed was [one more] general education class, [a beginning] level class—here I was a senior. I'd taken all my business classes, but I still needed this science credit, this general education credit. And I got to talking with this guy, and he was so excited—he just loved geology and explained to me that we were gonna go on field trips. We would learn all about how the Monument was formed, how the maze was formed, and what the valley floor was comprised of, and on, and on, and on.

And so I signed up for his class. And then I walked over to my next business class. [That teacher] was so unenthused about teaching that business class that I spent about five minutes there. I know my parents just think I'm crazy for this—I just walked over and ripped up my registration for my last year of business, and threw it away and walked back to the geology professor, Dr. Johnson, and said, "Here you go. Fill this thing out so that I can be geologist."

"Oh, my God," he said, "you can't do that. You're only—you're on your last year of business. You can't." And I said, "Yup, yup. That's what I'm gonna do."

It took another three years but I got my geology degree—and I got good grades. I ended up with nearly a 4.0 in my geology discipline because I was enthused. I had a horrible time in physics and some chemistry, but boy, it sure provided me a great lifestyle for 14, 15 years as a geologist. It was—I would say between my parents and Dr. Johnson, I got a real appreciation of what an education would do.

What do you think remains unfinished for you the arenas of professional success and in learning and education?

You know, as far as the welding company goes, I don't necessarily want it to get much bigger. Of course, it's always nice to be more profitable, because that way I can share and it would [benefit] my employees. I want to continue to give them good pay raises and a good standard of living, but I also donate thousands of dollars a year to different things, like the new screen and sound system at the Glade Park Fire Department for their "Movies After Dark," and to the Fountain System, and for the Memorial to Wayne Aspinall in Palisade. I donated this year to the Mountain Bike Association. I'm once again president of the board of that, and it allows me some freedom—having a successful company allows me to be able to get away from the office and do a few things like the grand opening of the big bike trail yesterday. A couple of hours here and there, I have that freedom and flexibility.

I want my company to be successful so that when it comes time for me to retire or sell it, that it will bring the resources to me and my family so that we can also donate money to nonprofits and charities.

That's the professional success that I'm looking for. Jen, the love of my life, does the same thing through [her] company. For both of us to be able to combine our resources and continue to support the charities around town we're very passionate about is where I see my success growing.

In learning and education, do you think there are things remaining unfinished for you?

I would love to go back and finish my business degree. Here I end up owning a business, and now I wish I had paid a little more attention in class. But you know, it'd be fun to go back to school. My daughter [and I] did a little trip up to Western State and Fort Lewis to look at those campuses. She gets exceptionally good grades and wants to go to school in the mountains. So we looked at a couple of campuses, and it was infectious. I wanted to go back to school. I wanted to go into art classes. I just wanted that whole experience again. I would love to just devote a lot of time to just learn, not with any particular point; just absorbing again.

I would like to further my education in geology, and one of these days, if I'm not working full-time or working at All Metals Welding, I would like to go back and take a few geology classes and get in to some of the geology clubs; and look at some of the studies of different things around the valley that are still kind of mysterious, like what the geologic cause of [certain canyons] was and things that are still not quite fully understood.

Tell us more about that.

Boy, if I had time, you know, to spend in places other than down at the metal shop—the world is your oyster, if you've got some time. And I would be certainly wanting to donate time to different nonprofits or boards. I'm on two or three boards right now, and that's really very interesting to me. It's kind of a fun way to impact something that you're passionate about, hopefully in a positive manner.

Chris, what are some examples of successful relationships that you've known?

Well…I've been married and divorced twice. Fortunately, I'm in a fantastic relationship right now with Jen and her boys, and my daughter. But the most successful has gotta be my parents. They've been married for 50 years. Gosh, I get emotional. They still travel together. They do everything together. They have their own activities apart, and that's healthy. They aren't [joined] at the hip at all times. And they really enjoy each other's company—they had been high school sweethearts.

My sister and her husband, just yesterday, celebrated their twenty fifth wedding anniversary. I was kinda kidding with her about my marriage successes [and told her] that for me to get 25 years of marriage I'd be on wife [number] seven. I'm very impressed [that] my sister and her husband have a great relationship.

I've seen many friends who have good, healthy relationships. They've learned a lot. I've learned a lot. I think it's unfortunate that so many people of my generation marry and divorce and marry again. But I think the good part of that is they've learned. And they eventually settle into very healthy relationships.

I've settled into a very healthy relationship. I now have somebody who I'm very compatible with, who is probably more into the outdoors than [even] I am. I didn't think I could find somebody that would just enjoy being out riding or, you know, camping more than I did. I found somebody who not only goes along, she probably drags me up half the time. So it's been a godsend to find somebody that I'm so compatible with.

Those relationships with my friends and my family that are really an example to live by are those where each partner really respects the other's viewpoint, whether they think they're completely wrong or not. It really does a lot for your own self-worth and well-being.

What else has life taught you about how to achieve success in relationships?

Not to settle for [who] happens to be in your life at the time but to actually go out and be picky. Be selective about the type of person you're with; try and understand yourself, but don't necessarily go for looks. To actually go for somebody that you're passionate about, not just because of their looks or their job, but because of them, because of what they do, how they are, how they treat you and your family and friends.

I've been handed a couple of real learning lessons. And to come away from that learning *what* I really need to have in my life, *who* I really need to have in my life, and *how* I need to treat my significant other, my daughter, my family, my friends—to show them my appreciation for having them in my life—is huge.

What did you learn to regard as being personally successful when you were growing up? And where do you think that came from?

I think my parents were able to instill in me that money isn't everything, and that family, and relationships, and friends are far more important than how much money somebody has. My dad would say, "Gosh, we go to these gatherings of business people and what's the natural first question out of somebody's mouth? What do you do?" And he would say, " I [don't] tell them that I own a welding and metal fabrication company, trying to make it sound like an important thing." He said, "I would just merely tell them, 'I work at a welding shop.'" Right then, you weed out the people that you want to know and the people you never want know. And he said, "The people you wanna know will ask questions. They'll say, 'Oh, that sounds interesting. What do you build?' " That's the best way of filtering out the people you need to know from the people you don't, that he'd ever seen.

I go to events and there's a lot of business and political people. When they ask me what I do, I say, "I work at a welding shop." And it works like a charm to this day. When somebody asks what [I] do, I'm more inclined to answer, "I mountain bike." "I ski." "I volunteer for [different] boards."

So, personal success for me and who really influenced it really comes from my dad and mom. Mom is very, very adamant that rich people don't really carry much weight with her unless they're wealthy people with a lot of charitable giving that comes along with them.

She donates to everything. She feels that if you are successful, you're obligated to share wealth with others. My view is much the same: if you've got enough money to afford a great big house, you can build a smaller one and donate to someone else. They [Mom and Dad] still live in the same house that I grew up in.

Looking back over your life as a whole, what areas of accomplishment give you the greatest satisfaction?

I would guess being a good dad to my daughter [Ellie]. We've gone through a lot, the two of us. Her mom moved to Denver, and so it was just the two of us here with my family. And gosh, she's just so well-adjusted and her mom and I worked really hard on that. She [Ellie's mom] moved back here and it's been good. We split time with Ellie. Ellie's 16 now, so she can pretty much make her own decisions as to how she wants to spend time and the amount of time. She's got a 3.7 or 3.8 grade average in high school, she's socially active with friends, and on a couple of committees —you know, social groups in school, civic groups, and honor society. [She's] probably my biggest success. We have a really strong relationship, and that's just the best.

And then, my relationship with my family, with Jen, with my sister and my parents—my grandmother's still alive. Dad comes down to the shop quite often and just checks in—makes sure he rubs in the fact that he's been out playing golf and not at work.

My best friend—we went to school together in Western State 30-some years ago—lives near Minneapolis. We still get together probably two, three times a year. We do an annual ski trip every year to Deer Valley in Utah. The guy's like a brother. His daughter's my goddaughter.

It's just a great privilege to have friendships that have lasted so many years. I would rather somebody take away the companies and, you know, the houses—I live here in a straw bale house on the Redlands with this kind of view. If you ask me to trade [my] friends for these really great things that I have—no way.

Have you found any downside to success—to achieving the success that you have achieved?

I don't think so. My mom always says that everything happens for a reason. And I truly believe that, [especially] after the kind of a health crisis that I've had. When I was a kid, I showed a lot of promise and potential in playing professional golf. I went to college on a golf scholarship. I went to nationals a couple of times, did well throughout the region, and won some tournaments. That was [even] after I wasn't [any longer] all that interested in it.

[Caddying] was only paying me a buck an hour and I remember Dad saying, "Boy, you ought to come to work down in the aluminum shop." And I did. Well, that was one of those times when [my] future could've gone in one direction or another, and it went towards learning the metal business. You always kinda wonder, "Gee, did I give up a dream just to make more money when I was 16?" But I know that I made the right decision. The people that I knew that ended [up as] pro golfers were just club pros. They didn't seem all that happy. A couple of them have become alcoholics; just—it's tough. And you know, as far as being on the tour, being on TV, I played a national golf tournament once. There were some guys out there that were so good. They eat, breathe, and sleep golf. I just couldn't give it all that much dedication.

When you look back at things, I don't think there's been a downside. Like Anne Frank said, "What a wonderful world that everyday you get another chance to improve the world around you." And still being here, as there was a time that it looked like I might not be here. Everyday is great, to get up and [off] the floor.

I'm far more emotional about this than I thought [I'd be]. This is hard for me, and that kinda surprises me. It has given me some [time] to really drill in on some of these questions.

Is there anything else that you'd like to say?

Yeah. Since this will be made into a CD that maybe my daughter will hear, or [she may read the] book, what I would like to say to someone else or to my daughter is,

"Just don't worry about the little stuff that happens everyday. Don't worry about, you know, somebody being grumpy. It's not your fault. You don't make things happen to others. Keep your eye on doing good not just for yourself, but for those around you.

"And treat people with respect, whether they are treating you with respect or not and I think you'll find that your life will be so full of warmth and love and friendship that the money will take care of itself and the world will provide.

"I believe in a higher power and if you treat others as you would like to be treated, the world will provide. It just seems to work, and don't worry about how big a house you have or whether you drive the right car. What matters is that you have a family that loves you, friends that love you, and [even] strangers and the opportunity to make them [friends]."

Dan Roberts

July 3, 2008

[One thing] has been huge, and it came through the steadiness of the family. "We still love you even though you may be doing poorly in an aspect.... You are not lesser because you haven't achieved."

I began to see where I fit into those personality types. It was an absolutely life-changing experience for me.... I understood then why they were doing what they were doing, which then helped me understand how to act and to react to what they were doing.

When you were growing up, what did you think it meant to be professionally successful? And what experiences led you to that definition?

Well, I grew up in Durango, Colorado. Born and raised there. We lived in a very modest family home. I had three sisters, so there were four of us kids, plus Mom and Dad, on a corner lot. Nice landscaping. I have fond memories of living there.

The successful, or professionally successful people in our time were the doctors, the lawyers, the individuals that lived on East 3rd Avenue. We lived on West 3rd Avenue, and they lived on East 3rd Avenue. So it was Dr. Lloyd and Dr. Burnett, for example. All had large homes on East 3rd.

East 3rd Avenue had a median in the middle of the street. Lots of trees on both sides. I don't think I made a distinction that these people were better than us. They just lived in bigger houses and probably had more education. I think that would be a fair summation.

Is there an experience that supports your thinking that those people were professionally successful?

Dr. Burnett was the family doctor and he lived in a huge, big block—or it was a rock?—house. It was a hewn rock, like sandstone, house that sat behind this big hedge and large trees. And he was a guy that was just bigger than life itself. He was a big fellow, and he had a wife and one son. And even as a kid, it was a bit of an enigma. Why do three people need a gigantic house like that to live in?

But yet, when you went to see him as a doctor, you never really had an appointment. You just went and sat in the waiting room until it was time to see him. He wore the white coat and smoked this massive cigar. He might be smoking it while he was talking to you. His place always smelled good. It was above the Penney's store in Durango, second floor—and very spartan. But he was just a very common individual.

He never portrayed himself as being better just because he was educated, had some money, and lived in a big house. And the same thing was true with Dr. Lloyd. His house was a big white house, kind of on the edge of the hill. But I never felt like they were lording it over us. It was those kinds of things in a relatively small town atmosphere that helped me form my opinions.

Then what is your definition today of professional success?

A professionally successful individual, now, is an individual of integrity—somebody that you can depend on, no matter what their station in life. So, talking about those individuals with the most common of jobs—the laborers, the finishers, who know their trade and do it well—these are people by and large with integrity.

But individuals with, generally, more education and opportunity, these are the individuals who probably have more opportunity to be more stealthy in their dealings, to mislead you, to make you believe something that isn't really fact. Because of that, my definition of a professional person now is probably more towards someone who has a degree in their field and can be depended on, if they're known as a person of integrity.

By your definition of today, in what ways are you already a professional success?

I started out going to a very small church college in Rock Island, Illinois. I was there a year and decided I was not going to be a music major; that just flat wasn't going to work for me. I was very interested in getting married at that time, even though I was still pretty young. So I did that and then began to pursue my education through some correspondence courses and some night classes. But I never really completed my degree. That has been somewhat of a stumbling block over the years. I think I have been hampered in my professional pursuits by the lack of my degree.

I did change my major to accounting, and I believe I am a good accountant—those that I work with would probably support that statement. But there are things that I could have completed, things that I would have learned and the development that would have come from more formal education.

Dan, what remains unfinished for you in achieving professional success?

Well, I used to think that I had to finish that degree. But a family, a very busy life, and a lot of involvement have changed that. I have since figured out that I don't have to have the degree to be successful, to be professionally successful. At my age, it is just not something that I am interested in pursuing—but I feel like I have achieved a level of success that has worked for me and my family.

When you were younger, what constituted success in learning and education? And who taught you that?

We had a very strong family. My mom had pursued a graduate degree but didn't complete it. She did get a certificate, if I recall. She has deep roots in Georgia and achieved that certificate while she was there. There was a level of—not pushiness, but constantly reminding us that we needed to get good grades; that we needed to do our best.

That wasn't always important to me. Even while my kids were growing up, they didn't have to maintain [a particular] level in order to for us to consider [them] successful. If you are doing your best and you are learning, that is all we were asking for. That was conveyed to me by both my mom and my dad.

My dad was a very well-known individual in Durango, largely because everybody saw him as a person of integrity. If Monroe Roberts told you that he would do something or that something was a certain way, you could stake your life on it. That example was huge to me. The rule in the house was [that if] you got a spanking at school, you got a spanking at home. If you made an F or a D, you got a spanking at home. Those were not acceptable grades, [regardless of] what I said earlier. You were not doing your best if you were doing that kind of thing.

I was very distracted as a youngster. There were just more appealing things to do outside the window than what was going on in the classroom. And it was hard for me to stay focused on anything.

I ended up taking the fourth grade over, and that was probably one of the better things that ever happened to me. [It was a] hard decision for my folks at the time. It was about the time that our school systems were [changing focus], moving students on through, even though they may not be achieving success. My test scores were always high—all of them, but especially achievement and SAT scores. Nobody could [figure out] why I would get high scores and not do any better on a daily basis than I was doing. That was always somewhat of a puzzle to my folks and me.

I believe I learn as much by assimilation as anything else. Somehow that stuff sticks. For me, [one thing] has been huge and it came through the steadiness of the family. "We still love you, even though you may be doing poorly in an aspect of what you are doing. You are not lesser because you haven't achieved."

Today, what do you think it means to be successful in learning and education? Is it any different?

Probably not. At Mesa State, I had a professor named Jo Doris. Jo was the Vice President of Student Affairs. She was a wonderful mentor, from the standpoint of allowing older students to work within their capabilities and within their time constraints. By then my kids were teens, I had a full-time job and I was involved somewhat in the community.

Jo helped me understand a science kind of learning and how to study at my age level. Most of the students were nontraditional, and some of us, who were more experienced in the business world than others, probably excelled in different ways than the more academic, younger ones coming up behind us.

She just brought a levelness and a method of learning to the table that I had not heard before. I would count Jo as one of those special individuals in my life who has helped me to define success, and especially professional success, in a different way.

Can you describe her method and how it changed you?

In the early '70s, the religious community of Grand Junction brought Tim and Beverly LeHays to the Valley for a seminar. I was the controller of a lumber store here in Grand Junction and had a very responsible position. I don't think I was struggling in my role as a supervisor, but I was certainly reacting wrongly in certain situations. For example, if somebody challenged me or if I felt like I was challenged, I was more willing to respond aggressively than after the LeHays were here. Well, what could they possibly have brought to have affected me that way?

Tim LeHays had written a book called *The Spirit Control Temperament*. And in that, he promulgated a theory, that Hippocrates had postulated years before, that there are basically four personality types: the sanguine, the phlegmatic, the choleric, and the melancholic.

And I began to see where I fit into those personality types. It was an absolutely life-changing experience for me in my professional development, and I think even in dealing with my family. I understood then why they were doing what they were doing, which then helped me understand how to act and to react to what they were doing.

That ties in to what Jo taught us, which was a systematic approach to study: if I give you an assignment, break it down into pieces that you can use; if you've got a lot of reading to do, break it down into pieces that may be relevant. Some of it you may not need to read. You just may want to scan.

Very simple. But I'm a very simple guy. And Jo just broke it down simply enough that, together with the LeHays, it made all the difference in the world.

How do you think it affected your children?

Our oldest [Dennis] was diagnosed hyperkinetic at about six years old—before I understood what hyperkinetic was. He is a good kid, vibrant and resourceful. But when it came to staying and learning, he just couldn't do it.

I have a very low patience level and he knew how to—I am not going to say he was purposely pushing the buttons—but he could get there faster than about anybody that I knew. I couldn't figure out that he just flat couldn't assimilate in his own mind what it was he was trying to learn. So I would yell at him, literally. I can remember one time [that] I am still embarrassed [by] to this day.

We were coming back from a trip to Arizona. He was sitting in the front seat between Jackie [my wife] and me. And his mom was working [with him] on some assignment from school. She was getting frustrated because he just flat wasn't getting it. It didn't make any sense to him. And I just came down on him and yelled at him. I mean, we are talking about a seven year old, for crying out loud. And I acted like something less than a seven year old. I can still recall the conversation—well, it wasn't a conversation, because he didn't know how to respond. And then we would just give up.

We had a really good family doctor who helped us put him through the testing to figure out what was going on. At that time, Ritalin was the drug of choice. It did enough to slow him down, to slow his mind enough that he could actually use his hands and the rest of his body to complete the learning experience. Dennis didn't have the capabilities, even at seven. My understanding of his personality, again, came from those learnings with the LeHays and Jo Doris. I think they made all the difference in the world [in] how I responded to my kids. [My kids] would tell you that if you talked to them now.

Is there anything that you think remains unfinished for you in the area of learning and education?

I would love to be more computer savvy. It is hard for me to just sit down and make myself learn. I can figure some of it out without help if I can just stay in front of the screen long enough.

What did financial success mean to you when you were growing up, and what personal experiences contributed to that understanding?

Well, financial success was the large houses and the nice cars and the good clothes. But I never felt like a distinction was drawn that they were better than us; because they had more to spend, we were less than them. As a kid, financial success was stuff. If you had stuff, you were financially successful.

What do you now think it means to be financially successful, and do you think most other people share your view?

I have a few friends [whose] definition of financial success would be the ability to flaunt their money. And that would be the massively large homes—the trophy homes, I am going to call them no—the sports cars, the name-brand clothes, attending the right events, being seen in the right places.

A long time ago, I moved away from making a connection between financial success and being able to give. We were trained from day one to give out of [our] resources whatever we had. Most of that was based around the church, as we paid our tithe. If we kids got an allowance, then we were expected to pay the portion of the tithe on that.

Every Sunday, we were given a certain amount of money to put in the offering, and that was Sunday School. What we were expected to give was to Sunday School. My parents took care of whatever offerings were given to the church. But each of us had a buck—and it was usually [just] a dollar—to put in the offering for Sunday School.

Once I decided I needed that money more than the church did. So I figured out these schemes to keep the money. And I was successful at doing it. Of course, my conscience got to bothering me, and I finally had to fess up. And as I recall I ended up paying that back. But the idea of giving is huge. You don't give to get: you give because it is the right thing to do and because Scripture instructs us to give. And the amount is not important. It is whether or not you are giving.

Do you think that you are already a financial success?

If it was bank balances, no. The reason I bring up bank balances is because we are getting to the age that retirement is very much on the horizon.

Coming through the '80s, there were some really severe medical traumas in our family, along with a few other things that wiped us out a couple of times. So financial success for me is learning to manage money; learning to live within our means, learning to stay and be content with whatever we can afford. And I think we learned that lesson.

Can you give me an example or tell me an experience that causes you to say, "I think we have learned that lesson"?

Well I have always had what I am going to call a "southern blue blood" streak in me. My personal preference is to live very well. But that is not necessarily the big homes, and I have never cared if we drove the latest car. But somewhere along the line, I learned that part of success was "stuff." I spent a massive amount of money. My wife came from abject poverty and had a better appreciation for money. If I had been smart, when we first married, I would have let her manage the finances. So stuff became important to me—you can spend an awful lot of money on stuff and end up with not much.

What are some examples of successful relationships that you have known?

Individuals that could go their separate ways completely and not lose their connection to their friends. We have friends who have achieved major success in the areas of finance and education, and still are very good friends. You can sit down and talk to them and feel like you are just picking up where you left off. That is very important.

And we also know some people that have moved on: "Oh yeah, we remember you," but it is not a warm relationship. It is, "I am a little better than you are" type of thing.

You mentioned a few minutes ago that Dennis and Jeff, your boys, are wonderful people. Tell me about your relationship with your sons.

Dennis and I have a different connection than Jeff and I do. Jeff is more intellectual [and] probably connects with his mom a little bit more than with me. But he and I have long and stimulating conversations. We can talk politics, we can talk religion, we can [even] talk computers to a degree.

Jeff is a computer guru with American Express in Phoenix and is involved in it on a day-to-day basis. So, early on, when we were developing systems in our company, we would have discussions on what he was doing—and still do to this day.

And he is just a joy, very well read, and just an intelligent man. He has two little boys, eight and six, Alex and Christian. And they are just a delight. He married a Greek national and she is becoming an American naturalized citizen. Just a beautiful family from the standpoint of whatever your definition might be of having it together. They live well, but simply. They are not looking for the constant push of making sure that they are experiencing the latest. It is just not that important to them.

Dennis, on the other hand, is a lot like I am. And I think that is why I probably relate more to [him] than I do to Jeff—in a lot of ways I can just see myself [in] Dennis, and that scares me. I am always thinking he is going to have to learn the same lessons that I have learned. I can't protect him from that, even though we may talk about it.

But again, good conversations. Dennis is a student of the Bible and he remembers things well. You can challenge him on different things, and he will have an intelligent, well-thought-out answer for you. [He] is highly regarded in his field, [of] construction testing and construction management. So we have that connection as well, since construction is my background.

I consider both of my boys as better fathers to their children than I ever was to them. And I mean that sincerely. They were able to catch the involvement with their kids. I have regrets for some of the things I didn't do with my kids that I could have done. I see both of them working toward making sure that they are involved in their children's lives to the level that they can be. They are my heroes—and I just thank the Lord for my kids.

> **You commented earlier that you had a strong family growing up. Can you tell me experiences that would describe the kind of relationship that you had within your family?**

A lot of it was built around the church. My dad was what would be known as a lay pastor, and though he was not regularly involved in the pastoral ministry of [our] church, he would supply other churches on occasion—if their pastor was on vacation or [a church was] between pastors, he would do some preaching.

There was a lot of musical talent in our family. My sisters played the piano; and while I took three years of lessons and still remember most of those songs, I never progressed much beyond that.

We had a lot of vocal talent, and so we were very active in the music ministry at the church. My mom had a beautiful singing voice [and] my dad played the saxophone. And while I could be terribly wrong on this, I remember—maybe it was more noise than anything else—but I think he played the accordion a little bit.

My mom quit singing early on, but she expected the family to still be involved. My older sisters were the accomplished pianists. And then Georgine, the middle sister, was a violinist. But when she got married, she put the violin in the case and that is pretty much where it stayed. Everybody loved to listen to June, my older sister, play the piano. And my younger sister is still very active in playing the piano and organ with her church.

At the same time, of course, we did have some very trying times. We've since come to find out, and this is difficult to talk about, that my mom has been diagnosed as schizophrenic. We never quite knew where her personalities were going to be or where we stood in situations. Her reactions could be down or they could be up or somewhere in-between.

I remember her as being an extremely loving individual and always somebody that I could depend on, and a praying person. I would come home from school and hear her in her private devotions. That instilled in me the importance of some things that are still very important to this day. And, as I have gotten older, it has helped me understand why some of the things in the family were the way they were. My mom was a very rigid individual. Jackie [my wife] and I were talking about this just last night. Monday was wash day—and, come hell or high water, the wash day happened. So if the weather was horrible, we still did the washing on Monday.

Then in 1956, my dad died as a result of an industrial accident. He would have been 44 that year, I think. I was 13 and my older sister was in her second year of college. My mom and the two oldest sisters had taken [my older sister] to Kansas City, Missouri, where she was going to school for her second year. [The] accident happened and my mom flew home. The company my dad worked for hired a driver to bring the car and my sisters back home. It was a very traumatic and tragic time and still has overtones to this day.

He was such a strong influence in our lives, all of us, that the family was never quite the same. And mom, with her mental situation, ended up in Denver General Hospital for several months. This was back in the '50s when they were still using shock therapy—there were some horrible experiences that came out of that for her. And, while it was reasonably successful, because she has remained mentally stable and very much able to function on a daily basis, it created a rift in our family that has never been completely healed.

Along with that, I think the death of my older sister contributed. [And while] as a family, I think we've worked through it all, and those things have made us a stronger family unit, they've created issues that we are still dealing with.

Dan, speaking of success in relationships, tell me about your relationship with your wife.

I met Jackie at a church camp in Maxwell, Nebraska; a brief encounter at that time. Then, we both ended up at the same church college in Rock Island, Illinois, and that's where I got to know her as a person. I left after that first full academic year, and she stayed on and was going to pursue her education. I went back to Colorado Springs and began to write to her. So largely, a lot of our courtship was through letters—and that in and of itself was interesting.

The church we were involved in at the time was extremely conservative—a "cultage" mentality, I regret to say—but we both learned some deep, deep lessons out of all of that.

I proposed to her on the telephone. She came to Colorado Springs and we were married there.

Jackie does not know who her father is. She's a war baby; she was born in 1943 in Phoenix, Arizona, in the hallways of what would have been the county hospital. She resulted from a,—and she would tell you this, if she were talking to you—one night stand. He was a Navy boy, in town for the night. I don't think this was Jackie's mom's style, but it happened.

She thought about aborting Jackie, and we have had the conversation about "aren't you glad that didn't happen." That's very meaningful to Jackie—that her mom did not do that and because, obviously, there was a decision involved.

Jackie had an older sister named Margaret who passed away recently. There were eight years between them. And this is one of the most convoluted [things] you could ever hear about in a family. Her mom was not into keeping records. Even though she worked for the state, and knew how to get a hold of the right people to get what she wanted done, Margaret never ended up on a birth certificate. Then years later, it suddenly appeared.

Jackie's kind of the same way. Her mother told her that her father's last name was: "...well lets get out the map.... How is that done in California? Berkeley. How is that spelled? That's how your father spelled it."

So she became "Jacqueline the Berkeley." [Hers] was a pretty dysfunctional family. If her grandparents had not been available to take her in at certain times, I don't know what would have happened to her. She would come home and [her mother would say], "Well, we're putting you on the bus and you are going to go see your grandparents" for who knows how long. Finally, when she was getting ready to go into the ninth grade, her mom just moved her to her grandparents' place in New Mexico, and that's where she finished high school. And so her grandparents had more influence on her than her mother did.

But Jackie is one of the most loving, agape loving, individuals you will ever meet. She loves you [as you] and not what you might be. Her mom lived with us for awhile toward the end of her life, and then she moved into an assisted care facility. I watched Jackie—she just loved her. And her mom was not necessarily a lovable woman.

Jackie just loved her because she was her mom, not because of anything else she'd ever done. Jackie not only loved her mother, she liked her, and she did her best to make her life as good as it could be for her remaining years.

She taught our boys to read and instilled that in both of them. They're still readers to this day. Dennis wouldn't have been if it hadn't been for his mom. Jeff probably would have been, because it's just his mental makeup—he loves to read, read, read.

Jackie's an artist—she paints. I could have been more supportive over the years, and that would've helped her. She'll do something fabulous and doesn't want to take any credit for it. Everybody loves Jackie. The other day, we attended the funeral of a friend and when Jackie gave the spouse a hug, he just broke down—and it's not that we had a lot of contact with these people. Jackie is the kind of individual that you could approach with just about anything. If she says that she's going to pray for you, she will pray for you. It's not just a comment. She doesn't see in herself that she has actually influenced, has made, and continues to make, a difference in people's lives. We've been together for 44 years and. like the Energizer Bunny, she just keeps going.

Looking at your life as a whole, what areas of accomplishment give you the greatest satisfaction?

My boys. I am so proud of both of them. So while I may feel like I missed the boat on some things, obviously some things were done right, and I guess I'm willing to take a little bit of credit for that, although I think most of it came from their mom.

The other areas of accomplishment would be where I am in my professional life, which is chief financial officer for a construction company in Grand Junction. That was never a dream; it was never somewhere that I really intended to be. I've always been in management. It just seems like wherever I was, whether working the stockroom at Sears while I was going to college or going to work for a JI Case dealer in Colorado Springs, I always ended up in management. I have organizational skills and I'm able to reason through things.

Can you tell me about the award your received— Citizen of the Year?

Yeah, this was in '06, I think—January of '06. The chamber always gives a Citizen of the Year award. Usually the recipient never knows that they've been nominated, and I certainly wasn't aware of anything.

I still don't know who nominated me or how that came about. We went to the banquet that year, as usual, and when they started making the presentation, [they talked about the] recipient being born in Durango in 1943. And then they began to go through the rest of the resume—well, they had gotten all that stuff from Jackie, who's typically not an individual to keep a secret. If I had had any idea that this was going on, I would have been able to wheedle it out of her, and she knows that. But she was able to keep the secret, and that was huge to her. Our boys had both been asked to make comments, which they did. When I was awarded that, it just completely blew me away. My comment from the podium was that I was speechless, and I still am to this day. I completely feel unworthy of the award. Obviously, we're very happy with receiving it, but it's just one of those magical moments that you might hope would happen in your life, but never expect it.

What remains for you to achieve or accomplish?

Well, I've come up with a motto or a code to live by, and that is: to be consistent, to finish the task, and to make a difference in someone's life.

That is where I believe I need to be by the time my life is over, to remain true to that motto and have it be more than just a motto. I haven't always been consistent, but that's [a goal]; I haven't always finished a task but, there again, that's a goal. And then to make a difference in someone's life, if nothing more than just being available and praying with them, trying to be a friend.

If I can remain true to those three things, that would be success; and, of course, my relationship with God is absolutely centered in all of that. I don't mean any of those to be just about me: it's all about Him, and my faith is number one. It's the guiding principle, and I trust that it will be that way through the end of my life.

Is there anything that you would like to say or add to all this?

There is one thing that comes to mind, and that [is] the metamorphosis taking place with me and Cliff Mays, Sr. I met him in 1975 when we returned to Colorado from Columbia, Missouri.

I met him at church, and I just knew that he was a concrete contractor. I worked for a lumber company as the controller or fiscal officer. Then in 1983, Cliff asked me, just in a conversation after church one night, "Why don't you consider coming to work?"

That was about a year after the Big Black Sunday in Grand Junction. Cliff had made a large investment in the future. He believed that the areas they were moving into were completely different than anything he'd ever done before in his business. It was all based on the fact that the economy was going to continue to be good here. So I came in as the finance guy—little did I know what I was getting into, and little did he know where we were going. Cliff has a very strong personality. He believes absolutely in what he believes.

One day, not all that long ago, he was sitting across the desk from me, and he says, "This has been kind of a love-hate relationship, hasn't it?"

And I think that's probably a pretty good description of our relationship over the years. You would never put us together knowingly. I'm opinionated and strong headed. He is, as well, and we didn't necessarily agree with all things [the other] was doing. So the love-hate would be that we loved to hate what the other was doing, and we hated to love what the other was doing. One day he walks into the office, and he's asking about a revolving line of credit and where we were with it. He wanted to know why we weren't paying it down faster and why I wasn't doing this or that. Well, I finally just got frustrated and I said, "Cliff, why don't you go do your work and I'll do mine." He laughed. That's one thing about him: rarely would we ever leave a conversation [without] both of us ending up in some kind of resolution—and it was usually a laugh. He said, "Alright. I'll go take care of that."

I realized, "Okay, I can talk to this guy and tell him what my feelings are in a situation." But we have grown together. He's like a brother to me, the brother I never had. I can tell him anything, and I don't have to worry about him talking to anyone else about it. He tells me the same thing. We have prayed together over the years, and we have fought the battles all the way and back again. And while the relationship would be, at best, tenuous sometimes and very strong at other times, it's just been a wonderful, wonderful thing. He's a business partner, a mentor, a friend—he's just so many things that you rarely come across in one individual. I love him dearly.

John McConnell

December 21, 2007

...We can do 25 kids in a workshop or we can do 25 teachers. But if we do 25 teachers and... each teacher has 20 kids, then we reach 500....

"STEM" means Science, Technology, Engineering, and Math. There's almost no occupation now that in some ways does not require a STEM education. If I can be a messenger talking to businesses, teachers, and parents, [I want them] to begin to ask questions of the school systems all over: "What are you doing to give my child a STEM education?" And maybe to the school boards, and [even] demanding, "You give my child a STEM education."

John, when you were growing up, what did you think it meant to be professionally successful, and what experiences led you to that definition?

Well, when I was growing up, I lived on a farm, and this was in the '30s because I was born on December 30th, 1930. You know, I did not grow up in times when you noticed great financial success around. That was at a time [that] you felt lucky you had food on the table, clothes, and everything else. This was the time of [my] living on a farm—a small farm like, you know, 120 or 160 acres in southeast Nebraska. And that was a time when you were pretty self-sufficient. You had gardens, you raised your own meat, you butchered, and a lot of the income that you had is when you went into town and took 30 dozen eggs and a can of cream, [sold them], and the money bought groceries that you needed for the week. So that was kind of a ritual on Saturdays—to take things into town.

So the idea of great financial success or having a lot of money was certainly not really very much in one's mind. It was a time when we "neighbored" a lot. That meant we helped one another, you know. You put up hay, you did cutting of grain, and things like that. It was maybe a term that's not used very much now. It's what is called "neighboring."

Success, in my mind at that time, was [that] you were pretty successful if you owned a piece of land, or you were able to have successfully raised a family, or if you were fairly self-sufficient.

Do you remember your grandparents and how they lived at that time?

Actually, I spent a lot of time with my grandparents when I grew up and lived with them a lot. So I know how they lived. Like I said, [it was] a rural setting in Nebraska, and so it was families getting together for Thanksgiving—and whole, big [entire] families, because you lived closer together than now.

[As an example], it was like [when I went to] school. I went to a one-room country school and there was one teacher, all eight grades—maybe six kids in school. You got to school in the morning and helped your teacher make the fire to warm up the building. And there was no running water, no electricity, and two pony barns outside, you know. If you needed a little light, you had a couple of gas lanterns that ran on white gas

What is white gas?

At the time, it was called "white gas." It may be that it didn't have any lead in it—I'm not sure. A lot of the gasoline had lead in it, and gasoline was actually sort of [a] red color. This was still [during] those times when they pumped it up in [that] thing that you could see [on the gas pump at the station]. When you got a gallon of gas, [you could actually see it when it came down from the] top. And the gas that you used in the lanterns was a different color. It was white. It was clear—not white, but it was clear.

How does your definition of being successful in your profession today compare to other people's definitions?

Well, my definition is really always, regardless of what your occupation is, doing the very best job that you can of meeting those expectations in your mind—doing the very best job that you can of it.

I met a guy one time when I was volunteering out at Cross Orchards who did a lot of maintenance [work]. And he said, "You know, my dad always told me [that] no matter what the job was that you had, you do the best job you can of it. And even though you may not like that job, you still give it everything you've got. You may be looking for something else to do but it's still, you know, doing the very best that you can with your abilities."

What experiences have you had to cause you to say that your definition of professional success is to do the best job you can?

Some of that comes from role models. One of the best role models I had, outside of relatives and parents, was a neighbor named Claude Glathar, and he was a guy that lived on the farm west of ours. And I worked for him sometimes in the summertime. He was a [worker]— he, you know, worked like crazy. Everything from in the crops that he raised to the animals—pigs, hogs. He was just a guy that you looked at, as a young person—in fact, all of my life—and I say, "Yeah, I've had some role models in life."

In about 1992, we went back to Nebraska to celebrate a friend's retirement and Claude was in the hospital. We went into Lincoln and we drove about 100 miles down to [the town he was in] to visit him in the hospital.

He used to write letters at Christmastime and they were so funny. I'd lost track of some of them.... So he was a guy that even [from] high school, [I] kept track of, actually, all my life—you know, until he passed away. And so we got to see him. He passed away about three or four weeks later. He had said, "You know, John, I haven't done everything right." [And] I said, "Well, you know, Claude, how many of us *have* done everything right?"

We were back in the Midwest again this September and saw his wife. She was in a nursing home. I was so glad I got to see her; she was one of those hardworking ladies that never went beyond the eighth grade, and raised a family, all of them successful kids. We lost her about two weeks ago.

And so those are some of things I think of that form our work ethic. It's part of that Midwestern, Protestant work ethic—whatever you want to call it—that comes along.

So actually, when I look at my life, I always kind of worked a couple of jobs [at the same time]. I was always doing something [else] besides. I was in the air force in Topeka, Kansas, and I worked at a TV station; then, I ended up going to college and working full-time, all at the same time. So I was always this, you know, driving and working hard to—so that I could do a little more, you know.

I went to trade school after high school, not college. I didn't go to college until eight years after high school. It was one of those things where I was working and saying, "This is not what I want to do all my life. So there's something else, another challenge, that I ought to go and do."

So you end up going to school and working full-time and have a family. Somehow or other, my ethic—work ethic—and what I deem [as] success and successes are not measured in terms of dollars, I think, at all. It was working and trying to be as good at whatever I did [as I could be].

So I always remarked that he's [Glathar] one of those people in my life that you [need to] meet really young. And I think people—kids—do need role models. It's one of those things now that we don't have enough of along the way.

By your own definition, in what ways have you already achieved professional success?

Well, I guess for me, success comes along two paths. One of them is that success in terms of the working career, and the other one I would term as that measure of success in what I'd call my retirement years.

In terms of the working career days, I always had lots of challenges. I was in charge of our electromagnetic isotope separator. We were actually doing something really new in the group—the group that I was in. I and my group leader, Ned, were looking at uranium and putting [it] in a small container and putting it in front of a neutron beam coming out of our reactor. [We were] actually fissioning the material, splitting the atom and looking at radioactive isotopes and half-lives that hadn't been looked at or [ever] seen before. And so that was exciting—the fact that [I was] part of a team of people that was able to achieve success in looking at and measuring things which hadn't been measured before.

And probably a lot of my role also has been somewhat like a teacher, even then, because we had young graduate students. So you were constantly helping young people get an education. It was probably, in terms of [my] working career, the happiest time of my life. It was sort of like going back to the "neighboring" thing: you are a part of a team, and you got to have all these pegs to make things work. And you were, you know, a part of a team. Not only that, but [we were also] developing and building things. That was a huge feeling of success—all of that.

And the other thing is [that] if you do a job well, you also find that people give you more freedom—more freedom to express yourself and to build or develop things.

At Los Alamos National Labs, I worked at a half-mile-long linear accelerator. That's, in laymen's terms, an atom smasher that's a half-mile long. [I was] running the front end of it—the injectors—which is where everything started out from. So it was another big effort that involved about, I don't know, maybe 360 people and was another one of those team efforts. The machine is broken up into sections the whole way along, and everything depended on teamwork, because it is such a complicated system. It's a miracle that thing ever ran properly, but it's another one of those things where you are a very integral part of making something run—it depends on you.

My work days [then and now] are a lot like volunteering: you're always on call and [that] means that you're a staff member [and] you don't get paid extra for working [extra time]. Your technicians get paid for coming in, but you don't. My usual work day was 7 [a.m.] till about 6 [p.m.], but I might get home, have dinner, get called back, and be there all night.

A lot of people won't do that because, you know, "If you're not going to pay me any more, I'm not going to do any more." Part of [the reason I do it] is pride in [a] work ethic, but it is also [being]part of that team. You know, you had a job to do and you had the talents and the abilites to do it. That was part of success—doing that.

There were lots of my workweeks which were 60 and 70 hours long, especially if the machine was running. That meant if I was in Santa Fe, 45 miles away, [and the] machine broke down—I always had a pager. [I] might be at a concert, [but I was] expected to get up out of the concert and go back.

Okay. So the other thing was retirement. I never was one who [worried] that much about [planning for] the dollars, because I was always—I guess I was concerned more about what I was doing with my job. I didn't pay a whole lot of attention to what I [could] be doing during this time to invest money or make money. I never had enough time for it, because I was always back at work.

So retirement ended up [with us] coming here to Grand Junction, and we had looked [around] for some period of time. There was a young man in my group, a mechanical engineer named Mike Borden. Mike grew up in this town. His mom still lives here [as does] a brother. Mike always said, "You ought to go up there and look [at] retiring there because it's a great town, and I would go back there in a heartbeat to work if there was just any jobs that, you know, are like I have now."

So we came and looked. And we had three criteria for a place: one was good medical facilities, one was [a] small college, and another was music. So it was medical, music, and college.

So Grand Junction fit all [three], plus Audrey [his wife] had problems with asthma. It fit good and we moved here in 1990.

For me, it was with the intent to do wood turning, and I was going to forget [all] that technical part that I'd been doing and shift to something else. If you go out and look at my shed out there, it's still full with turning blocks for the [lathe] to turn bowls and stuff like that.

But instead, my neighbor, who lived in the next house south at that time, talked me into coming to Wingate [Elementary School] and helping out with Odyssey of the Mind [an interschool problem-solving competition] in about 1991. Tom Parish was the principal down there, and he asked, "You sure you don't want to come in and help out with some kids in science a little bit?"

The teacher that I went in to help was named Gerry Wigent, and so, that was the beginning of another saga in my life—another whole thing that I didn't plan for. It's kind of saying to people that there are things planned for you, or that pop up, that you didn't quite think were there. It was not on your road map—not on your radar screen.

The Ryan Patterson Story

So in the midst of that, I found out that I really loved dealing with kids. Before, I'd not had time for that. This began a saga that Audrey and I didn't plan. Pretty soon, you know, it's like we were going around to other schools, out of the trunk of the car, down to Wingate with boxes and magnets and electricity, and things like that.

And at that time, I ran into this little boy named Ryan Patterson, who was in the third grade. He started coming to the house here, because in him was this glow in his eye, and an intensity and a focus and a passion—the first time I met him. Maybe that [reminded me] of some of the stuff I had—that passion, and focus. In addition [to] the other kids I was seeing, [he] was this little boy who would come over here and spend all day Saturday. And he would sit down there at the work bench at nine o'clock in the morning—most third graders by this time would say, after an hour, "John, let's do something else, I'm tired. Let's play." [But] this kid would spend the whole day there. He'd never say, "I'm tired." And he'd be there at five o'clock that night.

So this is something that went on every Saturday, plus other times, all day for between seven and eight years. [That was] in addition to seeing, at times, thousands of kids in a year. At the end of traveling around [and working] out of the [trunk of the] car, I was seeing about 4,000 to 5,000 kids. I could anticipate Ryan was going to be here all day Saturday. That was the beginning of another commitment in which you find out that kids need role models. And so, what you're doing, without really knowing it I think, is passing on your work ethic, your ideals, and your process—whatever it is. Actually, in a way, you're [molding] them a little bit, because they're around you enough. I'm sort of one of those guys who, if there's something that needs to be fixed, or needs to be developed, I'm going to do it. I may have to work like crazy at it and I might not be the smartest guy to do it but, as borne out by projects I [have been] given at Los Alamos that other people couldn't do, [I] know [I] can do [it].

So you [instill] into a kid like Ryan that ability and that drive and that showing that—maybe I would call it something like "stick-to-it-iveness"—that sort of says, "You know, I'm going to stick to this son-of-a-gun until I get it fixed or done." And I think a lot [of] that is what got imparted into Ryan in the midst of it all. It's helped him a lot.

More Ryan's Story

There's two boys who are in my life: [Ryan, and] the other one is Derek Vigil. I'll do them separately because they're two separate kids.

Ryan came as a quiet, very shy little boy who really—he had a speech impediment, and so he got teased a lot in school because his "robots" were "wobots" and things like that. And even through middle school, it was a really hard time. High school went fine. But it was part of those times of spending [time] with the kid. You know, he is learning circuits and you're starting to teach them, even in third grade, how transistors are working. And it's part of a time that, as you go along—I allude to it a lot as like that little [book about] Jonathan Livingston Seagull. You know, Jonathan really liked to fly and dive and everything. And I allude to the time with the kid like it's giving a kid wings and pretty quick you can—you find out they can fly. And you as the teacher—they can outfly you. They can fly a lot higher, faster, and everything else.

[It's] like we took him off to do things that might not [otherwise have happened]. One time when he was in the fifth grade, Audrey and I, took the trailer and went to Santa Fe for a week. There was a robotics competition down there and we took him. You know, he cleaned up on all the adults! Really, we took about [all the prizes]. They were giving away these little, kind of computers. They finally had to figure out some other way to distribute the prizes, because we had too many of them. They couldn't give them *all* to us.

You know, if you do a pendulum, you [can] look at the period of a pendulum [the time it takes to swing from one place to another]; it depends on the length of it. So they had this climbing robot that would climb a fish line. And you had [to] remotely control it and see how

258

high you could [get it to] climb. [Our] competition hardly got it up [the line]. And a PhD from Los Alamos was running the competition. So he asked Ryan to keep it going. So we gave it a *greeat biig swiinng*. And it was really high, and the thing cimbed all the way to the ceiling. You could see the period of the pendulum changing as his climber made it all the way to the top and then zipped back down.

I mean, it's always been a stitch with him, you know, to do this. It's one of those things in [my] life that's such a great joy to see. He started doing science fairs in seventh grade and he did [them] for five years—[grades] seven, eight, nine, ten, eleven. And in state competition, he was first place three times and second place twice. That's a pretty hard record to beat, you know.

We got to go to three international science fairs—in Philadelphia, Detroit, and San Jose. It's a joy to go to these things. There's about 1,200 or 1,400 kids, you know, doing projects.

The first high school one was a very hard one for him because he didn't win anything except an internship to a company called Axon in New Orleans. And he was 14 years old, I think, and it meant he was to go to New Orleans and work in a company for eight weeks. [His teachers were excited]—"Oh man, what an opportunity." But his parents and grandparents didn't want him to go, so I had the job of saying, "You know, if you don't let this kid go on, I'm going to be throwing brick bats at your house every day." I talked them into it.

He stayed with the lady that was the executive secretary to the CEO. So there's this little 14-year-old kid whose parents [couldn't] afford to go [visit him]. So halfway through the eight weeks, I flew down and spent about four, five days with him and saw the incredible things he was doing. That was probably the best thing he ever won in terms of those early years. He learned to lay out circuit boards on the micro level—microchip level— and that allowed him to go forward, then, two years later with the Glove [a project described later]. There were grad students [there] and they couldn't believe it—[Ryan was just] going to be a sophomore in high school. Those are things I look at as success—looking at what you can do with a child to help.

In his junior year, he was devising the Glove, [which] translates American sign language to the written word. That [project] culminated in [a trip to the Nobel prizes]. That kid won in more competitions than

259

any kid has ever won in the United States. He won the grand awards at the International Science Fair; he won the Glenn Seaborg award, which took him in 2001 to the Nobel prizes. He was one of 22 kids from around the world that got to go. He spent a week over there, got to go to the ball—the all-night dance. As a matter of fact, there were two guys, and I can't think of their names, who both won Nobel prizes that year. So [Ryan] got to see them over there, which was really incredible. [Ryan says that getting] to go [was] one of the highlights of his life. It took six hours of etiquette lessons, [but] he got to sit up [at] the banquet table, meet [everyone], and go to the dance.

But then he went on to win the Siemens Westinghouse Competition for $100,000,competing mainly with kids who'd come out of a lot of private schools and the Intel Talent Search. We were invited to Washington and he stood up in front of a bunch of doctors at the National Institutes of Health. He was a senior in high school—early senior in high school— and told them about what he did with the Glove. The joy that you have when you find out, you know, how worthwhile your time was spent is great joy. So I look at this as probably some of the most successful years of my life—helping to give a kid like this an opportunity to go and do something. And right now he's in his second year as an electrical engineer at Lockheed and doing very, very well.

And the other thing is that he is already giving back. He works on the board—has ever since he was a senior in high school—of the state science fair. He goes to the meetings, he goes to the science fair, he helps judge, he helps set up stuff. He was responsible for [the University of Colorado's] participating and giving, I don't know, $30,000 worth of scholarships.

The Derek Vigil Story

You know, that's [Ryan's] story. I have this other one named Derek Vigil who graduated [from high school four years ago].. He's a senior in college this year [2008]. He was a kid I started with a lot later. I found him such a remarkable kid, too. He was a junior in high school and came [in] need of a project. I needed somebody at the Center [The Science Center] to do a summer program for fourth, fifth, and sixth grade kids.

It was just awesome. He made up the whole plan, the questions—the whole thing. It's remarkable for a junior in high school to do this. [That] started a relationship between us. I remember, even though I had [many other] kids in the Center, that I went to his graduation. I stood at the fence because I had to go back to [the other] kids. He was the valedictorian that year and as he was standing up, giving his valedictorian speech, and he was naming off teachers, he said, "You know, the most important person in my life…" and he named me. And that was a—still brings tears.

Because of that [project] he did in the summer, he had a full ride to [the] University of Illinois at Champagne-Urbana. And at the end of his second year, end of his sophomore year, he had finished everything they had to offer in physics and math for an undergraduate.

He was through, [so] he did an internship at the University of Rochester that summer. His junior year, a year ago, he took all graduate work in physics and high-level math, competing with Chinese grad students. And this last summer, he worked at Harvard with a lady doctor, modeling brain aneurisms with fluid dynamics. Right now, he's in India in just humanitarian [stuff], because he's a kid who not only has this great vision and this ability to do high-level math and physics, but who's also worried about mankind and where the planet's going and what we're doing with [it] all. He wants to make sure he can make a difference in that world. So he's over there for a semester, learning. He calls me every so often, and emails. So next year he will be back, and he's going to spend it at the Center with me, doing lectures to other kids in between his undergraduate and graduate school—he wants to make a difference. Maybe success is a lot of how [and what] can you pass on to other kids—it's that *giving* thing. It has nothing to do with dollars, you know.

What do you think remains for you to do, John?

The biggest thing that I see now is getting things done with the Western Colorado Math and Science Center. And that involves both the desire to spread the philosophy and to spread the Center's concept—to see it built in other places.

We have reached a place in our society where I feel that hands-on science is so important and beginning in elementary school. It is a desire to see [to it] that science's part of the teaching tools are brought [together with those of] language, mathematics, social studies, and everything—that all these things are mixed. It's more of an integrated approach and so part of it is going to be a process to finish refining what we're doing at the Center.

That *means* things to me. Teacher preparation is very paramount. I realize that we can do 25 kids in a workshop or we can do 25 teachers. But if we do 25 teachers and I can get them to teaching the methods in the sciences, then that multiplies. If each teacher has 20 kids, then we reach 500 instead of 25. So, very important to me now is to put this process out [there].

It's the process of having a STEM education. "STEM" means Science, Technology, Engineering, and Math. There's almost no occupation now that in some ways does not require a STEM education. If I can be a messenger talking to businesses, teachers, and parents, [I want them] to begin to ask questions of the school systems all over: "What are you doing to give my child a STEM education?" And maybe to the school boards and [even], *demanding*, "You give my child a STEM education."

John, you've talked about the Science Center. What is the Center, and how did it start? And while you're at it, do you have a vision for the Center?

Well, when I traveled around all the time,—working out of the trunk of my car, going from school to school—my feeling was [that] I wanted to have a place somewhere where kids could come to me. And so that opportunity first arose in 1998 with Tom Parish [the principal] at the same school. Wingate had an extra room and Tom and I talked about it. That gave us an opportunity to take one classroom of about 1,000 square feet. [Someone talked] me into actually putting tables in, and thus began a version of the Math and Science Center.

It had all kinds of hands-on exhibits for kids to explore and to do things in, [but] I felt like it was a little small. So I asked the school district, mainly the superintendent, "Don't you have a little more room so I can make this a little bigger?" So in June of '99, there was room available in what was, previously, the Columbus Elementary School. The school district, without me [even] going before the school board, through the assistant superintendent, took me in there. It was about

6,000 square feet, and they asked, "Would this be enough?" I said, "Wow." It looked awful big. I really felt honored that the school district would give me 6,000 square feet of space and put no restrictions on it. No micromanagement; the only thing he said was, "Go do your thing."

And so in June of 1999, I started building this place. In January of 2000, we started seeing kids. The displays have changed and new tables have been built so that there is a huge display area of hands-on things, which changes. Over time, there have been, probably, 54,000 kids come through on field trips, and that doesn't include kids on weekends or summers. Kids come [with their] teachers and [other] people from a 160-mile radius of Grand Junction. It's an opportunity for kids to explore, and I think kids do have to explore to learn science.

We have a lecture room and, because of the generosity of the Coors Foundation, we have just [completed] $12,000 to $14,000 worth of renovation to the lecture room. So we can take the kids in, give lectures and hands-on displays. The Center is becoming a place for teacher workshops which we hold, workshops for kids, a mentoring outlet and, of course, the exploratorium [the hands-on room] itself.

We have a partnership with the University of Colorado. Every summer we have two students sent to us by the University. All expenses are paid by them and those students work for us. In fact, over this [coming winter/Christmas] holiday, the two from last summer are coming back to do some more work because they love the place. And it will mean [that] next fall, we'll start having between two to maybe five or six CU students assigned to us for a semester. They'll be going out into the schools to help teachers teach science, math, and engineering.

And so it's this expansion that we want to do—doing more outreach. We would like to be able to do some similar thing [elsewhere] on the Western Slope, like in Glenwood Springs or Montrose, or someplace where kids don't have to travel so far to come on field trips. The Center is really a multifaceted thing. One of the great joys about it [is that] we operate [entirely] with volunteers, and these are primarily seniors. One of the things [our schools] need to be doing is getting more seniors involved helping kids. It's what I call an intergenerational connection. It's these people [seniors] helping kids. You've got to have that kind of an experience out there. So it's getting seniors involved.

I think a good [analog to] why we need so much more hands-on science [is the experience of] United Parcel Service. They're finding out [that] with the youth coming to work, the only way they can really teach them to do the job is with a hands-on approach. It doesn't work to [just] read the manual. They've had to go totally to hands-on. The Center is an example—it's what we want to start. It's a way of connecting kids in school and keeping them occupied [learning] things of interest—and what better thing than science to tie all things together.

Can you think of an example here locally of that concept?

Carl Topper is a good friend of mine—Professor Topper. He has a PhD in soil sciences [and has] taught some in environmental and has taught teachers. He had a feeling that in order to be a good professor [teacher of teachers], he ought to spend some time in the classroom [teaching the children]. He was going to teach elementary teachers, so he took a year off and went to a school in Aurora [Colorado]. They gave him very low-achieving kids for the year but he had very good success with them.

He was doing science notebooks with them, and he said [that] at the end of the year, he had tears in his eyes when these kids graduated because of the turnaround they had. This year, meaning the fall of 2007, he decided to do one more year of elementary school. He decided to teach *first* grade in Frisco [Colorado]. To prove that you can do this with first graders, he starts them off with science notebooks and using science as a very responsive principle. He's now teaching in a dual language [school] and having to switch between the two [languages], and he says [that] because of this, he does not have [a single] discipline problem in his class.

These little kids absolutely love science; his kids will puff out their chests and say, "My teacher is a *real* scientist." I think that's really the proof in the pudding—we need to be starting out in kindergarten and first grade with those sciences. They can be doing that writing—those science notebooks—integrating literacy with it at the same time. So for me at the Center, [it's all about] promoting this kind of thing and trying to initiate [it] into schools.

John, what are some examples of successful relationships that you've known?

I think [there] have been a lot, both with kids and adults. I spoke of role models way back with Claude, and I, several times, have given talks on mentorship. You know, without realizing it, we're all mentored a lot and we may not recognize it as such. Mentoring means that there's somebody there who nudges, pushes, pulls, and tugs a little ways.

I'm thinking of a person—a Dr. Don Hagerman. Don and his wife live in Battlement Mesa [Colorado] right now. He was one of those people who came along and who really was a role model. When I was at Los Alamos, he was the division leader—and that meant he was the guy over all 360 people. He always had a special interest in you and [whether] you did a good job. If you were having trouble in the middle of the night trying to fix something, who ended up down by your side? He was also the guy who [would say] at seven o'clock in the morning, "You've been up long enough. You need to go home, because it's going to be unsafe for you on the road pretty quick if you don't." There are relationships that we make at work with people who we deeply respect.

Another one which I greatly admired when I was working there was a guy named Andy Broman, also a PhD out of—I believe it was—Columbia University. He's probably one of the smartest guys I ever knew. And so there was a lot of collaboration and [there are] good [memories and] feelings there.

Right now, I have a little boy named Austin who comes in. He's a little over four years old right now—I'm looking around for a picture—he's been coming in since he was three. He comes in and [I] send him home with projects. Maybe in kids like this you will see another Ryan or another Derek. It's another little relationship.

I was in the hospital recently—I had this surgery. And little Austin—his dad happens to be a nurse at the hospital—[and his] mom ended up visiting me. A couple of days ago, he was down at the Center. He walked in and the first thing he said was, "Where's John?" These are relationships you make, even automatically, with little kids.

[There are] seniors who help me at the Center. One guy is Allan Conrad. Allan has been my volunteer coordinator ever since we started in January of 2006. We met at the rector's house at a Christmas party, and got to talking. And out of that [it] started. It's a very close relationship and a friendship. We have a number of people—seniors—that come to the Center and you form a bond with all of them. They're people that have common interests with what you do. They wouldn't be there but to help kids. It's neighbors [too]. In this neighborhood, we sort of watch out for one another's house.

Where does it come from, John, this sense of community, of bonding?

For me, I think a lot goes back [to] that upbringing on the farm, as opposed to in town and sometimes not knowing your neighbor or anybody else. You know, that community of people—and part of it is that it goes way back. It goes back to your roots, I think.

Have you found any downsides to achieving success?

I don't really have any downsides. Maybe only that I haven't got enough done yet. You might talk about it that way. "I've got to get well and get with it." I haven't done everything yet with the Center [that] I want to do. Part of that is the fact that I was really, for all those years and until this last summer, running the place by myself. And now I have some help. I have Theresa Dwyer now, and she's a young lady that is very good. And so I feel like, with the support that I have now, we can go on and achieve a lot more. So if there was any downside, and I don't really look at it as a downside, I didn't get as much done as I wanted to get done.

What do you still want to achieve?

Well, I—I still want to see the Center flourish more, you know. I want to get across the value of STEM education.

And you know, I'd like to go to the International Science Fair when I'm about 80-some. I'd love to go again with another kid, you know, because that's so much fun.

If you find you have to retire from the Center, do you have any suggestions that you'd like to pass on about how to keep the Center going in light of your vision?

That's been of concern for me: what if something happens to me and I can't go on. I think a year or two ago, I would've been a lot more worried than I am now. Right now, as we speak, I've not been there much for a little over a month because of surgery, and I won't be there probably for the first three months of 2008 because of doing chemo. [And] that means having them run [it] four, five months without me. That's a good test; and I'm finding that it's doing quite well.

We have a board that's very much looking at this, because I'm not getting any younger. How do we direct and run [it]? And, what is that vision for the people who direct it? But I find out, [from] having Theresa, that there are certainly people that I feel very confident in—we can do something about that. So I'm not near as worried as I might've been two years ago. I feel very good about it now.

John, is there anything else that you'd like to add before we close?

First of all, you always have to say that there's somebody always behind you. And I'd say that's Audrey, my wife. You know, it really helps to have a spouse who really sees and supports your vision. She's had to be very tolerant because I spent an awful lot of time—a lot of time—at the Center. It has [involved, and] still involves, 60 and 70 hours a week over the years. And you know, we've been married 57 years. That's a long time for her to put up with me. That's very important. [Without that support, I couldn't] go on and do something like this. [She is] somebody who sort of jumps in and [is] very supportive. [Her] ideals and beliefs are the same as [mine]. That's a huge amount of help.

Conclusion

We ask a question—but are we really interested in the answer? And when the person launches into a story in response to our question, do we view it as an irritant? When we are sincere in our quest for an answer, we are blessed *many* fold if that person begins to relate an experience.

Stories matter and telling stories matters. They represent who we are. They disclose our life experiences, our values, and *why* we are who we are. And they help us to capture, preserve and then pass on our true legacy. Who we are is our legacy; our wealth is not much more than a piece of us, and for many, an insignificant piece.

The chapters in this book provide perhaps differing values for each reader. For me, to learn what each contributor believes about the meaning of success in learning and education is interesting. I am fascinated by education on all levels and am strongly opinionated about the different approaches taken to education by various politicians.

But the true value of these stories for me is just hearing the stories and listening to the person behind them. At some point, each reader of this book will finish it and put it aside. The book and its contents will gather dust. Ah, but what if a reader is the child or grandchild of one of those who freely contributed her stories to this adventure?

And what would that child or grandchild give, or pay even, for the opportunity to hear the contributor's stories in her own voice years and years from now? I remember my Granddad Graves sitting in his rocker pickin' at his banjo and singing some old Tennessee hill song. He had left Tennessee when he was a very young man with his big brother and on foot. Since his passing, I've heard a few stories about some of his life's adventures and lessons. But I heard none from him. I was too young and he was too old. I suspect many of us would look with sadness on our missed opportunities. What I would give to hear him talking again, and to sit with him while he talked about life growing up in the Tennessee hill country. I wonder how different my own life might have been had I learned from him, just as earlier generations learned life and death lessons at the feet of the old ones.

The libraries represented by your parents, your grandparents, and even yourself are at high risk. Let's get out the fire extinguisher! Purchase a small, inexpensive, digital recorder. Sit down with one of your important libraries and ask one or two very focused questions.

- When did you and grandma first meet and what initially attracted you to her?
- If this were your last day on earth, what would you want to tell her?
- Finish this sentence: I come from a people who....
- What are two or three of the most significant changes you've seen in the world during your lifetime?
- If you had an abundance of time, energy and money, what are some of the things you would you do with the rest of your life?

As you saw in this book, once someone begins a story, it goes on and on. Concentrate your attention on grandpa; let him know you are really interested, and be very careful not to interrupt him. Interruption will guide his conversation where you want it to go instead of where he wants it to go. Digression and "rabbit trails" are a blessing. Burn the recording onto a compact disc and pass copies among loved ones as gifts. It may take a short while, but they'll all soon recognize *the gift* for what it truly is.

Most of us never realize the fortune that lies within our library.

About the Author

Steve is an estate and business planning attorney in Fruita, Colorado who has limited his practice to basic and advanced wealth strategies planning.

He is also a nationally recognized teacher of strategic and tactical planning to lay persons and professionals alike and believes that effective modern planning can only take place in an environment that encourages people to think for themselves, to discover their own unique talents and the special goals that we all have for ourselves, our loved ones and our money.

A large part of his practice is devoted to encouraging people to preserve and then pass on their stories as a truly important part of their legacy.

Steve is married to Jan Gammill who recently retired from teaching kindergarten at Wingate Elementary School in Grand Junction, Colorado and has joined him in the Legacy Planning arm of his practice, called *Legacy by Stories*. They are members of Monument Presbyterian Church where they serve as elders and church leaders.

Visit his website at www.stevegammill.com and his blog at http:// Stevegammill.blogspos.com